James Woodward is a pastoral and practical theologian with a long-standing interest in people and what makes for health and well-being. As a priest, he has worked in a number of pastoral settings including hospital chaplaincy. This volume has emerged out of his work as Master of the Foundation of Lady Katherine Leveson, which supports older people in housing and care. He also directs the Leveson Centre for the Study of Ageing, Spirituality and Social Policy as a resource for thinking and practice.He has written widely in this area. For further information about his work and publications see his web page, <www.jameswoodward.info>.

New Library of Pastoral Care

Valuing Age

Pastoral ministry with
older people

James Woodward

First published in Great Britain in 2008

Society for Promoting Christian Knowledge
36 Causton Street
London SW1P 4ST

British Library Cataloguing-in-Publication Data
A catalogue record for this book is available from the British Library

ISBN 978–0–281–05779–5

1 3 5 7 9 10 8 6 4 2

Typeset by Kenneth Burnley
Printed in Great Britain by Ashford Colour Press

Contents

Part Three: The future of ageing

Foreword

There is nothing more certain, so it is said, than death and taxation. Now with equal certainty we are aware that before death and often with major financial implications there is old age. We live as an ageing population.

From the pastor's perspective it may sometimes appear that there are only older people with whom to do pastoral work. James Woodward takes us thoroughly through ministry with and to older people. They constitute a highly significant body in today's and for tomorrow's society. How many ministers, for example, lament the age profile of their congregation, especially that lack of youth and the preponderance of older people? Yet if they look closely at the age profile of the population in the area they may well find that their congregation matches it exactly.

This volume in the New Library of Pastoral Care covers the whole range of issues that an ageing population raises for the Church, for society, for carers and for older people themselves. It bases each section on stories and testimonies from older people. And it never loses touch with reality, whether talking about health and illness, or opportunities to try new aspects to living. There is no such individual as a stereotypic 'old age person'.

This book will be of great value to ministers and all those who work with older people. There are exercises to test one's understanding of the various dimensions of this period of life. 'What we must try and do is to befriend the elderly stranger within ourselves.'

Wesley Carr
Series editor

For Leslie Houlden,
friend and encourager

Acknowledgements

I am thankful to Bishop Mark Santer who as Bishop of Birmingham in 1998 encouraged me in this ministry among older people and to the Governors of the Foundation of Lady Katherine Leveson for their ongoing support. Bill Husselby, our Chairman of Governors, is a constant source of both encouragement and challenge.

The Leveson Centre has been a forum that has brought me into contact with a wide variety of individuals and groups working with older people. I am especially grateful to Alison Johnson, my colleague at the Centre, whose knowledge and expertise in this area have informed and challenged my own thinking. This book would have been much poorer without her. Thanks also to my other working colleagues in the Foundation: Jen Jones, Godfrey Chesshire, Jeanne Moss, Julie Fletcher, Chris Mundell, Sharon Roche, Dianne Truepenny and especially my inspirational Head of Care, Anne Atkinson, who shares my passion for quality and imagination in care for older people. I am deeply indebted to those older people whom I have worked alongside in Temple Balsall; their wisdom and experience shape this work at every level.

My congregation at St Mary's, Temple Balsall, have grounded my thinking and pastoral care in our journey of faith exploration. This church has seen an eight-fold growth in numbers, especially among the over-55s, and together we have reflected, taken risks and supported each other. Our children in the church primary school are a constant source of inspiration: they shape and form us in the spiritual life.

Some of the ideas have been tested out with a variety of groups across the West Midlands and beyond. I am particularly grateful to groups in the Universities of Warwick and Keele and training groups in the Dioceses of Hereford, Gloucester, Oxford, St Albans, Birmingham and Coventry. I am also grateful to the Lunar Society who invited me to give one of their lectures in May 2006.

Finally, thanks to Leslie Houlden, Mark Pryce, Alison Johnson and Colin Johnson for offering useful comments on the text.

Introduction

Over the past 20 years, much of the focus of my ministry has been health and human well-being. I have also been enriched by the privilege of pastoring: of struggling with and celebrating what faith means in the light of human experience. Pastoral care and practical theology in the light of age and ageing are the focus of this book. The writing emerges out of my work in the Foundation of Lady Katherine Leveson, an almshouse charity that offers care, housing and community to over 60 older people. I have lived and worked with the subject and, especially through the Leveson Centre, encouraged others to take a more positive view of the possibilities that ageing offers and what both Church and society can learn from valuing age.[1]

This book is written to help those involved in care, in a range of settings, to understand some of the pastoral questions and issues that older people face. In particular, it will attend to how the theories of age relate to our experience, and how experience might challenge and shape our theologies. It is this dynamic that all those who participate in care must attend to if we are to deepen our understanding of age and how best we might respond to it. As a young theological student, books in the SPCK Library of Pastoral Care gave me a broader sense of the range of information and knowledge needed to inform presence, engagement and response. Our shared commitment to this awareness of lifelong learning can help our ministry to be reflective and wise; it can broaden our imagination with sympathy.

I have particular concern with the nature of theology as a practical discipline. It is never quite good enough for ministry to be only concerned with human experience. For as Christians we must ask how, in our lives, from within the richness and diversity of experience, we might live and practise our faith. How does our faith enable us to grow old? What particular theological questions emerge as we consider the process of getting older? In what way and to what extent is the Christian tradition a resource for our third or fourth age; for our living and our dying? I hope that the theology in this book is practical without losing any of its challenges or contradictions. We need to keep on asking, 'What kind of God?' 'What does this mean for my faith?' 'How might I live more faithfully and hopefully?'[2]

One final theme completes this introduction. As well as offering the reader an overview of some of the themes and knowledge that undergird our understanding of ageing, together with a shared commitment to the liberating possibilities of theological reflection, both of these elements must be grounded in one thing: older people themselves. While I am writing, the older people I live alongside, the older people I have met and listened to, the older people I have read about, must never be very far away from the centre of my thinking. The text must be grounded in the experience of older people: their hopes and fears; their problems and possibilities.[3]

As well as providing a practical introduction to old age for those involved in pastoral ministry I hope this book will be of use to anyone who wishes to reflect on their own old age and even begin to plan for older age. In 2001 I visited Australia to see how New South Wales made provision for the care of older people especially in suburban retirement villages. I was impressed at the way Australian society had responded to the challenges of an ageing society and made appropriate provision. This was grounded in an economic response that enabled older people to achieve some independence and choice. There was a range of care and housing options, with a commitment to the development of quality and dignity for older people that one struggles to find in the UK. We have much to learn from the Australian context.[4]

Early in 2008, at a conference of managers who provide care and housing for older people in the West Midlands, I was surprised at how few of us had made provision for our old age. It seemed that most of us were in some kind of collective denial about the inevitability of old age and the necessity for us to make plans for it.

That seems an appropriate starting point for this book; a book that will help us think about the subject for ourselves, a narrative that is informed with what others have understood ageing to consist of, and that offers a theological coherence to pastoral care.[5]

This is not a textbook. Each chapter might warrant a book in itself. In each chapter I offer an overview of the subject area, sometimes with pointers for further reflection. I offer particular advice for those involved in pastoral care and reflection exercises for those who wish to work through what the chapter might mean for themselves or others from a theological perspective. I also offer some resource material in the Appendices. Each chapter is written to stand alone though the material is organized in such a way as to help the reader to digest the book quickly, thus providing the opportunity to turn back to areas of particular concern or interest.[6]

PART ONE

Understanding ageing

CHAPTER ONE

An ageing society?

LISTENING TO EXPERIENCE

I didn't much care for that – I didn't feel myself to be old and
I don't want to be reminded of my age . . .

(A 78-year-old Norfolk man to the author after listening to
a sermon on old age, October 2005)

It's not much fun getting older – just you wait.

(An 86-year-old resident of Temple Balsall to the author, July 2003)

Robert
Of course, old age brings its difficulties and challenges especially
with my body and its diminishments and also with the proximity
of death – I go to an increasing number of funerals these days . . .
but old age also brings its freedoms and fun. I have time free from
responsibilities to give and share with friends; time to listen and
think; time to read and ponder; time to write letters; time to give
something back to my community and family. I get less bothered
and anxious and gladder of the beautiful little things that make
up my life: meals shared; music; grandchildren; discovering new
ideas; laughter at my foolishness and anger that we human
beings can't always change the world for the better.

Elizabeth
In some respects I wish I had managed to prepare for old age. I
have never been good at managing change – 'middle age' hit me
and I hated not being young and attractive any more and suddenly I thought that I really was getting on! Retirement came
more quickly than I had anticipated and reconstructing my world

outside of the daily routine of work has been very traumatic indeed. Perhaps I have never been terribly good at dealing with my interior world of emotion but that's the way I was brought up and I have had to learn to cope as best I can. Looking back, I would have appreciated the opportunity to stand back and think how best to embrace my sixties and seventies. I especially wish I had made better financial provision for retirement – I worry how I shall be able to afford care if I ever need it. My own situation is an interesting combination of circumstance and chance. We 'doers' or 'activists' ought to be encouraged to be more reflective about old age and its opportunities.

Helen
I am now in my early eighties, though I am told that I do not look it and I certainly do not feel it! I am happy and active with a supportive and not overprotective family. My husband died ten years ago after a long illness and I was glad to be able to care for him at home. The small village community and church have been my salvation – I am blessed with an amazing mixture of friends and neighbours. I think my faith has helped carry me through life – it gives me a sense of meaning and purpose and wonder at the goodness of our world.

I have one thing I should like your readers to reflect on. I am sorry to sound like an oldie but I am now on my eleventh vicar and so you might say that I have seen some change in and around the church! My complaints (if that's what they are) follow:

I regret the lack of depth and intelligence in church life. I wish we could work harder at making sense of our experience and struggle more creatively with what faith is for us.

As an older person in my church I feel sometimes overlooked – and misunderstood. I don't feel that people make any effort to understand my pastoral and religious needs. I love the children and would like to help with Sunday school but there are other people in the congregation besides young families. From time to time I wonder whether the church is only interested in me when they want some money or support for the Christmas Fair! I wish my church could be more positive about us old ones.

Having aired those reflections I have to say that in some ways my age does give me a 'semi-detached' perspective which can't always be helpful. Vicars come and go; people drop in and out of church life; there are trends and fashions and the C of E is always having a row about something (it will ever be thus) – I let most of this wash over me because I want security, faithfulness, worship and discipleship without distraction and perhaps even much bother. Sometimes wisdom can emerge out of taking a longer view.

We are told that we live in an ageing society. By this analysis commentators mean that there are an increasing number of older people living in our society, combined with the fact that our average age expectancy has increased.

STATISTICS

Understanding statistics and their implications for us can be problematic! The demographics point to the reality that we live in an ageing society. Some facts are summarized in the box on page 6.

It is problematic to know what difference these statistics might mean for any one of us. We are unable to predict with any accuracy what shape old age will take for us or indeed how much old age we might experience before we die. When we age and how we manage the process of ageing may depend upon a range of factors, some beyond our control. Faced with the uncertainties and range of subjective judgements, it is understandable that many of us in our society do not wish to engage with age and ageing. Why anticipate challenges or difficulties before it is necessary? Perhaps our sympathies are with Elizabeth who has been too busy living her life to be overconcerned about ageing and her old age? The man outside that Norfolk church speaks for us when he resists any pressure to consider or give in to old age: 'I didn't much care for that – I didn't feel myself to be old and I don't want to be reminded of my age . . .' Many people simply choose to get on with living and pay little attention to their age, unless it presents challenges in the form of sickness or dependency.

There is another significant factor to challenge this distancing or even denial of the realities and inevitabilities of old age. Part of what it means to embrace human integration and flourishing is our preparedness to embrace and even confront our fears and anxieties. In a world that values the material and idealizes youth, we must consider the framework within which we construct our

An ageing population[1]

In the United Kingdom, in 2005, according to estimates based on the 2001 Census of Population, there were more than 11 million people of state pension age and over (11,244,000):

- 9,381,000 in England
- 975,000 in Scotland
- 609,000 in Wales
- 280,000 in Northern Ireland.

In 2005, the population of the United Kingdom, based on mid-year estimates, was 60,209,000. Of this figure, 18.7 per cent were over pensionable age:

- 7,100,000 were women aged 60 and over (of whom 5,505,000 were aged 65 and over
- 4,143,000 were men aged 65 and over
- 9,647,000 were people aged 65 and over
- 4,599,000 were people aged 75 and over
- 1,175,000 were people aged 85 and over.

A man of 60 could expect to live for another 20.5 years and a woman of the same age for 23.6 years, based on data for the years 2003–2005.

It is projected that by mid-2007, in the United Kingdom, 11,000 people would be aged 100 and over.

values and deal with those parts of our experience that cause us anxiety or fear. Elizabeth speaks for part of us when she expresses her desire to have lived her life in a slightly different way – that more time might have been given to the consideration of growing older and its widest implications. This is important for those involved in pastoral care because part of the pastoral task is to exercise imagination and compassion. It may be to ask: 'When I see an older person, what am I looking at? What is going on for this individual and their world?'

I remember reflecting on why the churches were so lacking in interest in older people with an Australian Roman Catholic nun who had worked for many years with people living with dementia. After reminding me that the Church so often reflected society and its prejudices Sister Margaret turned the generalization about the Church and its attitudes into a focused statement about the quality of pastoral care we exercise: 'What we must try and do is to befriend the elderly stranger within ourselves.' Unless we come to terms with the processes of ageing for ourselves, confront our fears and resistances, then we shall always marginalize older people, for they face us with realities we cannot or will not embrace. A necessary starting point for the consideration of ageing in society is the individual and our pastoral encounter with him and her. This will be the primary focus of this book, though this encounter will need to take into consideration some of the wider social, economic and cultural factors which impinge upon our ministry and mission for older people.

In much of the literature emerging out of the USA, social gerontologists struggle with the promotion of a new vision and practice of growing older.[2] At this point in the chapter I want to put this book's themes and practical support into this broader sociological understanding of the world we live in and the position of old age within it. There may be some readers of this book who want to explore what is unique or special about old age and in what different ways it might be possible to grow old. An older friend of mine asked very sharply, 'Does old age really matter?' At one level it seems that old age does *not* matter if one is fortunate enough to be able to enjoy good health, engagement and activity. Should we, however, explore the pastoral implications of our life journey as part of our growth and development? In doing so it would be helpful to know what are the universal characteristics, if any, of the ageing experience.

The statistics for the UK, quoted earlier in this chapter, seem to indicate that we are seeing the development of new kinds of societies, concentrated largely in the developed parts of the world, in which one fifth to one quarter of the population are retired, where fewer babies are born than are required to sustain the size of the population, and in which most people are living until they are over 80 years of age. From this perspective, put simply, there is a

strong case for saying that a dominant characteristic of the
modern condition in these societies is that of old age.

Upon what is our understanding to be based? How do we gain
knowledge about ourselves and our ageing? The cultural collective 'we' is shaped by dominant social and scientific understandings of old age. We are shaped by social, economic and political
institutions and we should bear in mind how these influences
shape the experience of old age. The challenge for those of us
preparing for old age is how far we can influence the future shape
and experience of the problems and possibilities contained within
the ageing process.

Old age becomes a meaningful concept in different ways and,
while individual ageing is universal, it has not hitherto coin-
cided with an ageing population. Ageing populations are a relatively new phenomenon in anthropological terms. For example,
in Europe, so far as we can tell, it is likely that from the time of
Roman civilization until relatively recent times, people were
lucky to live beyond their forties. Further, there were huge
troughs especially in times of invasion and epidemics. These
experiences fundamentally shaped the processes by which individuals and societies are said to age. On the one hand, there is
the experience that every individual who gets older has. Those
who reach old age have in common this individual experience of
getting old and being old, with its process of deterioration. On
the other hand, the ageing of societies is about population
change and reflects alterations in the relative size of age groups
in the population. We need, therefore, to be careful to differentiate between the experience of individuals ageing on the one
hand and the causes and social impact of such changing populations on the other. Some people have always aged, but an ageing
population, where the average age of the population is rising
steadily into middle age, is a new phenomenon. Growing old as
an individual in a young population and growing old in a population that already has a high proportion of older people clearly
result in different sorts of opportunities, problems, and kinds of
self-awareness.[3]

We should be careful not to confuse society with the individual.
Societies are not individuals and they do not have personalities
or personal attributes. They may have institutional practices and
common ways of behaving but a particular society does not carry

the characteristics of an older human being – in terms of attitudes, aspirations and capabilities. So it does not follow that societies with older populations should be denigrated as if they had the characteristics attributed to older people, such as being bound by tradition, unproductive and lacking innovative power.

One other reality needs to be borne in mind and it is that medical and biological conceptualizations of ageing have come to dominate our understanding of old age. From a Christian perspective, with its emphasis on the whole person and need to acknowledge the spiritual dimension of an individual, this dominance of a reductionist approach to care and support needs to be challenged.

Throughout this book we will come across ageism which we will see sometimes as prejudice or a set of attitudes, but also in terms of socially structured exclusion, institutionalized barriers for older people's full participation in society's benefits.

Put another way, we live in a society that confines and limits the possibilities of old age. How do and how can older people resist the pressure of some who wish to segregate old age, and thereby, according to some social commentators, subject it to deception, manipulation and control? Is it possible for old age to be a time of liberation as well as a time of constraint and decline?

We shall look at the question of retirement and how for some this period of life brings liberation. However, even in the liberation older people cannot escape the constraints of ageing. Some may go to enormous lengths to manipulate their bodies and resist the signs of ageing. However, some aspects of ageing bodies are open to mixed interpretation. Take, for example, the midlife end to female fertility. Although some construct this as decline and loss, for many women it has been experienced as liberation. Freedom from reproductive sex in many societies has enabled women to take on more senior or different roles. This has allowed some of the gender inequalities between men and women to be addressed. Some feminists have argued that women demonstrate the strength of their sex by ageing much more successfully than men. A closer conversation and mutual learning between the sexes is necessary for an enlarged and insightful appreciation of what the possibilities of ageing might be.

For many of my middle-aged friends, old age certainly looks to be attractive as a liberation from social constraints. The social obligations of middle age may be experienced as burdensome.

Thus in terms of the world of work, old age means the end of wage slavery, with retirement and the opportunities of a third and fourth age. However, for this to be a liberation there are some fundamental economic issues which have to be addressed if poverty is to be avoided. In terms of family life, we think of the empty-nest phase (note the negative imagery in this phrase). However, for some, no longer having dependent children offers the prospect of an expanded social life and greater affluence. Car stickers proclaiming 'Recycled teenager, spending the kids' inheritance' suggest at the least the potential for liberation in a post-child-rearing period of life.[4]

During my study trip to Australia in 2001 I was impressed by the attractiveness of retirement communities for many older people in the suburbs of Sydney as offering the prospect of new forms of social relationship. The baby-boomers, the age group who lived through the 1960s as teenagers, experience retirement as a time of social change and freedom. In the last part of the twentieth century, there was a much greater acceptance of the diversity of lifestyles, prompted by social movements such as civil rights, feminism, gay rights and the Green movement. It will be interesting to see whether the baby-boomer generation will also seek liberation from the cultural constraints of ageism. There are many fresh ideas for new forms of social relationships and new institutional arrangements in old age.

It may be that radicalism is a generational rather than an age phenomenon. We all know that people do not necessarily become more conservative as they grow older: the young are not automatically the radicals. Perhaps in the future, old age will be a time for rebellion and attempts, freed from previous constraints, to work together for change, while youth becomes a period of even greater conformity to its own groups' patterns of behaviour.

One of the challenges of writing this book is to appreciate the sheer diversity of the experience of old age. For some, old age *is* a matter of illness and decline and we need to accept and engage with the vulnerabilities of that situation. The movement known as the Third Age seeks to confront such assumptions by creating a positive image for old age as a period for personal development. The University of the Third Age has a significant effect in promoting a positive idea of old age as a stage in life which can be about growth and development.[5]

The construction of the concept of the third age uses the symbol of personal development available with increased leisure time. It stresses the possibility of an active lifestyle. While the emphasis on the retention of youthful characteristics and interests may revitalize the image of old age for younger retirees, it is simply not possible to retain for more than a few years this kind of independence and creativity for the vast majority of older people. Thus to retain the integrity of the idea of the third age, social gerontologists invented the notion of the 'fourth age', namely a period of life after pre-work, work and post-work that constitutes a final stage of dependency. Thus, despite many benefits, the third age formula does not overcome the problem of old age; it merely postpones it and puts a positive shine on its earlier phase. It also raises the unfortunate possibility of people being blamed for their failure to age properly and not to stay fit and have active lifestyles.

This has led us to see that the way people think about old age in Western society can be problematic. In particular, the medicalization of ageing and death has curtailed other possible routes to understanding old age. In the fourth age people often lose control of their bodies to the medical profession. In Western society to be truly old is predominantly to be seen as sick. Concentration on ill health in old age is not natural; it is not a wholly inevitable process, but it is a product of the way we organize our society, including how we organize and use knowledge. It may be that old people are stereotyped as ill and as a burden on the health services, because they are objects of other people's 'knowledge' and investigative interest – from medical research to television documentaries. It may also be possible that old people are stereotyped as unattractive because they sometimes like to hold on to property and power. An alternative might be an old age which is seen as an access route to the spiritual power of our ancestors, or as a source of knowledge about our common humanity. The older person as the wise person deserves more visibility and attention than our Western society sometimes gives it.

What shape old age might take in the future remains to be seen. There are particular social and economic challenges that are dealt with in Chapter 15 of this book. Certainly there is hope for a healthy, dignified and revalued old age lived in material comfort, within a sustainable environment. However, there is a view that when the population time bomb explodes there will be poverty, no pensions, social division and conflict, and ecological disaster. But there may also be resilience, transformation and fun in old age. Older people, as we shall see, should be seen as a repository of cultural wisdom and expertise, craft skills and local knowledge – things that are valuable to us all. However, it is important to avoid romantic stereotypes of old age, since older people can be repositories of prejudice and ancient animosities as well as the positive side of tradition.

The point has been made that old age is not something that can be avoided and so perhaps it is important to distinguish liberation *from* old age from the liberation *of* old age. The first is represented by the dream of eternal youth, while the second can be achieved through the construction of a meaningful third or even fourth age. Or, put another way, the first works with a picture of ageless identity, while the second represents freedom from the constraints of middle age. The first is an illusion, the second a distinct possibility.

So we may conclude that ageing is not just something that happens to people; it is also something that is done to them – and may, even can, be 'managed' by them. The alienation from old age which is felt by so many in our society may not be a reaction to biological processes, but rather a rejection of the social constraints imposed on older people and an alienation from the negative cultural perspective with which old age is so commonly understood. In fact, old age can be a valued time of life and we shall need to think about it in that way as deliberately as we can.

While not wishing to underestimate in this book about pastoral care with older people the range of challenges that they may present, I also want to offer a more positive and realistic view of age and its opportunities. Painful physical decline is not inevitable and creative adjustments can be made with appropriate help and support. While loss and change are often features of older people's lives, they can offer the possibility of depth and growth that can bring peace and fulfilment. The spiritual and religious dimensions of age are especially important and I want to show how our lives are enriched by older people. Older people like Helen have much to offer and to share with us if only we will listen to their experiences, their hopes, and their valuable insights and reflections on life. A wise society – or a spiritually mature church – might usefully describe itself as an intergenerational community where the distinctive contribution of older people is integrated and valued. While we might have some sympathy with the warning that old age 'is not much fun' (older resident to the author), that should never be the last or defining word for our understanding of what it can mean to grow older. This creative view of ageing will depend upon a more imaginative grasping of the positive opportunities of old age. It will also depend upon our attending to the inner, non-physical, essentially spiritual dimensions of the ageing process as well as the physical adjustments and changes that ageing presents to us as individuals and as a society.[7]

FOR FURTHER REFLECTION

Exercise 1

Defining age for ourselves

Fill in the gaps with reference to yourself

I feel ____ years old.

My ideal age is ____.

The age I would most like to be is ____.

I look ____ years old.

The age I would least like to be is ____.

My actual age is ____.

Exercise 2

Reflect on the place of older people in your local community and church.

Exercise 3

Consider yourself to be living within the last ten years of your life. What might your needs be?

Exercise 4

Take some time to listen to an older person. What strikes you as you listen to their experiences? What do you consider their pastoral needs to be? Does faith help in the process of ageing?

CHAPTER TWO

Theories of ageing

LISTENING TO EXPERIENCE

Mark

In one sense, although I am 84, I deny that I am old! I refuse to give in to the inevitable changes and diminishments that ageing brings. I totally agree with the philosophy that says we should use it or lose it. Determination, positive thinking and a full and busy week are part of my approach to old age. The secret, if that is the right way of looking at this subject, is inside: mind and soul over matter. I take regular exercise. I keep my mind active. I love company and have regular visits from friends to enjoy good conversation and my modest cooking. When my wife died, my children wanted me to move into a retirement community but I think it was for their benefit rather than mine! I'm not giving up my life or independence without a fight.

Joan

I live in a large council estate on the outskirts of Glasgow. I am old (88) and feeling very frail and lonely. My mobility is poor and I cannot get out of my flat without someone coming with me. I try not to feel sorry for myself but life is tough. I am a survivor – my husband died ten years ago and I have had to endure the death of my two children. Weak hearts seem to run in the family.

Money is tight. I have £140 a week which has to cover everything. I make it stretch but I have to be very careful. I have meals delivered to me but I miss cooking and sharing meals with other people. I don't believe in complaining – in many respects I have had a good life. I hope that I don't have to live on for a long time!

Harriet

Ageing is a strange business. I am now 78 and I don't know when it was that old age started. I retired at 60 after a lifetime in teaching. In some ways I was glad to retire – I didn't really like the way teaching was going – but I missed work terribly and still do. I regret not picking up some part-time work or study. The time and space and a good pension have given me lots of opportunity to travel, keep up good friendships and do my voluntary work with the National Trust. If you pressed me, it has been difficulties with my mobility (they started about three years ago) that have made me feel my age. I am stiff in the morning. I can't get in and out of the bath any more and have had to have a number of mobility aids installed in the house. I think other people treat me as old – I especially hate the way some people patronize me. I wish my vicar wouldn't call me 'dear' – she should know better!

Brian

I am a retired clergyman and I have had ten years of wonderful retirement. Travel, learning French, getting to know my grand-children, offering time to people who need support and advice have all been part of these years. However, despite my best efforts to keep my brain active I have experienced some significant decline in my intellectual functioning. My memory is very poor and some of my friends get impatient with my repeating myself! This is a worry and I am undergoing health tests to see if I have the early stages of dementia.

Edna

I am 86 and live in residential care. I cannot move and need help with almost everything. My severe arthritis has left my body in a very poor state. I even have to have help to eat my food and take drinks because of my twisted hands. I am surrounded by wonderful care here and the steady, patient and forbearing support of the care staff. By almost every definition I am not healthy, but I don't see things that way. I feel very alive and fortunate. I have had an amazing life that has been full of opportunity and activity. I believe my own life to be healthy despite the definitions! I enjoy listening to people and taking an interest in the ups and downs of their lives. I spend some time praying for others and help run a prayer group here. I listen to the birds and keep an eye out for the changing seasons. We live in a beautiful world and we should cherish and delight in this wonder with awe and joy. While my body seems to deteriorate, I feel more alive; healthier inside. Some of this is related to my spirit but a good deal of it relates to living in this special place alongside people who care with love and attention.

This chapter seeks, as necessary background information to pastoral practice, to offer an overview of some of the theories that undergird the processes of ageing. Ageing is a universal process and in humans a perfectly natural one that follows a particular pattern. While the pattern may be common, the way in which this pattern expresses itself is peculiar to each individual.

It has already been indicated that culture shapes ageing and it follows that our own views will be determined by how we see the shape of ageing. Inevitably some of these views may be implicit – others more informed or explicit. From a faith perspective we have affirmed an approach to all people as whole persons but this chapter concentrates on physiological and physical circumstances. One of the tasks of this book is to ensure that we can see how the various dimensions of ageing shape the lived experience. For example, there is a significant economic element in our picture: anxiety about continuing welfare makes it impossible for a person to maintain any sense of self-worth and to develop personally and spiritually.

How old is old? Whatever age we choose is bound to be artificial and we will always think of others and even ourselves as exceptions. Gerontologists agree on the age of 60 to 65 as marking the threshold age for ageing because during this range the physical changes associated with age are taking place. Others argue that this range is increasing, with substantial numbers of the population being able to access better health at an older age. But common experience seems to suggest that at least there is no plain correlation between chronological age and how old a given person actually feels at a particular time. In other words, it is a subjective matter, no doubt shaped by the particular circumstances of health and general well-being. The danger that all who accompany older people fall into is to assume that decline in one area of a person's life is necessarily matched by a decline in other areas. The voices of Harriet and Edna (pp. 16–17) remind us of the unique individuality of each older person and how easily our pastoral behaviour can disempower them. Our pastoral attentiveness certainly needs to respect the diversity of experience. We have much to learn from the stories of older people.[1]

THEORIES OF AGEING

There is no single theory or account for ageing and no one is quite sure, with precision, what factors contribute to successful ageing. There is certainly a genetic element: our genes set the limits to our longevity by determining the number of times cells can successfully replicate themselves. The ageing process involves 'errors' in the process of cell replication, building up to a point where the system or a particular organ can become dysfunctional. This process, complicated as it is to conceptualize, is called the somatic mutation theory.[2]

Another explanation suggests that the body begins to attack itself, directing its defences against its own cells rather than against infections. This is called the autoimmune theory. Linked with this explanation is a further suggestion that over time the body's system becomes clogged with 'cellular' waste which cannot be cleared. This then results in a breakdown or illness.

The programme Senescence maintains that the body has a genetically inbuilt propensity to decay after its reproductive phase is completed. A popular version of this approach suggests that older members of a species need to die off to make room for the younger, breeding members.

There is a genetic basis for each of these explanations and some scientists believe that the genes responsible for the breakdown in the ageing process will be discovered, which might enable us to control ageing. The dream of very long life may be attractive to some but, as will be demonstrated, there are other significant factors which influence the shape of ageing and these may seem to be less desirable.

MODELS OF AGEING

When most of us think about ageing we see loss, change, decline and eventual death. This is, of course, the model of ageing which predominates in society. So the life cycle goes something like this:

we become fully functioning towards the end of our second decade and continue on an even course for the next 30 years or so.

We then begin a decline which is gradual but may become accelerated somewhere in our sixties and ends in an old age where we have to cope with a number of challenges to our health and status, and general loss of capacity. From this perspective it is not surprising that age should be resisted or even denied – something we put off thinking about or planning for until we absolutely have to. If this is the picture of ageing that we hold, pastoral care will be about support and consolation rather than seeking to encourage change or further development.

However, in recent years a different model has been developed which contrasts markedly with the established one. While it acknowledges age as bringing decline and loss, it argues that this decline is not as steep as might be thought and that a number of measures can be taken to minimize, delay or even reverse it. From this perspective the inevitable losses can be more than compensated for by advantageous gains. Seen thus, ageing is a process of change rather than only or necessarily a process of loss.[3]

For some older people, age brings a liberation. Work and family can be constraining and retirement and age can offer an opportunity to redefine ourselves with all of the resources that experience, wisdom and age can bring. There may be an increased ability to tolerate diversity and ambiguity, which can lead to a relaxation of defences with an enhanced appetite for living in the present moment and doing all kinds of new things. Take a look at any of the colour supplements to the weekend newspapers or an established magazine, such as that produced by the National Trust. The advertisers target this group of people offering them a range of leisure, recreation and holiday opportunities denied to those in work.

Ability to respond to this new freedom will depend in part upon a person's economic status. But, from the perspective of pastoral care, within the model there are all kinds of opportunities to promote spiritual and personal development. This model is often described as the compensatory model. Not surprisingly, it is a model which most gerontologists prefer.

ASPECTS OF THE AGEING PROCESS

The basic features of the ageing process may be summed up in the following way:

- *Slowing down* Apart from sometimes obvious changes in appearance, the sense of slowing down at a physical level (that is, simply not moving as fast) and at a psychological level (our reflection time increases) is probably the first indication of feeling older.
- *Loss of flexibility* Older people notice this chiefly in their joints but also as it impacts on their ability to modify approaches to a problem or adapt to unexpected changes in their lives.
- *Reduction in spare capacity* This reduction is demonstrated in a number of ways, particularly a slower recovery from either exertion or illness. Older people comment on their reduced capacity for doing more than one thing at a time! Put another way, older people get more tired.
- *Impaired capacity to replace losses* Viewed from one perspective, the life cycle is a process of change and loss and we are required in a number of ways from infancy onwards to replace losses of all kinds of things, for example, abilities, relationships, jobs, homes, status, possessions. Some individuals show a tremendously flexible capacity to cope with these losses and changes, but we see that the capacity to engage with them tends to decline as we age. This does not mean that older people cannot change but that the ageing process makes it more difficult for them to do so.

We should note that none of the above features are pathological or disease processes – they are all consequences of a normal ageing. We should expect to experience them ourselves and in some ways be ready to anticipate them. Some of the afflictions associated with ageing, for example, arthritis, may exaggerate some of these features, but they are distinct from them. So the pastor must not confuse ageing with disease.

MYTHS ABOUT AGEING

Maggie Kuhn (the founder of the Gray Panther Movement in the USA) suggests that our thinking about ageing is bedevilled by myths that are based on misunderstanding or distortion. These myths might be summarized in the following way: old age is a disease that no one admits to having; old age is mindless; old age is sexless; old age seeks to disengage from society; old age is a personal and social disaster. Issues relating to learning and sexuality will be dealt with later in the book, so we concentrate here on some of the other features which Kuhn has highlighted.

INTELLECTUAL FUNCTIONING

A feature that I have observed among pastors who work alongside older people is our tendency sometimes to exaggerate the effects that ageing may have on their intellectual powers: intelligence, memory, ability to learn and reason. We have noted that ageing has some bearing on all these functions and it varies from person to person, but is normally much less than is commonly imagined. An older person's ability to live creatively is as much influenced by low expectations of others and self; a lack of stimulation, opportunity and challenge; or poverty, with the effects that it can have on diet and living conditions; and other external and artificial constraints.

When psychologists measure intelligence they find that performance across the age range improves to a certain point (probably at the age of 30), holds steady for a couple of decades, and then begins to decline. It is not surprising, therefore, that there is a long-held belief that we lose our wits as we grow older. These results were challenged by a different method of investigation which clearly demonstrates that while there is some decline, it has been greatly exaggerated by many.

The most significant finding of this latter work is that of the plasticity of intellectual abilities. Encouragement, opportunity, environment, support: these all improve our intellectual performance, just as we have seen that our functioning can be inhibited by a very wide variety of factors.

A later chapter will deal with the question of sexuality, but one of the dangers of pastoral care alongside older people is to forget that as living growing human beings, emotion still plays an important part in their life. Some older people, liberated from constraints, become less inhibited and express their emotions and opinions very freely. Others, sometimes as a result of depression or loss of confidence, may become more reticent. They may be unfortunate in living in contexts where there is little opportunity to express emotion. Do we allow older people to express frustration and even anger? What opportunities for self-expression do older people need in order to continue to bring out their unique experience of life? If negative or potentially frightening emotions are suppressed, then an older person can feel very isolated.

A number of theories have been promoted about ageing and one of them, popular in the 1950s and 1960s, was the disengagement theory of ageing. This suggested that as people aged and retired (often at an accepted and fixed time), they withdrew from responsibility and involvement with public affairs and retreated (literally) into a quiet life. This theory of disengagement does not attract widespread acceptance, though elements of it still pervade our culture. Among a younger generation, in the heat of a demanding work role, there can often be a longing for retirement as a giving-up of responsibility in order to enjoy the 'luxury' of endless quantities of time to do all those things that one might have been putting off! One of the reasons why retirement homes are less popular with some is that they seem to disengage older people from the community and from active presence and relationships.

Some people, as they age, take on more commitments and responsibilities – retirement offers an opportunity of re-engagement rather than disengagement. Knowing when and why to give up is a very difficult decision for older people to make, but we should be clear at this stage that removing challenges, opportunities and risks from people's lives may be debilitating for them. There is a danger of boredom, a feeling of uselessness and lack of meaning which can result in despair. We should try to allow older people to face challenges, even undertake new adventures, as part of our commitment to their creative growth.

Some writers have referred to the concept of the *mirage* of health when considering older people.[4] In other words, it is a mystery why older people consistently rate their health as good when other evidence suggests that the health of older people is not so good. The fact is that one's experience of well-being is subjective and if society holds a range of perspectives and opinions about the nature of age, people certainly embrace a wide variety of understandings of what it might mean to be healthy. As we have seen with theories of ageing, people draw on a mixture of official and 'folk' accounts to weave their own explanation of what health means. There are different ways of seeing the matter which affect ways of knowing and consequently shape how health might be measured.

Undergirding this book is a belief in the coherence of what has been described as the biographical explanation of health. This account explains a person's health in terms of their biography or as the product of their life story and it has very clear methodological implications for understanding the health and the health needs of older people.

The biographical explanation is concerned with the whole person and is part of a holistic account of health which emphasizes the person as a unique individual. The older person is not seen as a collection of bodily ills, but as a thinking, feeling, creative being who has strengths and weaknesses of body, mind and spirit. It is possible to be healthy in mind and spirit even though the body may be frail.

Holism is often linked with equilibrium or a state in which bodies, minds and spirits are in harmony. Critics of the holistic account of health argue that it ignores the impact on the individual of the wider physical and social environment, but it is a useful framework within which pastoral care might operate.

Measuring health, fascinating though it may be, is not an end in itself, nor is it a purely academic exercise. It has its uses. It is important to be aware of the ways in which health is evaluated and, in pastoral care, to place the pastoral conversation in the context of a wider framework of factors.

It may be helpful to take an overview of some of the particular challenges that face older people. These activities of daily living (ADL) form part of the attempts to assess a person's functioning and resources they may have to enable them to maximize their independence.[5]

Understanding an older person's needs in context

Activities of daily living
- Physical activities of ADL, i.e. maintaining basic self-care.
- Mobility.
- Instrumental activities of ADL, i.e. being a functioning member of society and coping with domestic tasks.

Mental health functioning
- Cognitive.
- Presence of psychiatric symptoms.

Psychosocial functioning
- Emotional well-being in a social and cultural context.

Physical health functioning
- Self-perceived health status.
- Physical symptoms and diagnosed conditions.
- Health service utilization.
- Activity levels and measures of incapacity.

Social resource
- Accessibility of family, friends and, where needed, a familiar professional, voluntary helper.
- Availability of these resources where needed.

Economic resources
- Income as compared to an external standard.

Environmental resources
- Adequate and affordable housing.
- Siting of housing in relation to transport, shopping and public services.

Source: Standardized Assessment Scale for Elderly People, Royal College of Physicians and British Geriatrics Society (1992)

WHAT IS THE MEANING OF HEALTH FOR OLDER PEOPLE?

We must now turn once again to some of the ways that older people understand what constitutes health. There has been some significant research into lay accounts of health in Britain and the following represents a full range of concepts of health used by respondents and representing diverse views:

- Health is not being ill.
- Health is absence of disease or well-being despite disease.
- Health is a reserve (strength).
- Health as behaviour, health as 'the healthy life'.
- Health as physical fitness.
- Health as energy, vitality.
- Health as social relationships (relating well to others).
- Health as the ability to function.
- Health as psychosocial well-being.

There is some indication that both men and women engage in a number of activities in order to keep healthy. Men engage in more active pursuits such as gardening, sports, leisure and walking, although walking is also a major pursuit of women. In surveys, doing housework was mentioned more by women, and so was a healthy diet. Within each category, for both men and women, numbers engaging in such activity diminish with age.

Health as energy or vitality was a category used by many older people, like one 74-year-old man who described it in terms of tackling jobs: 'You feel ready to get on with anything that needs doing. You feel that you can tackle any physical work.' For older women health was interpreted as being able to do one's house-work.

Maintaining social relationships and having enough energy to help others were also important to older people. A 79-year-old woman, disabled with arthritis, said, 'To be well in health means I feel I can do others a good turn if they need help', and another 74-year-old woman said, 'You feel as though everyone is your friend, I enjoy life more, and can work and help other people.' The research shows that many older people associated health with happiness and this has important spiritual implications for the pastor. One 74-year-old farmer's widow described health in very enthusiastic terms: 'I've reached the stage now where I say isn't it lovely and good to be alive, seeing all the lovely leaves on the trees. It is wonderful to be alive and be able to stand and stare!'[6]

Clearly physical explanations were linked to functional ones with good health described as: 'when you can get about and get your own shopping and not depend upon people to run and get your errands and run and do this and that and you have to plead with somebody to do something for you'. Yet another woman described her health in terms of moods: for her it was an emotional state: 'Sometimes you'd think I am so cheerful, 'cos I'll have a mood and I'll start singing for no reason. I just happen to be.'

So it emerges that there are three major ways of viewing health for older people:

1   Being free from illness or disease.
2   Having a source of strength to resist illness.
3   Having the capacity to function in everyday life.

Other elements of research indicate the immense resilience with which older people cope with illness or the threat of it. While illness is acknowledged as a threat to normal living and often a continuous struggle, many older people spoke of the necessity to endure and to bear it positively with a sense of stoicism. The moral aspect of older people's attitudes to health and illness is a common theme. A study in rural Wales of both working- and middle-class older people found that 'good health is associated with the right attitudes and moral fibre and complaining or talking about health is seen as self-indulgent'.[7] That older people have a tendency to minimize health problems is also found in their response to ageist attitudes. Older people deny or play down their physical ailments in order not to fulfil negative images and be labelled in stereotypical ways. For many people (and this is a critical point) 'old' was not a chronological term but was actually synonymous with ill health. To have ill health is to be old; therefore to be in good health is not to be old, even if one is 70, 80 or even 90. Old age represented failing strength and lowered resistance to disease. 'The blood is thin', 'the body runs down', and loss of energy and spirits: these were the images associated with 'old'. The belief that age brought illness was sufficiently entrenched to make it possible, eventually, to make illness the grounds for seeing oneself as 'really' old.[8]

In a further piece of research, in a book called *I Don't Feel Old,* respondents do not believe that actual age determined if someone was old.[9] Being old was to do with their physical condition – they had internalized the cultural stereotype that old is synonymous with decline and ill health. Common descriptions of old were:

- When people are incapable of doing what they used to.
- It's not what you look like. There's nothing nicer than an elderly lady with white hair. It's senility, when you lose control of your faculties.
- No age when people get old. It's to do with health.
- When one becomes unwell.
- Depends on health and physical ability.
- Well, I think old means when you are incapable of doing what you used to do. I think of this one as old because she is a bit helpless at times, but there's another lady more or less as old, but she's capable, so I don't think of her as old.

To deny ill health is to deny the negative stereotype of old age. It follows then that older people are under great pressure to cope stoically with ill health and not to complain. They are also under great pressure not to make too many demands either on the health services or on others and thereby become a burden to society. Maintained within this brief overview of older people's voices and perspectives on illness are contained some ageist attitudes within society but also within older people too.[10]

FOR FURTHER REFLECTION

- Make a note of the physical activities that you have been engaged in today. This includes washing, dressing, eating, walking and sitting, hearing, seeing, and talking.

- Which of these activities were the most important to you and why?

- If you could engage in these activities to a limited extent, and needed special support or equipment, what things would be difficult for you to do?

- Think about the plans that you have for the rest of the day, or tomorrow. What would be impossible, difficult, or just as straightforward if you had limited mental or physical abilities?

CHAPTER THREE

Images of old age

LISTENING TO EXPERIENCE

Ethel and her library

I had the opportunity recently to view Ethel's library. The books were to be sold as she moved to different accommodation which had less space. Now in her mid-nineties she was embracing a diminishment of ageing and memory with quiet strength and letting go of her books. It was a wonderful collection of volumes, each inscribed with a date and a place. Often the books had been presents from the husband and wife to each other. The breadth and range of interest gave rise to a deep sense of richness and wisdom of the life of an individual lived to the full – some of this fullness hidden by age. The volumes, carefully looked after, revealed an interest in poetry from across the centuries, anthropology from a global range of cultures, a splendid variety of novels and short stories, books on art, cookery and history. There were travel guides reflecting many miles of journeys across Britain and abroad. Knowledge and spiritual wisdom aren't always obvious or immediate in older people, but if we look more carefully we can uncover their existence in abundance.

Bloom – an exhibition of flowers

A Welsh photographer, Steven Hopkin-Jones, represents, in a group of very vivid, colourful and rich photographs, a number of dying flowers. On immediate viewing, they revealed very little but, as so often happens with art, the more attention these images were given the wider the variety of thoughts and reflections that emerged. The floral portraits displayed a power to confound and change expectation but, in the end, presented images of beauty hidden within ruin and change. These photographs of domestic blooms took on an unrecognizable form in death. In death, tulips twist around themselves. Similar in life, they now each take on a unique identity, abstract forms full of mystery and colour emerging as they wither.

I was reminded of what most people do when flowers are brought into the home. Once they have lost their bloom they are discarded. They are no longer any use to us. It was at this moment that the photographer found these blooms at their most appealing. It is as if the pictures challenge us to see that these flowers still have character, perhaps even more character! They are almost striving to remain beautiful. How can we unlock our appreciation of the character that lies within older people?

In this chapter, I want to open up a kind of conversation within which we might imagine ourselves as artists – those charged with representing or painting age. This pastoral and practical book will seek to enable us to explore what age means in terms of knowledge, experience, wisdom, or indeed prejudice, fear or sheer unpreparedness to have our presuppositions broken and reshaped. I am reminded of a comment by one of my best theological teachers who used to say (and he was in his fourth decade of teaching Christian doctrine) – 'The truth is out there somewhere, and I am not completely sure where.' The reason that this is so helpful is that it expresses a humility and a preparedness to open ourselves up to new possibilities of truth, especially when that means turning around and looking at something differently.

It is puzzling to hear people discussing normal ageing or the natural ageing processes. We are all biological creatures, but does age hold much meaning beyond the cultural gloss we paint it with? And if it does, has not science enabled us to manipulate our destinies? This is important in terms of images and beliefs that have circulated about the ageing process. Clearly increasing age cannot reduce the biological changes of decline but, although these affect us all, they occur within a social framework which superimposes a series of cultural codes, symbols and expectations that vary with the chronological time of the individual's life course, historical period, and particular societal settings. Is it more normal, therefore, to grow naturally or, conversely, to resist the process and attempt to defy the shape our ageing may take?[1]

This conversation is important because we ourselves need to work out what it might mean to age successfully (as the gerontologists put it) – or to age well, a concept which is perhaps preferable.[2]

You might at this point think about a particular image of an older person. It might be an image taken from art (Rembrandt's work of painting older people, including himself, is an obvious example) or an image captured in an advertisement or magazine. When we look at an image of an older person, what do we see? In the box is an exercise that you might want to engage with.

Learning to paint (figuratively)

- List the feelings you most associate with age.

- List the adjectives that you most associate with age.

- Paint a picture of an older person – describe them and their life.

- Can you paint a picture of yourself in old age?

There is much to see in, for example, Rembrandt's art. In the details of the face and the eyes, Rembrandt manages to capture an older person's loneliness and doubt, together with a presence and tranquillity at this particular point of their living. There is an energy between the restlessness and the absence; reflectiveness and wisdom; pain and death. These are not easy images to stay with. At one level the artist is spent and unable to struggle any more. At another there is both stillness and searching: it is not easy to know whether the artist is looking backwards or forwards. Rembrandt was capable of drawing age in its fragility, dependency and closeness to death.[3]

What is extraordinarily skilled about Rembrandt and other artists is that they are in touch with their emotional and spiritual worlds. Perhaps one of the reasons that age and old age is something that we tend to deny in our Western culture is that it is something that we most fear. It follows then that what we most fear can have power over us and shape the way in which we think about, respond to, conceptualize and paint age.

There is a powerful tradition within the artistic world that the best work of artists is often done at the end of their lives. This was certainly true of Jacob Epstein who believed that his best sculptures were created during the last two years of his life.[4] It was in old age that Monet was at his prime as an artist. Pissarro, again, was at the height of his creative powers towards the end of his life. Matisse, Titian and Turner all give us pictures which are characterized by a triumph over matter, whether the stuff of paint or the palpability of people and things, that shows us that the work of their last years represents the final development of their talent.

Let us see if we can develop these thoughts by offering some general sociological theory relating to the process by which we have come to have some knowledge about ageing and our attitudes to it. I remember going to talk about the work of Temple Balsall to a local Women's Institute group. It was a cold winter's evening and a large group of over 50 people asked me to sit quietly while they conducted their business – which meant I didn't get started on my talk until just before 9.00 p.m.! As I proceeded with the talk, the room got warmer and a significant number of the group took refuge in sleep. However, the first question was from a perceptive woman: 'I don't really understand why anybody would want to work with older people unless they had to – why do you do this type of work?' The comment was even more remarkable because I guessed that the woman was at least 70.

We've already seen in this chapter that it is important to unpick the presuppositions that undergird our attitudes to age. I am not old. I am not long into midlife and, while I wish for many more years, I do not wish to grow old if that involves a major constriction of opportunity. I am aware, therefore, that some of my thinking arises from contradictions. Why is it that this baby-boomer, born in the middle of the twentieth century, a potential pensioner, wishes to remain for ever young or, at least, non-aged, and what may be the implications of this thinking, assuming that I am typical of my generation?

So, one of the things that pastoral care needs to nurture is humility. However hard we might try, it is not easy to enter into the world of those who are older. And while we may be content to live with some of the gaps in our understanding, it has profound implications for the way our (or my) generation begins to plan for the economic, social and spiritual provision for older people.

In much of the work of the Leveson Centre, especially with the churches, I have become a keen advocate for seeking to change the prevalent culture which marginalizes and disempowers older people. Though it's easy and generally splendidly provocative to say to groups of clergy (especially when a senior cleric is present), 'We should sack all youth workers and start to employ older people's workers', this provocation generally does no good and it certainly does not shift the prevailing culture in which we work. On the whole, in the painting of age, churches prefer to put at the centre of the picture children and young people, believing they are the future of the Church. This lamentable approach is not confined to the churches. Dealings with social services often reveal a functional approach to older people which refuses to anticipate problems and plan accordingly, but rather prefers to respond to a problem after it has arisen. Financial constraints are inevitable, though the dominant values have a powerful shaping influence over the ways in which we do, or do not, prioritize older people and their needs within the health and social care economy.

In this respect the work of Berger and Luckmann is helpful.[5] It helps us to understand the unexamined taken-for-grantedness of ageing which is deeply embedded in our culture. We should be aware that each individual is born and socialized into a ready-made cultural environment and that environment will to a large degree condition the way we perceive things. This book reminds us that world views, including our view of age, are thus partially inherited but generationally distinct at the same time. This seems to me a crucial point if we are to understand how people make sense of their ageing and how they act on the basis of these interpretations.

While perceptions and evaluations of age are socially created the ageing process is itself ultimately a biological one. Like every organism, the body goes into a state of irreversible decline following maturity. What is contentious is how the social frame impinges upon this fact. In other words, maturity itself is a term

capable of many and varied definitions – and social 'flavours' –
and the biological is but one of these.

So all of us must manage transitions within a specific culture
and there are particular challenges associated with certain stages.
Erikson has asked us to think about life as a map with stages.[6] He
argues that a series of appropriate tasks have to be fulfilled before
moving on to the next stage or phase. So an interesting further
area of thought is about what the task of old age might be. Erikson
argues that the task of old age is what he calls 'the late goal of ego'
– 'integrity', that is, an assured sense of meaning and order in one's
life and the universe.

As we have seen, other writers refer to the third and fourth ages
and while these terms might be helpful, it is hard to describe them
without being aware of some of the difficulties of slotting people
and their diverse experiences into such sharp categories. The pictures – and the people we know – may not easily conform to the
formal categories. In this respect we must resist the constant tendency to oversimplify and be careful about our speech, aware of the
way we may fall into language that promotes ageism.[7]

Why does it appear that it is still acceptable to make fun of
people on account of their age, describing them as wrinklies, crum-
blies, or oldies whereas it would have been totally out of order to go
on about their gender, race, sexual orientation or disability? In the
public perception fuelled by the media, older people are seen as
insignificant because they are not regarded as prime consumers or
producers. There is a bleak public image of ageing. Many appear to
think that all older people are sick, confused, useless, complaining,
unintelligent and incompetent. They fail to notice what the older
generation can offer to society as a whole. Where, for example,
would many working parents be without the vast contribution that
grandparents make to childcare?

Sadly this ageist attitude is rife in the Church as well. We apol-
ogize for our ageing congregations, we put endless money into
youth and children's work, but almost never into work with older
people. Most dioceses have youth and children's workers and very
few workers with older people. Consider the timing of services. In
many churches, the only traditional 1662-style services take
place at 8 a.m. or in the evening after dark while the prime mid-
morning slot is reserved for so-called all-age worship or other
modern guitar-led celebrations. All this means that older people

get the message that they are only tolerated rather than respected for their contribution.[8]

How this ageist attitude contrasts with the biblical view of old age where older people are seen as wise, as elders and as people to be honoured rather than ridiculed. It was Simeon and Anna, both mature in years, who first recognized the significance of Jesus in the temple. Consider the roles of Nicodemus, Joseph of Arimathea or Gamaliel in the New Testament narrative. And what of the fifth commandment?

The task we face is to identify the underlying assumptions that keep older people in the churches marginalized and challenge the shortage of positive pictures of ageing as opposed to ageist stereotypes. Where would the Church be without the contribution of its members over 60? How many church posts, for example as church warden, youth leader or treasurer, are held by older people? How many of the pastoral visitors and informal carers of both the young and old are themselves over retirement age?

Far from being a drain, a joke or a burden, older people have so much to contribute to society and to the Church and they do not deserve to be the butt of ageist jokes. Older people have been released from the pressure to justify themselves or to be successful in the working world. They are often more secure in who they are, less defensive and have an ability to live in the present. They can have a crucial role in pointing younger people to ways in which they might make better sense of their lives. They can contribute time, prayer, wisdom, experience and competence. They are more tolerant of contradictions and paradoxes and less concerned about finding the right answer to questions.[9]

The really strange thing about ageist attitudes and poking fun at older people is that whereas the other categories of people who benefit from anti-discrimination legislation make up no more than half the population in any one case, we shall all be old (unless we die an untimely death). If we are careless in our younger days about how older people are regarded or treated we shall surely reap the harvest of our own prejudices one day.

To talk of 'the elderly' is to create a category of people definable by their elderliness alone: 'They can possess no existence independent of their elderliness, and are thus considered not fully human.'[10] According to such a position, 'elderly' is acceptable when used as an adjective, but less so when used as a noun. We need to look further at the use of 'independence' and 'dependence' and the notions associated with these concepts. Do we not all belong in both categories all through our lives?

We have already noted the diversity of representations of older age. Here are some of the things that we might discover from popular representations of age. The first is that we undoubtedly live in a world or a culture that is obsessed with youthfulness. Indeed, when older people are represented they are often shown as eternally young: Joan Collins is often portrayed as a 'young old person'. Perhaps one of the results of this is that old age suffers from a greater distancing, stigmatization and denial. This positive ageing discourse effectively eclipses consideration of illness and decline, and then, in total contrast to Rembrandt's portrayals, final decay and death take on a heightened hideousness. By contrast, there is a haunting picture of Marlene Dietrich in a wheelchair looking like a little old lady in constant pain. There is another image of Rita Hayworth who suffered long and hard from Alzheimer's disease, with her face revealing its ravages in mind and spirit.[11]

We are offered some very idealized views of retirement, where 'whoopees' (well-off older persons) and 'glams' (grey, leisured and money) shape the picture. We will see in Chapters 13 and 15 that from an economic perspective such a retirement is only likely to be achieved by the few who are wealthy. This is sobering news for a generation that may be denied final salary pension schemes. The question here for pastoral care is whether we can or should refashion identity in later life.

We have sought, therefore, in this chapter, to put our pastoral care into a broader context. I have argued that we need to shift some of our cultural perceptions by rescuing age and older people from their marginal and sometimes invisible position. This will only be done if we ourselves are prepared to engage with some of our fears and see that this area of thinking and representation is significantly nuanced, open to paradox and contradiction. It will simply not do to try and fend off old age as an act of defiance against our inevitable change in identity. If sex was the taboo subject of the nineteenth century, and death that of the twentieth, perhaps old age will be the great prohibition of the twenty-first century? It is time to celebrate; in this book we listen to the stories of older people and capture and learn from their spirit.

FOR FURTHER REFLECTION

Exercise 1

Think about an older person whom you really admire – what terms would you use to describe this person?

Contrast the following words:

> freedom, generativity, possibility, desire, urgency,
> hope and relationship

with

> finished, bored, smelly, withered, useless, blank,
> passive and drab.

What words do we most readily use in relation to older people?

Exercise 2

What adjectives would you use to describe your current age group? What adjectives would you like to apply to yourself in old age? How do you express your freedom? How do you share your wisdom?

Exercise 3

Imagine yourself on your sixtieth birthday. How did you or how do you feel about this birthday? How would you describe your hopes and fears, your attitude at 60? (Those of you maturing nicely, please adjust the age!)

Exercise 4

Is there an art to growing old?

Exercise 5

Where do we learn about growing older? Whom do we learn from? Who are our role models?

CHAPTER FOUR

Health and well-being in age

LISTENING TO EXPERIENCE

Malcolm

I am 82 now and keep reasonable health. I feel fortunate to have a good constitution and enjoy the outdoors. I was a manual worker with the local council for most of my working life and I am not afraid of hard work. I don't think that I should have lived quite as long as I have. I have not led a healthy lifestyle. I have been a steady drinker and heavy smoker all my life. By today's standards I have eaten all the wrong sorts of food. I find food particularly tasty if it is fried! I believe that health is a matter of chance and luck. What will be will be – that is my philosophy.

Elizabeth

I have reflected on Malcolm's thoughts (above) and I find myself in disagreement with his fatalism. Our health is directly related to our choices and our lifestyle. I have taken great care with my diet – in my twenties I decided to become a vegetarian and I enjoy a regular pattern of exercise. My yoga helps me to be in touch with my body and its rhythm. I never drink alcohol or caffeine.

Colin

My wife died years ago and my health hasn't really been the same since that time. I just don't feel myself – part of the reason for life has gone and I will never get over it. I think sometimes people just imagine that I should get over it and that I should be able to get over my loss. It's very lonely being surrounded by people who don't want to understand one's pain. I don't sleep well and while I eat I have never enjoyed good cooking since my wife died. Sometimes I feel real despair and long for the time for me to join her.

Max

I live in a suburb of Birmingham in a house that has been my home for 70 years. The city and its community has changed beyond recognition and, for my wife and myself, much for the worse. I don't feel at home here anymore. There is no sense of security or community. My car keeps getting vandalized and since we have been burgled seven times we are very apprehensive of leaving the house. The neighbours are unfriendly – we don't really have anything in common – many of them don't even speak English. We don't feel we belong. Since the buses changed, getting out and about is much harder. The corner shop closed three years ago and we get our food from the supermarket about four miles away. I hate complaining like this but we feel alone and afraid living here.

We have already acknowledged some of the complex subjectivities that surround age. Age is personal and related to a range of beliefs, values and life experiences. Chapter 2 offered some theoretical information about aspects of the ageing process and its relationship to the concept of health. The meaning of health for older people is diverse.

In this chapter we shall build upon these theories and experiences to open up the concept of well-being in age and explain how it is multidimensional. This contextualization of health and well-being is an important part of understanding older persons and their pastoral needs in a broader perspective.

The reader is familiar with two statistics relating to old age: that we are all living longer and that women tend to live longer than men. In the consideration of these two statistical facts we need to explore a little further what makes for health and wellness in old age. How are we to understand what makes for a healthy old age and is it possible that we may come to understand more why it is that women seem to be healthier in old age than men?[1]

The major causes of mortality for those who are 65 years and over remain broadly similar across the range of groups that live in society today (heart disease, stroke, malignant diseases and respiratory diseases) – though there are distinct ethnic variations. A good deal of the Health Service's innovation has been directed towards health promotion and disease prevention. An obvious example of this is the successful attempt to prevent smoking which has led some health experts to conclude that mortality in later life will probably continue to fall, as efforts to prevent premature deaths throughout the lifespan continue. We shall also see later in this chapter that health and well-being need to be put into the broadest of perspectives. For instance, those older people who are better off in society (in terms of income, geography and housing) have better health chances than other 'classes' of the population. The medical profession is to be commended for its attempts to work with others in understanding particular conditions that threaten quality of life for older people and in their efforts to provide preventive action to improve the quality of life.[2]

The term 'quality of life' has gained some currency over the past few years, often without being well defined. Those who have researched this concept with older people show that, for those living at home, its meanings include good health and the opportunity to maintain family relationships, social contacts and activities. The conclusions from this research highlight the need for health to be seen within the social context and show that quality of life needs to focus as much on the ability to maintain social contacts as it does on functional competence.[3]

Another factor needs to be considered in the light of a burgeoning interest in health matters in all sections of society and the rise of consumerism. The latter led to a growth in the self-health movement and an increasing focus on holistic health. Future generations of older people are more likely to be informed about health and health choices and will seek greater autonomy in healthcare and a more participative role in decision-making. For those involved in pastoral care, some individuals are less likely to want to respond to an approach which does not allow the diversity and richness of their experiences and convictions to be attended to.[4]

We should acknowledge here that although individuals of all ages have strong ideas about health, there is no general consensus among lay persons about its meaning. Some regard health as a resource for living, a valuable asset to be sought and held. To others it represents a means of fulfilling roles and responsibilities. A number perceive it as synonymous with 'coping', which implies an adaptive response to the pressures of life. Studies of older people show that frequently they regard health as 'possessing strength', as functional fitness or independence. Some see it as the capacity to enjoy life or an ability to enable others to enjoy it.[5] Edna's reflections (pp. 16–17) demonstrate how a strong sense of health is not necessarily related to physical ability. Health is understood here as an inner strength or even an attitude to life. Of course, the notion of health as freedom from disease and disability is also common.

An exploration of professional definitions reveals similar diversity. For those espousing a rational-scientific perspective, the perception of health as a disease-free state seems to be logical. This idea has formed the basis of the customary medical model for many years. It gave rise to professional medical strategies concerned with the diagnosis and treatment of diseases, each with cure as a goal. Consequently, this led to a strong focus upon classification of disease and the development of specific therapies.

Over the last decade or so those involved in thinking about and defining health have wanted to offer a definition which stresses its multidimensional nature and places the individual in a socio-environmental context.[6] Attending to Max's negative experience of his social environment (p. 39) demonstrated that we live in a world where 'community' is a complex reality with signs of real breakdown in some areas. His sense of vulnerability and isolation have a profound impact upon his health and well-being.

The idea of health as a fluctuating, dynamic experience, with wellness as its constant goal is one that has a strong hold over those working in this field. Health and illness are envisaged as an upwardly directed continuum, ranging from a peak of high level wellness at one end to very poor health and possible death at the other, but with the individual constantly endeavouring to move upwards along it, in spite of occasional setbacks.[7]

Maslow built upon this perception when he introduced the term self-actualization as the peak of his 'hierarchy of needs' model, arguing that it is the drive towards the fulfilment of cherished personal aspirations and potential which provides the motivational force towards wellness.[8]

There are many other ideas of health and well-being. In

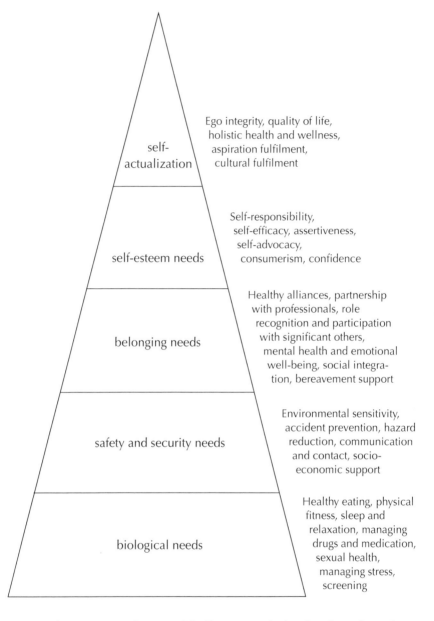

Figure 4.1   Maslow's model of human needs showing dimensions of health and well-being[9]

general, they regard health positively, defining it as 'soundness of structure and optimum bio-psychosocial functioning, a balance between one's internal and external environment'.[10] Wellness is depicted as experienced wholeness – as growth towards maturity and personal development, while contending with adversity in a manner appropriate for each individual. Such traits frequently characterize older people, who have often learned through experience that they are experts on their own wellness or well-being status.

Compare and contrast Malcolm's view of health with that of Elizabeth (p. 38). Both share a basic sense of well-being. Malcolm expresses a fatalistic view of life and health. He does not accept any personal responsibility for his health, though he may underestimate the effects on his well-being of his physical exercise through his occupation. Elizabeth gives voice to the importance of personal responsibility for balance and choice in life and health. She expresses a holistic view of the interrelationship of body, mind and spirit.

Wellness or well-being is more an attitude, an aspect of one's life, a philosophy. It embodies a zest for living, a desire for 'becoming' which involves one's whole being. It assumes both perceived quality of life and behavioural competence. Characterized by the exercise of autonomy to the highest level possible within one's circumstances, it represents interest and involvement which are orientated towards maximum function and development.

Two writers have offered this definition: 'A balance between one's environment, internal and external, and one's emotional, spiritual, social, cultural and physical processes.'[11] It is not an artificially contrived or spurious condition, but a state of being which takes account of realities and works within them to achieve potential. Many older people are successfully striving towards their wellness goal without recourse to any professional help. In this process, empowering older people to regain their health, develop competence, self-care and greater self-efficacy, enhance their fitness, extend their life skills and make informed choices about their well-being becomes important in maintaining and promoting good health.

Within this context of understanding well-being and the promotion of health, there is a medical dimension, an educational dimension, an economic dimension, a political dimension, and a philosophical or spiritual dimension. This is represented in Figure 4.2.

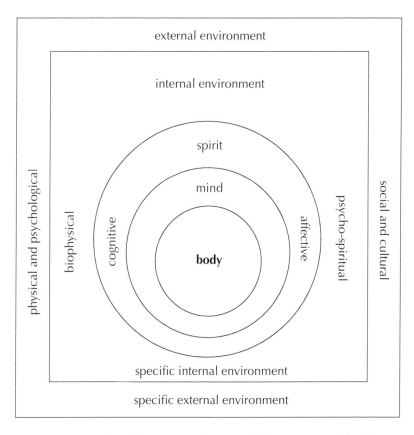

Figure 4.2   The older person at the core of the promotion of health and well-being[12]

Amalgamating these various concepts and applying them to the individual, one suggestion is that at the heart of the matter are older persons with their unique heredity, and varying ages, race and gender. Each older individual is seen as a bio-psycho-spiritual being, with each part contributing to the whole person, who in turn is essentially socially interactive. However, as Figure 4.2 points out, older individuals must be placed in their bio-socio-cultural environmental context, because influences from these environments impact constantly upon them. As each older individual progresses through the lifespan, the interplay of their heredity with their distinctive cultural and life experiences produces their lifestyle, develops their personality and dictates both their age changes and age differences. It also brings about each rich biography, which then constitutes a heritage for others. It is at this level of the older individual that an emphasis can be placed upon the need for healthy lifestyle to maximize functional ability and to develop self-care.

Further, we should note the interplay between a person's unique heredity and specific internal and external environments which produces *personality* and *lifestyle*, and thereby determines the rate and character of ageing.

It is important that from this perspective pastoral care takes into account the multiplicity of factors influencing health and wellness in later life. Just as no individual can exist in a vacuum, so older people's health cannot be promoted without reference to their social context. This means we need to take account of their families and other relevant groups, their local communities and the wider society of which they form part. We need also to be aware that each level influences the health behaviours older people adopt and the health choices that they can and do make.

One factor that should not be underestimated in the consideration of health is a person's ability to cope with change and especially loss. Colin expresses some of the significant challenges that many older people have to face (pp. 38–9). Pain and sadness are significant influences on health and the possibilities of well-being.

Traditionally pastoral care has often been individualized and failed to take account of the wider social context.[13] Research in this area has demonstrated that healthy, integrated intergenerational or older families, which practise health-promoting behaviours, will impact favourably on community wellness. Similarly, strategies aimed at community wellness can, in turn, make it possible for families in smaller social groups to practise health-promoting behaviours. Examples include community provision for healthy leisure: parks, gardens and safe cycleways; swimming; education, libraries and information centres; advice agencies; luncheon clubs; and social groups of all types including churches. Healthy neighbourhoods and communities make up healthy societies. Figure 4.3 looks at two layers of the factors influencing health and wellness in later life (family and group influences, and community influence).

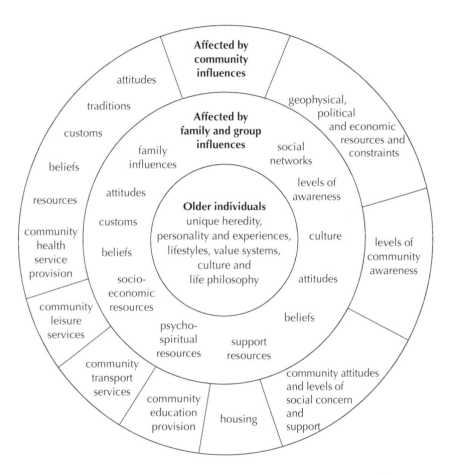

Figure 4.3   Factors influencing health and wellness in later life[14]

In addition, pastoral care of older people should look at wider societal influences.

- National resources and constraints.
- National policies on equality, social justice and citizen involvement.
- National food protection policies.
- National social security policies.
- National environmental protection policies.
- National policy for control of drugs, tobacco and alcohol.
- National education policies.
- National leisure policies and provision.
- National transport policies and provision.
- National health policies and resources. Government attitudes and beliefs.
- National social policies and provision.
- National social economic policies.

CONCLUSION

As we have engaged with the experience and reflections of older people at the beginning of this chapter, we conclude that the concepts of 'health' and 'wellness' are complex, multidimensional and even contradictory. All care, and pastoral care in particular, must put the older person at the centre. They must be empowered to shape ways in which health might be improved.

Health and well-being are multidimensional and embrace medical, educational, economic, political and philosophical perspectives. Wellness includes self-responsibility and that may include an awareness of diet, physical fitness, the management of stress, healthy sleep and the embracing of change and loss.

In the promotion of health and well-being in old age there is still much work to be done in understanding what shapes ageing and what makes for 'successful ageing'.[15] There still exist significant levels of inequality among older people. Pastoral care and its possibilities are much shaped by the wide range of influences. These influences can combine to shape very different experiences of health for an older person.

FOR FURTHER REFLECTION

Exercise 1

What is the role of religion and spirituality in promoting health and well-being?

Exercise 2

Ask older persons with whom you come into contact what they mean by the terms health and well-being.

1   Discover what they include as components of well-being.

2   Compare these with your own perceptions.

3   Look at and explore the difference between these accounts.

Exercise 3

Consider how you might help to reduce inequalities in health within and between groups of older people with whom you come into contact.

Identify ways in which these older people who are more vulnerable or at great risk might be more effectively helped to achieve higher levels of wellness.

CHAPTER FIVE

Diminishment: age-related changes

LISTENING TO EXPERIENCE

Roger

I am now 84 and I manage to maintain my independence with a little bit of external support. I get help with shopping, cleaning and transport. The changes in my ability especially my mobility have been gradual. I have some pain and discomfort in my knees and legs and this means that getting up and down stairs can be difficult. It takes me quite a long time to get going in the morning. I take regular walks and sometimes wish I could leap over the gates! I don't feel frail but my doctor keeps reminding me that I am.

Susan

I am sitting at my table looking back at some old photographs. How age changes the body! In what way? Well, I am fatter than I was 20 years ago. My hair is thinner and now has lost its natural colour. My skin is very much drier, thinner and wrinkled. Of course I regret some of this loss and change but there is an inevitability about all this. Nothing in life remains static.

Nancy

I had a massive stroke about eight years ago that nearly finished me off. The National Health Service did a wonderful job and put things back together. It took some time. I have lost some mobility and I can't use my left arm. This makes eating rather difficult but my husband is a patient carer and a very good cook! My doctors are concerned about my heart and blood pressure but it seems to be controlled with medication. I am not frustrated by what has happened to me and try not to be over-preoccupied by my health. I know that I am living on borrowed time and I try to make the best out of each day.

Peter

I hate old age – it is a terrible process of slowing down and things packing up. Life becomes an increasing trial and I don't find that people understand or try to appreciate the shape of old age. I have coped with diabetes and gradual difficulties with my mobility. I get around but I don't think it will be long before I have to give up driving. About two years ago I had a long period of feeling down and couldn't concentrate on anything. Eventually I was diagnosed with depression and that is managed with medication. I really don't want to go on living for much longer. I have a poor quality of life.

Alice

I feel less and less inhibited as I grow older. I am much less bothered about what people think or feel. I don't mind giving people a piece of my mind. My views on living have become much more firmly held in old age. I am much less patient and get very frustrated about things that I disapprove of. I really don't like change and feel regretful about matters that I can't exercise any control over. I sometimes think that others find me bad-tempered and grumpy.

It is important to understand how people interact with each other and function within their environment in later life. We need to understand the normal changes that occur within individuals across the life course. Change takes place at different rates and to varying degrees. These changes influence functional capacity, interaction with others, everyday life and the quality of life in our later years. They may also influence a person's health, especially in middle and later years. From this perspective, ageing involves a process of change, from birth to death, in our interacting biological, physiological and psychological systems. It follows that while there may be varied patterns of ageing, health and dysfunction, we are all individuals, who may choose whether or not to adopt safe, healthy, personal habits in regard to diet, drugs, alcohol, smoking, sex and physical exercise. These have been shown to slow the process of ageing, increase longevity, maintain independence, and help us to adapt to age-related changes in later life such as loss of muscle and strength.[1]

Both genetic factors and environmental factors of socio-economic status (inadequate housing, for example) can speed up the normal changes in ageing or health for those who are predisposed to what doctors call disease states. This chapter will focus on continuity and change in biological, sensory and personality systems across the life course. Issues relating to memory and cognitive functions will be discussed in Chapter 8. The changes or diminishments in view now, involving both decline in vision, hearing and mobility and growth in wisdom, experience and knowledge, result in either cumulative advantages or disadvantages in later life.

It is beyond the scope of this chapter to present cellular-level explanations of changes that occur to human organisms. It is also not possible to explain such major diseases as heart disease, stroke or cancer. The causes of these are as yet mainly unknown, though they are likely, as in other situations, to be a result of a combination of genetics, injuries, environmental factors and living habits.

A disability is a reported difficulty in performing some of the activities of daily life, such as dressing, getting out of bed or using the toilet; or in performing instrumental activities of daily life such as shopping, banking, cleaning and maintaining a home, and driving a car. A physical or mental condition or a health problem is responsible for the kind or amount of activity that can be completed. Older people report more disabilities than younger people, and more older women than older men report one or more disabilities. The number of disabilities and their severity increases with age. Among people over 65 years of age, the disabilities reported most often are mobility problems, pain, declining agility and confusion. Although these disabilities restrict functioning in later life, whether they increase dependence or lower one's perceived quality of life depends on such factors as tolerance of pain, energy levels, personality and self-esteem, available support, type of environment and whether one lives alone.

Frailty is often associated with ageing, but is less well defined. It is not an inevitable consequence of ageing. Frailty is characterized by muscle weakness, especially in the legs; by fatigue and diminished energy reserves; by decreased physical and social activity, loss of weight, and a slow or unsteady gait. Frailty is strongly related to increased risks of falling, social isolation, dependence and institutionalization, and nearness to death. The causes of frailty include genetic traits related to metabolic, cardiovascular and immunological systems; the onset of disease or injuries that limit physical activity; poor nutrition; sedentary living. Lack of regular physical activity in later life leads to loss of muscle strength and endurance in the legs.[2]

Disability or frailty are two possible outcomes of individual ageing. It is important that pastoral care has an awareness of some of the physical changes which occur in individuals as they age, and especially the decline in health and the gradual losses of physical, motor and cognitive efficiency and ability. Most people do not spend their later years in a state of acute dependence, but for people in very frail old age there can be changes which result in both disability and frailty. We must appreciate differences in response which can be accounted for by genetics, social and environmental factors, including socio-economic status, gender, diet, race, ethnicity, occupation, geographic location, body type and age cohort.

As we age, visible changes occur in the skin, the hair and in the shape and height of the body. During middle years the skin can become dry and wrinkled as it becomes thinner, loses elasticity and subcutaneous fat. Similarly hair becomes thinner and loses its original colour. Not surprisingly, a profitable cosmetics industry has evolved to respond to these particular changes. There are many who actively market anti-ageing gimmicks, programmes and products.

Ageing adults are faced with a cultural ideal of a youthful body and an active life. To cope with the changes observed in one's appearance and with the inner changes that are felt, such as less efficiency, decrease in energy and aches and pains, older adults adopt various cognitive strategies. Some studies have identified two types of adaptors. The 'active copers' continued or had begun a programme of physical activity and were conscious of how they dressed and appeared. The 'reactive copers' reported that they knew they ought to be active and to pay more attention to appearance, but for various reasons did not invest in physical activity.[3]

Some of these external changes, such as change in body shape or a shortening of stature, influence how people perceive themselves and how others perceive and interact with them. For those who are secure and live in a supported social environment, physical changes are seldom traumatic. However, for those whose identity and social interaction are closely related to their physical appearance, attempts to alter the presentation of the physical self may become a time-consuming battle, particularly people who are separated, divorced or widowed and anxious to date or attract a new partner.

INTERNAL CHANGES

The most significant influence on the performance of physical tasks is internal physical changes. Such changes might include the following:

- A decrease in water content and an increase in fat cells in relation to muscle cells.
- A decrease in muscle mass and elasticity.
- A decrease in bone mass and minerals so that bones are more brittle; this increases the likelihood of fractures.
- A deterioration in the range, flexibility and composition of the articulating surfaces and joints, which enhances the likelihood of fractures or arthritis.

Many of these realities can lead to degrees of immobility, changing leisure activities, and an inability to perform household tasks in the latter years. It follows that the physical environment that an old person lives in is very important.[4]

CHANGES IN PHYSIOLOGICAL SYSTEMS

Over time, most physiological systems become less efficient and less capable of functioning at maximum capacity. The central nervous system slows down with age, as evidenced by a longer response or reaction time, the earlier onset of fatigue, hand tremors and a general slowing of the automatic nervous system. These changes can influence a person's movements and behavioural reactions.

Age-related changes in the muscular system result in a decrease in strength and endurance, although the rate and degree of loss depends on the frequency and intensity of physical activity. These changes reduce the ability to engage in endurance tasks or in tasks requiring repeated actions of the same muscle group, such as digging in the garden or washing windows. A decline in muscular endurance also reduces the efficiency of other body functions, such as the respiratory system.

Perhaps the most noticeable and significant forms of physiological change are those in the cardiovascular system. There is a decrease in the maximum heart rate which results in changes in output and stroke volume, and associated with this is an increase in blood pressure. These factors combine to lower the efficiency of the system and to hasten fatigue during physical activity.

It is more difficult, however, to retard the onset of arteriosclerosis and atherosclerosis. In these conditions, loss of elasticity in the arterial walls restricts the flow of blood to the muscles and organs, and they are characterized by a hardening and narrowing of the arterial walls. These cardiovascular diseases, which are especially prevalent among men, are difficult to prevent or treat because their pathology is still not fully understood.

The efficiency of the respiratory system decreases with age for a number of reasons. These include decreases in elasticity of the lungs; in vital capacity; in diffusion and absorption capacity; and in maximum voluntary ventilation and oxygen intake. The changes reduce the efficiency of intake and inhibit the transportation of oxygen to organs and muscles.

It is not surprising, therefore, that physical activity has a number of benefits for the ageing person. Many studies have found a positive relationship between the amount of participation in physical activity at work or play and the level of physical and mental health and mental performance. Similarly there is an inverse relationship between the degree of physical activity at work or play and mortality rates.[5]

MOTOR AND SENSORY SYSTEMS

Earlier in the chapter we have noted that changes in the central nervous system occur with increasing chronological age. The most noticeable of these changes is a general slowing of motor, cognitive and sensory processes. A number of explanations for this phenomenon have been proposed, including a loss of neurons, which are not replaced; a decrease in the size and weight of the brain; diseases such as manic depressive psychosis; coronary heart disease; strokes or depression; hormonal changes; or loss of motivation and concentration.

Whatever the cause, a general decline is observed in the speed of psychomotor performance, cognitive function and sensory and perception processes. This is more pronounced as the required action becomes more complex, for example, in abstract reasoning or when rapid decisions have to be made while performing certain tasks. The observable slowing down has a direct effect on social behaviour and leads to stereotypes of older people such as the slow, overly cautious driver. In fact, with advancing age there may be a slowing of speed to ensure accuracy. This cautiousness, a generalized tendency to respond slowly or not at all because of the possible consequences of a mistake, occurs in many situations where a decision must be made. Regardless of the underlying mechanism, this slowing down reduces the chances of survival when fast reaction time is required, as in heavy traffic. It may also limit complex thinking because the mediating processes slow down to the point where some of the elements, or even the goal of the task, may be forgotten.[6]

Reaction time, the period from perception of a stimulus to reaction, is a complex phenomenon and is not well understood. A slower reaction time has been explained as a physical problem resulting from a number of possible physiological processes. These include a decline in signal strength as neurons and nerve cells die; an increase in reflex time for skeletal muscles; a loss of efficiency in central processing mechanisms so that more time is needed to monitor incoming signals; and a general deterioration in the sensory motor mechanisms. Loss of reaction time can be offset by practice and sometimes a strong desire to succeed at the task. In fact, some people have argued that with unlimited time to monitor stimuli, an older person is often more accurate than a younger person.[7]

SENSORY PROCESSES

Communication with others is essential throughout one's life, be it face to face or indirectly, for example, by television, telephone or the Internet. To interact with the physical environment and with other people, an individual sends and receives information. This ability depends largely on sensory receptors (eyes, nose, ears) that permit information to be received by and transmitted to the brain. As we age, greater stimulation is needed in order to send information to the brain.

Changes with age in the major sensory receptors and processors reduce the quality and quantity of information available to the person. The efficiency of the receptors also influences the interest in communicating and the capacity to understand information. Changes in these systems are seldom abrupt and may not even be noticed at first. If an impairment is not severe, the person compensates for the loss by a variety of means: a person may use a different sense to a greater extent, such as lip-reading to compensate for loss of hearing; or intensify the stimulus (for example, with a hearing aid) or correct it (for example, with spectacles) or use experience to predict or identify the stimulus (for example, recognizing a 'stop' sign by its shape). If two senses decline simultaneously, as vision and hearing often do in later life, a person may have difficulty with their tasks, with walking or with social interaction.

By about the age of 60, there is a higher threshold for all four taste sensations: salt, sweet, bitter and sour. In addition, there is less saliva and a loss in the number of taste buds. These changes are compounded by smoking, wearing dentures and by taking some prescription drugs. Furthermore, the ability to detect or identify odours declines with age.

When the sense of taste and smell decline at the same time, a person may enjoy food less and may start eating smaller amounts, with a consequent decline in nutrition. In short, mealtime is no longer so enjoyable a social or culinary experience.

With advancing age there is a loss of sensitivity in touch and vibration in some, but not all, parts of the body. Indeed, some older people who singe their fingers on a hot stove do not notice the pain or damage. However, the prevalence of pain increases with age; the main sources of chronic pain in later life are arthritis, rheumatism, angina and vascular disease. Chronic pain has a serious effect on physical and emotional well-being, and when it becomes severe it affects all aspects of our everyday lives.[8]

Although complaints about pain often increase with age, it is unclear whether pain thresholds remain constant or decrease with age. Part of this uncertainty stems from a failure to separate the physiological variable of the pain threshold from the social and psychological elements of pain. It is not known whether observed age differences in pain perception are related to the processing capacity of the central nervous system, to changes in the peripheral receptors, to the source of pain, to the personality and motivation of the individual, to changes in the cognitive processes interpreting the source and nature of the pain, or to some combination of these factors.

PERSONALITY PROCESSES AND AGEING

To explain changes in behaviour with age, social scientists have tried to determine the relative influence of personality factors. Perhaps nowhere else is the interaction of the personal system with the social system more evident than when considering personality as a factor in the ageing process. Personality involves individual differences in diverse human characteristics such as traits, emotions, moods, coping strategies, cognitive styles, goals and motives that are unique to an individual who interacts with others in a variety of settings.

Most personality research focuses on the early developmental years of childhood and adolescence. It tries to describe and explain characteristic ways in which individuals think. Two questions dominate personality research:

1 Is behaviour determined internally by personality traits or externally by the social situation?
2 Is personality stable, once established, or does it change as people grow older?

To understand the influence of personality on behaviour throughout later life, we need to try to answer two questions.

SOCIAL BEHAVIOUR: A FUNCTION OF PERSONALITY TRAITS OR THE SOCIAL SITUATION?

Is behaviour determined by personality traits or by the social environment? According to the *trait approach*, individuals, through a combination of heredity, early socialization and interaction with significant others, develop personal traits and characteristics, a cognitive style and a temperament. These behavioural dispositions are thought to be stable over time and they enable individuals to respond consistently and predictably to their social and physical environment.

In contrast, a *behavioural perspective* argues that behaviour is determined by the social situation. According to this perspective, personality per se does not exist. Or, if it does, it has little stability since the behaviour of an individual is determined by external social norms and sanctions unique to specific situations, such as the workplace, the home, or a leisure situation, or perhaps one's time of life. It follows then that through an interactive process involving personal and social systems, individuals, lifestyles and, indeed, choices evolve.[9]

PERSONALITY: STABILITY OR CHANGE ACROSS THE LIFE COURSE?

The question is still being debated, although the available evidence suggests that after early childhood, people demonstrate reasonable consistency in such personal characteristics as preservation of self, attitudes, values, temperament and traits. Many individuals make a conscious effort to maintain consistency in the behavioural and cognitive presentation of the self. When behaviour and personality are assessed and averaged over a large sample of situations, stability is the normal pattern, in the absence of confounding health problems.

However, some evidence suggests that personality changes occur at or beyond middle age in some people. First, some people exhibit changes over time in some traits, even though a person's relative position in the group may not change. The most dependable person at the age of 20 is the most dependable person at the age of 50, perhaps because dependability has become a more esteemed and important culture value. Of course, some people will change more than others. These changes are perhaps inevitable and sometimes very unpredictable.[10]

How are these changes to be explained? A developmental perspective argues that people alter and adapt as their individual lives evolve. A relatively new concept in personality research is generativity, a process that begins in midlife when individuals become less concerned with self-identity and more concerned with mentoring and helping others – such as their co-workers, older adults, children or young colleagues. This is achieved by becoming a leader, mentor and contributor in the broader community. Self-concept is a subset of personality: it is the outcome of our motivations, attitudes and behaviour relevant to our self-definition (how we define and present ourselves to others) and our personal meaning in life. This 'self' has three basic components:

1 Cognitive (who we think we are)
2 Affective (feelings about who we are)
3 Connative (actions on the basis of self-perceptions).

There is both stability and change in the self-concept as we age. We use our physical, cognitive and social resources to maintain or change our self-concept as social or cultural situations change. Historical and cultural trends influence the self-concept and self-motivated actions. Life-course events shape the self, and the content of the events influences life-course experiences. Moreover, the self is influenced not only by care and social circumstances, but also by culture and our place in the social structure earlier in life, which may or may not change later.[11]

There is some evidence about the way the self attempts to understand and how adults cope with stressful situations that emerge in later life – retirement, widowhood, death of friends, daily health, dependency and institutionalization. Coping is sometimes defined as 'constantly changing cognitive and behavioural efforts to manage specific external or internal demands that are appraised as taxing or exceeding the resources of the person'. In the self-evaluation process we cope and adapt, making social comparisons and noting the discrepancies in how we react, behave or think compared to others in social situations. This process involves social cognition; that is, we focus on the content and structure of social knowledge and on the cognitive processes involved in accessing such knowledge.[12]

Demonstrated changes in personality reflect underlying latent needs and characteristics that could not be or were not expressed in earlier life. People's social situations may change with age, and people become less inclined to present the self in a traditional, outmoded or inappropriate way. For example, as a person who is striving and ambitious in early adulthood moves into middle or later life, he or she may devote less time to work, become more relaxed in interpersonal situations, and demonstrate a different presentation of the self in all situations. Change is more likely to occur if career goals have been obtained, especially at an earlier age than expected.

Another factor leading to an apparent change in personality is the lack of opportunity to demonstrate common traits. For example, the need to be aggressive or achievement-orientated continues, but opportunities to satisfy it are no longer as readily available at work or at play. In addition, the physical and psychic energy needed to continue a pattern of aggressive and achieve-ment-orientated behaviour may no longer be available.

Finally, emotions are at the heart of social relations and they influence how and why we care about outcomes. Joy, fear, anger, shame, guilt, disgust and love are expressed to varying degrees across the life course, depending on the social context. In later life, emotions may be felt but not expressed, or only expressed for or against certain people. Age does not affect emotional intensity in itself, nor does it bring with it a generalized negative mood (as in the stereotype of grumpy old men) or a decrease in positive mood.

In conclusion, does personality change as people age or is it stable? The answer to the question is both yes and yes. The evidence increasingly supports the co-occurrence of persistent traits and unfolding development linked to changed life tasks. While most people do not experience major personality changes with age, some change their patterns of social interaction as situations or demands evolve. Similarly, others, aware of changing norms among younger cohorts, change their behaviour or cognitive pattern to fit with con-temporary lifestyles. Some personality changes may be related to physiological, medical or cognitive changes; others reflect latent character traits, fewer opportunities or a change in social environ-ment.

Many psychologists have tried to measure single or multiple personality traits to determine whether differences exist by age, or age is a more significant factor in personality differences than other social variables, in particular, gender, socio-economic status, race, ethnic backgrounds or birth order. Some common personality traits are aggressiveness, anxiety, authoritarianism, cautiousness, conformity, conservatism, creativity, decision-making style, egocentrism, ego strength, emotionality, extraversion, happiness, introversion, irritability, need for achievement, passivity, perceived lack of control, reminiscence, rigidity, risk-taking, self-concept or self-image, self-esteem and sociability. For most such traits, the evidence in favour of the prevalence of either age differences or age changes is equivocal. For example, despite some inconsistency in the findings, it seems that the current cohort of older people are generally more conservative, cautious, egocentric, introverted and passive and less emotional than younger age groups. But it isn't clear whether these differences are due to lifelong characteristics or changing interaction patterns with younger cohorts.[13]

The early years of gerontology were characterized by attempts to identify personality types that would explain life satisfaction or successful ageing. This body of descriptive research generated many labels for older people who appeared to think and behave in similar ways – stable, rocking-chair, passive, dependent, integrated or un-integrated, disengaged, active, or competent and husband-centred (for women!). The labels were thought to describe lifestyles that had been built over the life course, persisted in later life and explained adjustment to the demands of ageing. Most of these types were derived from a single research study, usually with men. This perspective on personality is not well accepted today: labelling is considered ageist and inaccurate, and unable to account for diverse personalities in later life. Moreover, lifelong stability in personality is considered less likely as generativity and changes in the self occur across the life course in response to all kinds of influences. Of course, if successful ageing could indeed be defined or explained, it would involve many other factors, not just personality.[14]

As people go through life they experience inevitable changes in physical structure and the whole range of other dimensions which bear upon their experience. There are constant variations both within and between individuals, in the rate of loss or gain in most domains of life because of personality factors (hereditary, health, education, gender, lifestyle) and environmental factors (work, housing and neighbourhood). All these factors require coping strategies and adaptation. These normal changes take place with age, influence, personal behaviour and lifestyles as well as the way others react to the ageing person.

FOR FURTHER REFLECTION

Exercise 1

If you think of two or three older people in your family or circle, to what extent do personality, lifestyle and health distinguish those who are adapting well to growing older from those who are having some difficulty?

Exercise 2

Develop a plan to enable more older adults to share their wisdom for the betterment of society.

Exercise 3

Looking ahead 20 or 30 or more years, to what extent do you expect that you as an individual will have changed and in what ways? Consider appearances and characteristics you have observed in your parents, and reflect on whether this will be you in the future – why or why not?

PART TWO

Responding to and learning from older people

CHAPTER SIX

The religious and spiritual needs of older people

LISTENING TO EXPERIENCE

Michael

I am sympathetic to religion. My parents were occasional church-goers and I attended a church school. I want to lead a good life but haven't found religion much practical help. I do not understand how to read the Bible and find some of the language of hymns and liturgy strange.

I taught art in an inner-city comprehensive school for nearly 30 years – not the most popular of subjects in the school! It was a tremendous source of satisfaction for me when I could enable my pupils to express themselves and to appreciate the energy and imagination that artists can express. I often expressed my view that effective education could be achieved through 'pictures' as much as 'words'. Some of my happiest memories were taking pupils to the City Gallery and working with them to uncover the shape and depth and texture of a picture. I hope I shared with them something of how art can help us to see life and its possibilities.

In some ways I have always been on the edge of things – shy and introverted but a bit of a rebel. Most of my head teachers found me fairly unmanageable! Retirement came as a relief with plenty of time (and money) to pursue my painting and journey across European city art galleries.

I go to church from time to time but as a single man I feel excluded by some of the talk of belonging and family. I am curious about the shape of meaning and the inner workings of a person's spirit or soul. I would appreciate the chance to reflect on these matters; to be listened to rather than talked at. I am told that

older people become more spiritual as they age – I am beginning
to want to reject this assertion – it doesn't bear out in my experience.

Violet

I have been part of the Church for all of my 82 years of living. I am
deeply committed to our village church and do all that I can to
support its work. I don't think that I have a very strong faith – I try
to live it rather than think about it too much. I have always been
concerned to do my best to help people in the community who are
frail and vulnerable – especially older people. The Church must
always look outwards and serve people as best it can.

The Church has always been there for me at important times of
my life. I remember the love and care that surrounded me when
my husband died some ten years ago. Baptisms and marriages;
harvest suppers, summer fairs and the celebration of Christmas
and Easter have shaped my life and sustained me.

I have one daughter and it's a cause of some regret that we no
longer speak. We had a nasty argument and have never had any
contact since that time. I feel a terrible sense of shame and guilt
because I was responsible for the conflict. My daughter said some
terrible things about us, her parents, that I shall never forgive
her for. It is sad and hurts me deeply but I don't know if it is
something that will ever be put right. The confession and absolu-
tion in the service is very difficult – nothing can take away my
deep shame. We talk about forgiveness but it is difficult to practise.

Malcolm

I am 92 and I think that I have probably lived too long – I am a
frail old man! Life isn't very easy and I need assistance with most
things, for example, I am dictating this to a carer. I loved to cook
but can no longer do that. I liked to read and write but my eyesight no longer makes that possible. I have great pride in my
family but my wife passed away 20 years ago and two of my three
children have also died. I am tired and frustrated.

I am a Christian and if I ever needed help it is in this time. I
need help with prayer; help to reflect; help to move beyond self-
pity and regret; help to prepare for my death. Please pray for me
and I hope that you won't have to live as long as I have.

Helen

I shall be 84 in April, so I have well exceeded the biblical three score years and ten. Every day, therefore, is a bonus, 'something given above what is due'.

As I get older, I feel increasing cause for celebration in the seasons. Indeed, creation has an added significance year by year. Seemingly simple things take on an added meaning, for example, the bird table, the ever-changing trees, the bowls of spring bulbs, enjoyment we can share with other people.

One can take the enjoyment of the world on to a much more mundane level. Like many older people, I find that much more of my life is involved in domesticity. Here I am very blessed because my husband and I are able to work in partnership. I now look on cooking as a creative process as I am handling created things, the lovely colours and textures and shapes of fruit and vegetables, for instance. You may recall the words of Brother Laurence:

> In the noise and clatter of my kitchen . . .
> I praise God in as great tranquillity as if
> I were on my knees at the Blessed Sacrament.

We desperately want to hold on to our belief in prayer, but we are often embarrassed by our own inadequacy. I regard prayer as being an important responsibility and privilege in old age when I have more time and more experience than in the past. But I think that by now I should be better at it, and it is not easy to admit that. Physical health varies and spiritual health is just the same. Times of spiritual depression come to most of us. Sometimes it is linked with an inability to forgive. We all know the costliness of forgiveness and that coming to terms with it can be an important part of the unfinished business with which an elderly person can be struggling. There are now two aspects, forgiving and being forgiven. We have all been hurt; we have all hurt other people. In the Lord's Prayer, we say, 'Forgive us our trespasses as we forgive those who trespass against us.'

I meet many old people who still live adventurously. But it is hard to be adventurous all the time, and the temptation can be there to give up because it is all too much of an effort now, and we can't change the world as we thought we could when we were younger. But even though we are limited by age, we can still make a difference. We can pray; we can keep ourselves informed; we can collect paper to help the environment; we can write to our MP.

Throughout life, we need a sense of humour, and perhaps more so in old age when there are inevitable difficulties. I have noticed that in some old people a sense of humour seems to diminish and that is a real loss. It helps to have a companion with whom one can share a joke, so old people living alone may be disadvantaged in this respect. When we are old, we tend to make stupid little mistakes. Perhaps, for instance, we take longer to get coins out of our purse than we used to. This irritates us. It might be better if we responded in the spirit of the person who wrote, 'Blessed are we who can laugh at ourselves, for we shall never cease to be amused.'

I have a certain amount of fear of the process of dying, but not death itself. In the case of death, we are all aware that we know so little about what happens after death. But if we trust God and his love for us, as far as I am concerned, I can feel secure, even though I do not know what form life after death will take.

As I have found in my personal experience, old age has drawbacks, but it also has strengths, one of which is a quality of detachment that leads to a sense of perspective. That will help, but it will not take away the darkness altogether, far from it. For example, old people in particular feel very let down by world affairs, including September 11 and all that it symbolizes. Yes, we had to agree that the world was a wicked place, but we thought that on the whole there was some improvement. And now we seem to have encountered a new intensity of darkness.

I try to hold on to the words said to have been scrawled on a wall by a Jewish lad in prison in the 1940s:

> I believe in the sun even when it is not shining,
> I believe in love even when I cannot feel it,
> I believe in God even when he is silent.

I claim that for me a prayer attributed to Niebuhr is particularly appropriate in old age. Here it is: 'God grant me the *serenity* to accept the things I cannot change, *courage* to change the things I can, and *wisdom* to know the difference.'

The concept of spirituality means many different things to

different people and requires some unpacking and interpretation if there is to be any deeper understanding of expectations and needs.[1] While working with the concept of spirituality in ministry over the last 20 years, in a variety of settings, I have come to share the belief that the word spirituality runs the danger of becoming a vague and diffuse notion, functioning like 'intellectual Polyfilla', which changes shape and content conveniently to fill the space its user has devised for it.[2]

For the purposes of this chapter we must note that the many modern writers on this subject (by no means all of whom are care practitioners) regularly insist that spirituality is not the same as religion but refers to something much broader. The word spirituality, once chiefly used within a Christian setting for the understanding and practice of the devout life, has now widened its use in the light of modern circumstances. This understanding of the theory and practice of spirituality and spiritual care is certainly embedded in the present understanding of health care chaplaincy and its work but is also held by those working in palliative care. For example, Tom Gordon, working in Marie Curie Cancer Care, confidently asserts: 'We must understand the basic principles – that spirituality is common to all, and that it is not always synonymous with religion.'[3]

In an article entitled 'Helping to create a personal sacred space' Moffitt writes that using the term spiritual 'frees us from being tied down to any one-faith tradition'.[4]

McSherry, writing from a nursing perspective, expands this point:

> Spirituality is often viewed as being synonymous with religion and a belief in God. Yet to adopt such a narrow definition is to exclude a multitude of people, atheist, agnostic, humanist who may not share such beliefs, but who nevertheless have a spirituality that is real.[5]

So it follows that any reference to religion in common parlance will generally be understood to refer to its rules and regulations, rituals, beliefs and traditions, whereas usefully spirituality is understood as that which constitutes inner life or unseen workings – the forces and powers which propel it. This can be described as character and ethos, ideals and intangible beliefs which hold all together; even values and norms. Thus it follows that both individuals and particular organizations or cultures may have a spiritual character. Many have rejected the concept of spirituality precisely because it is so often used in the context of religious thinking and practice. Alyson Peberdy offers a simple distinction: 'Perhaps it may help to see spirituality as a search for meaning, and religion as a particular expression of that. (One that usually involves God-language.)'[6]

In pastoral practice, however, it is much more problematic to separate spirituality from religion than these statements suggest. At this point readers might like to discover this for themselves by looking at Exercise 1 at the end of this chapter.

The interconnections between spirituality and religion for older people will be demonstrated later in this chapter but, for present purposes and providing an overview, here is a list of the definitions of spirituality that have emerged from my work with health and social care professionals who seek to respond to an individual within the context of a holistic approach to support and care. Participants at workshops were asked to define what immediately came to their mind as a short definition of spirituality. These definitions emerged:

- inner peace and well-being;
- purpose;
- love, warmth, understanding;
- is incapable of definition;
- a dream or vision that gives meaning;
- a wholeness from within;
- unconditional love for one another;
- contentment;
- being taken beyond oneself;
- completeness;
- the searchings of the inner being;
- that which gives meaning and purpose to life;
- what matters most;
- individual or unique value;
- connectedness;
- togetherness;
- hope or faith;
- relationship with God;

- faith in inner self and religion;
- communicating with God's spirit;
- peace of mind;
- satisfaction.

An overview of these definitions indicates a broad consensus around how spirituality may be sensed and thought of, and its inevitable connectedness with religion for those people whose spirituality has been shaped and nurtured in and through a faith tradition.

The findings might be summarized as Figure 6.1.

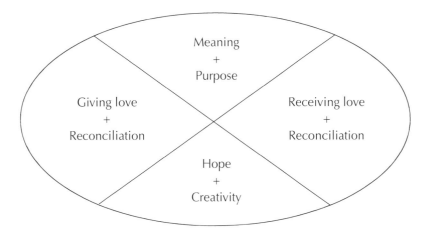

Figure 6.1   Spirituality

WHAT ARE SPIRITUAL NEEDS?

Travelbee offers this definition of spirituality: 'to assist individuals and families not just to cope with illness and suffering, but to find meaning in those experiences'. Another doctor, teaching medical students on a busy surgical unit, offered this important insight:

By teaching skills of knowing, hoping and trusting we should enable patients to trust experience or anticipate meaning. People need to make sense of their circumstances and to find a meaning in the events of their day, their relationships and their life.[7]

Amidst this range of sometimes rather diverse definitions it is not surprising that when it comes to practice, many individuals and organizations have given up on the practice of spiritual care or have preferred to narrow the subject to its association with religion. This is particularly the case when considering the care and support of older people. In a busy and demanding day it is difficult for a care worker, charged to carry out a number of personal tasks for an older person, or indeed a friend or relative, to have any practical sense of how they might best respond to their non-physical needs. However, a good working definition of spiritual needs is vital, for it helps us to understand the integrating factor which can empower and facilitate good care. And, more basic, it helps us to keep this dimension of care firmly on the map.

There are five considerations implicit in the above which might be summarized as follows:

- Addressing that which is inexpressible.
- Awareness of things greater.
- The sense of the transcendent that allows us to understand ourselves in context.
- What counts most?
- What helps us to make sense of life?

In this perspective, we can see that all of us are spiritual beings and that some of us express our spiritual needs through religion. This broad approach to spiritual needs and spiritual care affirms our interconnectedness as whole people and acknowledges that our spiritual lives can often be underdeveloped in a reductionist and materialist culture – whether by our own neglect or by their deliberate suppression. For most of the older people that I have worked with there is some residual sense of the Church and religion. If this volume is rewritten for *my* generation in their third age in 20 or 30 years' time, this chapter will certainly take a very different shape.[8] The capacity to find words to discuss the subject may simply have been lost.

The following three short extracts from writers best summarize this approach to spirituality:

- To care sometimes, to relieve often, to comfort always. (Strauss)

- If I as a doctor spend an hour of my clinic time talking to a woman who has only a few weeks to live I am making a clear statement of her worth . . . I am affirming the worth of one individual person in a world in which the individual is at risk of being submerged or valued only for his strength, intellect or beauty . . . It is a prophetic statement about the unique value of the human person irrespective of their age, social class or productivity.[9]
- As you ought not to attempt to cure the eyes without the head, or the head without the body, so neither ought you to attempt to cure the body without the soul . . . for the part can never be well unless the whole is well . . . And therefore, if the head and body are to be well, you must begin by curing the soul.[10]

In other words, spirituality, from this perspective, is about enhancing, enriching and expanding humanity. It embraces an ethical and social dimension as well as a person's opportunity or ability to be resilient in the face of change and disaster. It must also always have the older person as its focus and it must be committed, as we are in this book, to listening carefully to the diversity of experience that older people inevitably bring to those around them.

The Leveson Centre has been organizing seminars relating to the spiritual needs of older people for some time and it is a constant pressure and challenge for facilitators of such conferences to encourage professionals to put older people at the centre of their focus and practice. We need, all of us, to be more sensitive and imaginative about how we care for and learn with older people. This was brought out by a comment from a matron of a nursing home who, unable to be at the conference, wrote, 'I am concerned about wanting to meet the spiritual needs of older people, many of whom do not ask or tell you what they want.' I think the comment characterizes some of the difficulties in understanding and defining spiritual care, but it is also a spur for us to listen more carefully to older people. Evaluating and understanding an older person's non-physical needs can rarely be done in a short interview or assessment – it is a more radical, longer-term commitment to the person in all their mystery and richness.

There is much evidence to suggest that when people get older (beyond 55, to set a rather artificial marker) they do indeed become more open to the spiritual dimension of life. I have experienced some wonderment at the abundance of spiritual gifts so evident in people who are in their third and fourth age. It is my opinion that older persons are essentially faced with two choices: to turn in on themselves and the health problems that they may have, becoming set in their ways with fixed and relatively narrow patterns of thought; or, alternatively, to acquire a lifestyle based on openness to others, knowing how to welcome and understand partialness and difference and taking on board what is new. It is interesting to reflect in what way these choices are shaped by religion, culture, education and upbringing. Certainly the person who chooses (if that is the right word) the lifestyle of openness has already learned in earlier years how to grow old; this is someone who accepts and lives through this phase of life as a time of continuing growth, a process of evolution rather than involution. As an old man, George Bernard Shaw affirmed in the Postscript to his play, *Back to Methuselah*: 'Physically I am failing . . . yet my mind still feels capable of growth, for my curiosity is keener than ever. My soul goes marching on.'

Paul Baudiquet, in his study of the artist Rembrandt and his paintings, concluded: 'Since his youth, Rembrandt had but one vocation – to grow old.'[11]

Rembrandt had discovered early in his life the inner beauty that lay beneath the failing physical powers of older people. Much of his work consisted in portraying this in his graphic paintings of older people showing the depth of tenderness, serenity and inner strength that could still radiate through the gnarled hands and bent form of so many of his subjects. There was something about this inner life which attracted Rembrandt from his youth, showing him that the end time of life could be one of promise and fulfilment rather than despair and loss of dignity, even when it showed all the outward evidence of the latter.

There is an inevitable agony and ecstasy of the older person, which we need to attend to, to listen to and to learn from. The spirituality of ageing includes meeting and facing fear at an age when one is expected, or at least hopes, to be 'wise', 'settled' and 'integrated'. However, confrontation with and questioning of the ultimate meaning of life and death is, for some, an everyday experience – and it brings with it wonder and fear, light and shadow, agony and ecstasy. This is no mere 'retirement' agenda, for it embraces life, time, experiences, memories, hurts, money, status, achievements. Life may become more simplified but it is also more focused. If older people pursue their search for meaning with intensity and support, so opportunities for spiritual development continue.

One might summarize spiritual needs therefore, in the following ways. These needs are rooted in an understanding of spirituality as the way in which an individual responds to and makes sense of the raw experiences of life. They can be interpreted within or without a religious framework. There is a need in all of us:

- To feel valued and affirmed.
- To love and to be loved.
- To hope in something in this life and beyond.
- To have faith and trust in someone or something.
- To know peace, security and tranquillity.

We should note that spirituality is not a separate component of life and is not confined to moments of prayer and of conscious awareness of God or 'the other'. It underlies the whole of our lives – our aspirations, desires, fears and self-searching. It is the ground of our friendships; delight in nature and all creation, our relationships with others as well as God. These needs or longings or yearnings are satisfied in all kinds of ways and in all kinds of 'cathedrals'. For some, their essential spiritual needs are met through relationships and especially the family; for others through the satisfaction of consumerism; for others through sport and leisure and recreation. These diverse longings colour our aspirations and our hopes, our values and our choices. But like plant seeds, they need to be nurtured and sifted so that the best are able to grow stronger and to blossom.

One of the opportunities that growing older gives us is to attend to this dimension of our life. From this perspective, one could argue that mature age is part of the all-wise and all-loving plan of our Creator and can hold within it special blessing. It is this blessing that older people are called to find and to celebrate; for these can be wisdom years. Life can be a journey towards wisdom, but it will not be complete until we come to terms with what Erikson calls 'the un-alterability of the past and the un-knowability of the future'.

In a somewhat different perspective, one might think in terms of a range of needs put like this:

- The need for community.
- The need to be needed.
- The need for celebration and laughter.
- The need for recognition of individuality.
- The need for acceptance.
- The need to *be* rather than to *do*.

Older people can become a reservoir of values to transmit to new generations. Experience has shown that wherever older people are valued, included and enabled to participate, the community is a richer one. For example, older people can show us that accepting limits is part of human life and there is a value in *being* rather than *having* and *producing*. Certainly old age often brings with it losses; yet I have seen how older people with a number of medical conditions, who were nonetheless positive about their state of health, lived longer than those, who, although being less ill, had a negative attitude towards the situation they were in. This shows that a person, even with a number of physical illnesses, can in reality be healthier than another, perhaps with none, if that person accepts their limits and sufferings, living out their condition as an opportunity for spiritual growth. Spiritual needs, which generally become more intense in older people, can become gifts in the context of reciprocal relationships. It is the spirit of fraternity that makes us come out of isolation and weave a network of relationships in esteem and solidarity in which every stage of life can acquire a new understanding of its own beauty and at the same time of the beauty of the other. This particular approach is summed up in the reflections of Alison Johnson in *The Collected Writings of David Wainwright*. David reflects on the need in retirement and the third age to 'let go', to learn to accept the bereavement that comes with retirement from work and loss of status, to become aware of what he calls the 'zone of perpetual human maintenance – always something medical to attend to, always some clinic to go to!'[12]

David writes of the acceptance it is possible to find in the fourth age of life:

We are the elderly foot-soldiers of the church with a job to do. I believe that if we offer our diminishment to Christ on behalf of the church and of the world, our activity will draw the sting of suffering and will also help us remove some of the fear of old age and reveal instead the riches of God.[13]

Sheila Cassidy builds on this as she reflects:

It is the lavishing of precious resources, our precious ointment on the handicapped, those with mental illness, the rejected and the dying that most clearly reveals the love of Christ in our times. It is this gratuitous caring, this unilateral declaration of love which proclaims the gospel more powerfully than bishops and theologians . . . It is a particular form of Christian madness which seeks out the broken ones, people with dementia, the handicapped and the dying and places before their astonished eyes a banquet normally reserved for the whole and the productive.[14]

So, we acknowledge that a person's spirituality manifests itself in a very wide variety of ways. It is a complex phenomenon shaped by many factors, touching as it does on fears and aspirations, hopes for life and reflections on death. It is deeply personal and, while some diagnostic or assessment tools can help appreciate a person's spiritual need, it is best quarried through ongoing relationship, conversation and trust.

Before dealing with some specific pastoral issues I wish to comment on four particular questions that older people often ask in relation to diminishment. First, what is the meaning of vocation? Or perhaps, put in a more theological way: what does God want of us at any particular moment of our being or living? For some of the people that we live alongside, the loss of work remains an abiding cause of grief. It is very difficult to give up the status that comes with our work role. All of us have to learn, at some point or other, to give up and give way. This loss of work can result in a loss of our primary source of value and meaning. As Martin Luther put it: 'That to which our heart clings is our God.' How then do we reframe the sense of self and worth apart from the work role?

Second, how do we embrace finitude? We all have to face the

gradual limitations of life and the choices placed upon us. These limitations take all kinds of shapes and forms: physical, financial, social, spiritual and vocational. Part of our spiritual task is to achieve and nurture faith and values that enable us and others to work with, hold and yet transcend the immediate limits of the self. We can find within this process the possibility of hope, mystery and depth.

Third, how do we embrace anxieties around non-being? The ageing process, combined with the death of those closest to us, can make us more aware of our own death. How do we understand who we are and what our ultimate destiny holds for us? When did we last freely talk about our own deaths either with ourselves or others?

Fourth, how do we enhance autonomy? This is about power and control and how we empower older people to live as fully and richly as possible. We should always talk about work done *with* older people and not work done *for* them. Part of the challenge of spiritual care is so to connect with those we work with that together we can discover and rediscover the unique opportunities for growth and possibilities of our living at whatever age. This affirms the bonds of the human condition and our desire to live in a community where all can both belong and participate.

There is a story of a woman who came across Michelangelo in his studio chipping away at a beautiful block of marble. Shocked by the waste as the pieces of marble piled up, she rebuked the sculptor. He looked at the stone and her and then replied: 'The more the marble wastes, the more the statue grows.' This story reminds us that in addressing the spiritual needs of older people we should attempt to ensure that as the wasting takes place, older people are valued, and something of greater value is being allowed to grow.

I wonder sometimes why many people avoid deeper and more meaningful relationships with older people – something that happens at all kinds of levels. Carers can care without engaging; worship can happen without engaging those taking part. Perhaps there is a part of us all that denies the ageing process and fears what older people represent. We need then to come to terms with the 'elderly stranger' within ourselves, to face our fears, and thereby free ourselves to respond, to listen, to learn and to grow in dignity towards our ultimate destiny.

FOR FURTHER REFLECTION

Exercise 1

What do you understand by the concept 'spirituality'? What are your spiritual needs at the present time?

Exercise 2 – Exploring how our needs and values change

Complete these statements on your own; then reflect on them, either alone or with others.

1   My idea of a perfect day is

2   There was a time when

3   Young people never think about

4   I really dislike it when

5   I hope I never have to

6   I wish older people would

7   The one thing I could never do without is

8   Why don't churches

9   What I want most from life is

10   My biggest fear about getting old is

Exercise 3

This exercise may produce a range of answers and possibly some surprises. Be careful with the strength and possible complexity of what emerges. The aim of the exercise is to demonstrate how our needs and values change as we get older. We need to pay attention to this and perhaps even ask for support in helping us to relate our changing needs to our faith.

You are marooned on a desert island

- What object would you most want to have with you?
- When you are rescued, which place would you most want to be taken to?
- On which day of the year would you most like to be rescued, so that maybe you could join in a celebration?
- While you were on your desert island what life event, or turning point in your life, did you think about most – say, an event (other than being marooned) that changed your life the most?

This exercise encourages us to be reflective about our life, what we have come to see as significant and how our particular life experience may shape our beliefs.

Exercise 4

For your own understanding write down your present definition of the meanings of the terms *spiritual* and *spirituality*.

Exercise 5

Consider the following experiences:

- attending a funeral of a close friend who has recently died;
- going to listen to classical music being played live by a large orchestra;
- watching birds sing and feed their young;
- worshipping with a large group of people;
- sitting with one other person on the warm sand of a beach as darkness falls.

Which (if any) of those would you consider spiritual experiences?

Exercise 6

Here are some reflections from older people that have emerged as they explore their spiritual needs.

- Confusion is part of life.
- Don't try to be an expert in anything!
- Listening is a gift.
- Don't manipulate me with comforting words.
- Don't judge me – I can't help what I am.
- My feelings are important.
- Pay attention to things – it can be amusing!
- Learn to receive graciously.
- Learn to be comfortable with silence.
- Be willing to learn new things about yourself.
- Don't compare yourself with others – you will always lose!
- Find out what nourishes you.
- Use your common sense.

In exploring an older person's spiritual needs here are some questions which might be useful triggers to conversation and reflection:

1 Are you conscious of your age?
2 What keeps you going in life?
3 Tell me how you spend your time.
4 How would you like to be remembered?
5 What do you get angry about?
6 What are the qualities you think your parents gave you?
7 What were you doing when the war began?
8 Do you think that others understand being old?
9 Are there advantages to getting older?
10 Do you pray?
11 What most upsets you about the world today?
12 What gives you most pleasure?
13 Do you think we should try to be good?
14 Do you feel hope?
15 Do you feel wiser now?
16 In what ways do you sense God?
17 Would you like to go on for ever?
18 Has your spirituality changed since you got older?
19 What do you see when you look in the mirror?

FOR FURTHER DISCUSSION

- How would you define spirituality for yourself?

- Does your church community take into consideration spiritual needs?

- Can you think of any examples of good practice in the area of spiritual care?

- What prevents us from meeting spiritual needs – in ourselves and in others?

CHAPTER SEVEN

Worship *with* older people

Worship usually refers to specific acts of religious praise, honour, or devotion which are directed to God. It is the informal term in English for what sociologists call 'religious cultus', or the body of practices and traditions that correspond to theology and religious belief and express or embody it in corporate action.

The central ritual for most Christians is the Eucharist. This act of worship commemorates the Last Supper, with the use of bread and wine, connecting the community with the mystery of Christ's death and resurrection. It is a sacramental act of worship that brings hope and strength to participants.[1]

Prayer and the reading of Scripture are also important aspects of Christian practice. Christian traditions have rituals for other occasions, for instance, celebrations of stages in a life journey, closures and death. Ritual and symbol are important conveyors of meaning and help the individual within a community to connect with a sense of identity and meaning. So much for a rudimentary introduction to how one might define worship. How does this relate to practice? This chapter will outline what needs older people bring to worship and how we might best respond to them. First, let us look at some experience shared in the following case studies.

LISTENING TO EXPERIENCE

Claudia

I couldn't imagine my life without worship; both Sunday worship at my church and my personal prayers and devotions. At 86, I have been going to church for most of my life – it has shaped me in so many different and wonderful ways. As I grow older my faith has changed and, in prayer, I appreciate the space to offer the complexity and pain of life to God. I also need to celebrate all that is good and praise the God who is at the heart of this goodness. I especially appreciate the prayers that I know by heart, and I also enjoy singing. Many hymns and psalms have been faithful friends and guides to me. In worship I know myself to be deeply loved by God and ask for grace to express that generosity to others. In worship I hope to be given the strength to live my life within the present moment, aware of the limitations of my vision. I am much less bothered these days about knowing or believing the right thing. Simply being is a delight and I am glad that age has liberated me from the activity and 'busyness' of so much of modern life. I love to sit and watch and wonder and smile and pray.

Michael

At the grand old age of 76 I don't think that I have aged terribly well. I am one of those unfortunate people whom others think to be older than I actually am! I keep going to church but don't find it easy. The church does not seem to be the place of serenity that I once experienced. I don't think that I am resistant to change but I find too much change difficult. I feel the loss of the familiar services – finding your way around service books can be very bewildering. None of this is helped by my partial loss of sight, and I cannot hear as well as I could, despite my hearing aid! I enjoy children and keep cheerful but feel very marginal to the church community. I support the church financially but it never seems to be enough, given the ongoing decline. I have welcomed our new woman priest who is wonderful, but I wish I had the chance to talk about my faith with someone. I know that they are very busy. I will keep going to church for as long as I can – it is my Christian duty and wonderful to be nourished by Communion. I know that I am at the end of my life and I pray for the grace and love of God to help me die well. I don't expect the church to adjust for my sake – time moves on – but I wish someone would listen to us 'oldies'.

Joan

I will attend any service that is offered. I love to sing; I love to pray; I love to listen and learn. I need God's guidance and love every moment of the day. I enjoy God and all that the Church brings to worship. I have a trusting and unquestioning faith – the words which best sum this up are: spirituality, goodness, joy and praise. Sometimes those who lead worship overlook this. They can have a tendency to go on too long and make things too complicated. I wouldn't dare say that to my vicar's face!

Intercession is very much an important part of my Christian pilgrimage. One of the things that I can do is pray for others – to be still in the presence of the Lord and offer them up in prayer. I also love those familiar hymns.

Chris

My husband is living with dementia and I am speaking on his behalf. We are both lifelong Christians. We both believe in the power of God to reach out and touch each person individually, to share his love in abundance and be in relationship with us. These beliefs are especially important as we have struggled with the progressive diminishments of dementia. We have had to embrace confusion of time and place and personality.

We have had to withdraw from church worship because of the embarrassment and awkwardness as the illness has advanced. We know it is hard to understand what is going on. Alas, familiar church worship is meaningless and ineffectual. I know that my husband sometimes feels very alone as 'religion' in the formal sense of worship, prayer and ritual is fading away.

Richard

I belong to a generation that didn't really 'do' feelings. I was taught that they are best kept to oneself. Worship speaks for itself – it needs no voice or explanation. Sometimes I think that the words and forms of services suppress rather than support worship. I regret the emphasis on cheerfulness and humour rather than duty and devotion. I appreciate silence, ritual, music and mystery in worship: the world of the Book of Common Prayer, Keble, Herbert and Traherne. Loving God and following him for his sake only.

The individuals represented above clearly demonstrate the considerable diversity of perspective and experience to be found among older worshippers. They remind us of the danger of generalizing and, indeed, ever imagining that any one community will be in a position to meet everyone's needs. Imagine all these individuals in one congregation. What pattern of worship would enable their needs around worship to be met?

There are a number of factors to be borne in mind when reflecting on the provision of worship for older people.

First, and most obviously, we need to listen carefully to older people and their experience of worship. We need to dig deeply into the ways in which worship is shaped and formed. And through this conversation we need to get a balance between affirming that which is treasured, and challenging those perspectives which are either distorting or limiting. In this process we shall surely learn from older generations and the ways in which community and companionship have shaped and reshaped their lives. It will be important to know why some people hold such firm convictions; for example, why Richard is so loyal to the Book of Common Prayer, its language and associated rituals. Through these conversations we shall discover the need for silence and space and how older age brings with it a need for more reflectiveness, depth and even wisdom. These needs are shared by all Christian disciples so that as an 'all-age church' we may nurture reflectiveness and so grow in wisdom. As pastors, we shall have an enlarged sense of what is relevant and perhaps irrelevant; how people engage or listen to teaching and instruction and what kind of sermon best helps people to engage with the story of faith and salvation. We shall also note that some people find change difficult and may even be alienated from the Church and its worship by particular practices. A healthy community will want to listen to their sense of displacement or even anger, acknowledging its force without attempting to dismiss it or even transform it. After all, old age does not carry with it dictatorial powers!

Second, there are a number of practical issues associated with older people and worship that need to be borne in mind. These relate to those older people whose sight or hearing is diminishing and also those whose mobility is restricted. Churches need to think about their sound system and provide large-print orders of service or guides to help older people find their way through the liturgy. The physical layout of the church needs to be borne in mind when accommodating wheelchairs. Is it possible to accommodate wheelchairs within the main body of the church so that older people may feel at the centre of worship rather than at the margins? What kind of support might very frail older people need during Sunday worship, which may last up to an hour and a half? Many older people express their delight in children. Is it possible to encourage interaction between older people and children during worship and afterwards?

Third, this conversation about worship, its shape and place within the life of the church, is an important one for everybody to participate in. A pastoral church will want to give every person an opportunity to express their views and perspectives. A pastoral church will want to help individuals to understand their spiritual life and what might best support them to grow in faith at whatever stage of faith or life they may be.

Fourth, we must never forget what an enormous resource older people are. They contain a church's and community's corporate memory (which may often be inaccurate!) – both for good and ill. While older people may often be experienced as blockers of change they are not always so. They have experienced change and responded to it. They often have unique insights into the building and people. They want to support and encourage the work of the church. They are often the most significant financial supporters of the work of the church. They appreciate the pressures and difficulties resting on church leaders. Like Joan (pp. 84–5), even though they are not physically strong, they can be drawn into other kinds of participation, like prayer and intercession, that can enrich the whole community.

We now turn to specific acts of worship designed to support older people either at a weekday service in church, a residential care or nursing home, or at home. Whatever the setting, chiefly care homes of one sort or another, but also parish groups, services are often fitted or squeezed into a tight schedule as far as residents and staff of homes are concerned. The service, however, is very important for those attending – it is likely to be one of *the* events of the week (or the month). Is it, however, something provided by those in charge or something done with the glad co-operation of the old themselves? In other words, where do we stand in relation to older people in this particular context? Busy clergy or others responsible for leading worship are used to the former view of their role, if not in theory then in the practical matter of the production of worship. But it is important to cultivate the latter approach. Why? Because older people often have too few chances to express themselves, to present views or experiences, despite often feeling replete with 'experience of life'. We might argue that this runs the danger of turning worship into part of a therapy programme! Well, perhaps there is no harm if it is. And anyway, is not worship better if the worshippers can really be enlisted into the act and not simply left passive? Wherever possible, a collaborative and participative approach should be preferred. We should never underestimate the importance of the act of worship and how older people want to be celebrated *with* and not *for*. They express a desire to engage and express themselves and their experience.

In Temple Balsall this takes the shape of a 25-minute Communion service at 11 o'clock each Wednesday morning. The form of worship is derived largely from a traditional Anglican rite. However, there is enough informality within the service to enable others to feel at home in the group and with the service.

The ways in which older people can be enabled to participate must depend on circumstances, but it may include, for example, choosing hymns or tunes; offering intercessions; reading Scripture; bringing a discussion element into homilies. People value structure and habit, so there is no virtue in too much anarchy or unpredictability. For even though some value participating vocally and all will profit from the stimulation offered, there is also value in the familiar format. Music and silence have roles too. Here are some of the things that older people value: listening and learning about faith, especially the questions that old age poses; the opportunity to sing together and to offer prayers for situations or people.

In this context, at Temple Balsall we have generated a cycle of Bible readings for the liturgical year.[2] These readings are designed to fit in with the seasons of the Church's year but are deliberately chosen to be short and readable within the particular context. They also offer an opportunity for further reflection or discussion. So the passage is read, always by a resident, and this poses a question to which the group are invited to respond. Sometimes the question is connected to a bit of reminiscence or reflection; or it may often be contained within an experience of the community (the illness of a member of the care staff or a wedding or a death in the community). The address offers a special opportunity for engaging with what people have to offer. Many are likely to be shy, modest or unused to uttering in public (perhaps especially in this setting of worship); but not only is it good for them to have the chance to think aloud about matters of faith (and perhaps a new experience), it also gives the worship leader a sense of who these people are. One never ceases to be amazed at what is said, for good and for ill. Sometimes there is fun. The process takes time, especially in encouraging confidence to grow. A warm welcome can usually be counted on and people grow in confidence in their readiness to take part. The support and presence of friends and family can often help. The care staff or others who work in the place can also usefully participate. This can become a process of deepening faith and of enlarging horizons. It can be done within the context of eucharistic or non-eucharistic worship. It is a model to be explored and experimented with.

To think further about the possibility that the liturgy offers to encourage, listen to and value older people: on a number of occasions I have been invited to churches to conduct or preach at a morning or evening service which is given over to asking the congregation to think and reflect upon ageing and the spirituality of ageing. These services offer an opportunity to give older people a voice, to encourage the whole congregation to engage and support older people both in church and community, and to pray for those who are involved in working with or supporting older people in a variety of ways in the community. They offer an opportunity to express gratitude for the role that older people have played in church life and also an opportunity for older people to be given a voice. One may use these services to interview one or two older people from the congregation about their life, their faith and their reflections on the mission and ministry of the Church. A yearly service to celebrate age gives a community and church an opportunity to redress some of the imbalance in its priorities and perspectives.[3]

CHAPTER EIGHT

Older people and memory

LISTENING TO EXPERIENCE

Michael

At a conference I was asked to spend some time getting in touch with my perceptions about old age. Specifically I was asked to articulate what it is that I most fear in old age. One aspect of loss and change emerges with complete clarity. The thing I most fear is the loss of my memory. The loss of memory can be a source of real frustration and anxiety. For what are we without our memory? Our whole character, the personality we have built up over the years is made out of memories. To have no memories is to become a ghost.

Barb Noon

> Sometimes I picture myself
> > like a candle.
>
> I used to be a candle about eight feet tall –
> > burning bright.
> Now, every day I lose
> > a little bit of me.
> Some day the candle will be
> > very small.
> But the flame will be
> > just as bright.[1]

I felt depressed and defeated. I tried to pick myself up for visits to the doctor but otherwise I just stayed in the house and didn't do anything. I became a recluse. I was so ashamed of the way I talked. I felt stupid because I couldn't seem to put even a simple sentence together. The efficiency and organizational skills, which people once paid me for, had all but disappeared.

People just don't seem to understand that you can't relearn things . . . But it's not all doom and gloom. I can live with it quite nicely as long as people don't expect too much and aren't constantly trying to convince me that there's nothing wrong . . . Don't overprotect me or act like it's some terrible thing that we should pretend isn't there.

THE IMPORTANCE OF MEMORY AS WE GROW OLDER

As we grow older, memories seem to play a larger and larger part in our lives. There is not much we can do to change the general shape of our story. There are fewer things we can expect to achieve. What we have to offer depends much more on the sort of people we are; and the sort of people we are is very much a matter of how we think and feel about the past; what we have done, the people we have known, the cards life has dealt to us. And so remembering is important. All too often it happens that when people get to the age at which they need more physical support and comfort, they have a rougher time of it than ever before; when they need security, they can be worried about money; when they need company, they are sometimes left alone. How in this situation might memory be used to connect with happier days? In well-known lines, Tennyson wrote:

> This is truth the poet sings,
> That a sorrow's crown of sorrow is remembering happier things.
> ('Locksley Hall')

In spite of this, happy memories can be a source of courage and comfort and a spring of gratitude for all the good things that life has given. This cherishing of the positive can enable hardships to be more easily borne.

But often memories are not happy. There are things in all of our lives which haunt us. Some of these memories might relate to grief or pain and these leave their mark. Looking at older people one can sometimes detect a kind of quiet shadow behind the eyes of some who have suffered significantly – a shadow which never quite lifts even in the midst of laughter. But perhaps more difficult to cope with are significant experiences of shame and remorse. Perhaps how we failed to be patient, to give sympathy or understanding; how cruel we were with our tongue or how we have borne so many grudges for real or imagined wrongs. Perhaps there was, years back, a scandal in which we were involved, or a court case or even a prison sentence. A deep desire for forgiveness pervades our memories. We need to ask what kind of help, support or space we might require to deal with such memories.

Our ability for self-deception is, perhaps, more significant than we might allow for. All of us, to some greater or lesser extent, alter the story and perhaps even retell it to ourselves in a way which places us in a more favourable light. It is difficult to have the courage to face the darker side of living and of our own lives. But surely it is important to remember the bad things, and to remember them honestly and accurately; to face the truth about ourselves and others. Few of us can look back and not say with John Henry Newman, in the words of his famous hymn, 'Pride ruled my will.' Integrity, peace and wholeness can only be achieved if we learn to forgive and be forgiven. All of us make mistakes but we can learn from these mistakes, even if only in the act of facing and remembering them.

Learning to admit to our faults and to say sorry is an important part of memory. We may not succeed in putting everything right but if we refuse to remember things as they really were, then there will always be some diminishment in our attempts to live creatively and truthfully with the memories of our lives.

PROBLEMS AND MISCONCEPTIONS ABOUT MEMORY LOSS

We live in a world that places high value on cognitive skills. Societies are layered and fragmented in a way that results in unprecedented dependency on others. It is rare for people to be self-sufficient if they do not know how to manage the machinery of social and cultural life (nutrition, recreation, shelter, transport and so on). Think about the whole range of quite complicated tasks associated with food and eating. We need to go to a shop, make choices, and then operate machinery to cook, and to have a body which is capable of chewing, swallowing and digesting. With this particular core task there is a significant dependence on cognitive skills to undertake what is complex and technical.

This complexity of society contributes to reducing the functional ability of people with memory problems. In the developed world, those experiencing memory loss can easily be outpaced and outplaced in the functional machinery of society. Some have argued that the capacity to accommodate cognitive change is greater in the developing world where there is no stigma associated with memory loss and societies have so far found ways of coping with change in this way.

For the majority of people, full cognitive function is maintained as they grow older, with modest, age-related changes in memory which begin in maturity and develop gradually. Dementia is *not* a part of normal ageing: and it is very unfortunate that a myth of growing old is that an inverse relationship occurs between grey hair and memory! This myth, which is essentially ageist, portrays the older adult as senile, foolish and confused. Although there is some evidence to support the view that general cognitive ability slows in old age, this slowing is often measured in extra milliseconds needed for processing and does not impinge upon the everyday functioning of older adults. Indeed, the CRS (Can't Remember Syndrome) may actually peak in middle age when the stresses of life can be at their greatest: as do so-called 'senior moments', for example, when one goes upstairs and then wonders why!

WHAT THEN IS DEMENTIA?

As we have already seen, dementia is not an automatic part of growing old and we all begin to lose brain cells as we age. In dementia, the cells of the brain die more quickly than in normal ageing. The brain experiences holes like those in a sponge, tangles like a ball of wool, and transmitters zapped out in a random manner. The causes are complex and perplexing and are not yet understood. Diagnosis is difficult and can only be established with certainty through examination of the brain after death. Before making a diagnosis, the doctor will need to rule out depression, a urinary infection, poor diet, over-medication and constipation, all of which can result in confusion!

Sadly there is as yet no cure, although many believe that a high standard of specialist care may help to maintain quality of life. There are now drugs available, such as Aricept, which may delay but will not cure the symptoms. However, a decision by NICE in 2007 has limited their use to those in the moderate and severe stages of dementia. This has been a real blow to people with dementia and their carers as there is much anecdotal evidence that the prescription of Aricept in the early stages has given people a chance to discuss and plan for the future.

There is often confusion with terminology. Dementia is the term for a group of diseases which includes among others Alzheimer's disease.[2]

Alzheimer's disease (55 per cent of cases) changes take place in the brain leading to the death of cells and a gradual and slow decline.

Multi-infarct or vascular dementia (20 per cent) mini strokes destroy small areas of cells – step-like progression.

Lewy body disease (15 per cent), **frontal lobe** (5 per cent), **others** (5 per cent) (these include Korsakoff's disease, Pick's disease or related to Parkinson's or Huntington's disease, AIDS , CJD or alcohol, and increasingly Down's syndrome).

The major symptom is loss of short-term memory. People remember all about when they were children, but forget that they've turned on the gas or that they asked you the same question ten minutes before. It is now thought that rather than losing their memory, they may only have lost *access* to their memory. In the early stages this access may come and go with occasional or even frequent lucid moments. As someone with dementia said, 'On a good day I am still capable of writing a reasonably coherent letter and yet other days I have a hard time constructing a single sentence.'[3] It is often only when looking back later that one can see when the disease first began.

There are numerous other symptoms and it is unlikely any one person will develop all of them. The overall impact of the disease may depend on what the person was like before and on the type of dementia. Some people become disagreeable and difficult, others become passive and docile.

People with dementia may:

- Become confused about relationships, for example, believing that their daughter is their mother.
- Get muddled about time or place or confused about night and day, for example, getting ready to go to the shops in the middle of the night or asking to go home when they are already at home.
- Have difficulty in communication, for example, forgetting words and repeating the same question over and over again.
- Become unable to make sense of things, for example, how to use the kettle or a knife, fork or spoon.
- Have problems with familiar tasks, for example, putting on clothes back to front or inside out, or burning saucepans.
- Develop inappropriate behaviour, for example, eating with their fingers or swearing, going outdoors in nightwear or singing out loud in church at the wrong moments.
- Hide, lose or collect things, for example, collecting up all the towels in a care home, taking other people's handbags.
- Become angry, aggressive or upset (these are not now seen as true symptoms of the disease but rather a result of frustration at being unable to make oneself understood).
- Walk seemingly aimlessly round and round; but this behaviour is now thought frequently to be for a purpose, for example, looking for a parent or child. The challenge is to discover why.
- Experience hallucinations, for example, being convinced that they are being robbed, or watched.[4]

HOW CAN WE SEE THE PERSON BEHIND THE DEMENTIA?

Until the early 1990s the future for people with dementia was bleak – there was little alternative to the medical containment model of care, where the person with dementia was looked after, but often in a depersonalizing manner. People were 'warehoused' in old-fashioned mental hospitals, were kept fed and clothed (often in other people's clothes), kept quiet with drugs and simply waited to die. Dementia was known as 'the death that leaves the body behind'.

Tom Kitwood of the Bradford Dementia Group made a breakthrough in developing the idea of person-centred care. He saw dementia in the context of a person's life history with their personality, their specific illness, their general health, their network of relationships and their physical sensory environment. He believed that the crucial factor is to treat each person as an individual and to approach them with a knowledge of who they are (who they are, not who they were). He identified a 'malignant social psychology' which in its treatment of people dehumanizes and depersonalizes them. Hence the person with dementia is deceived, disempowered, treated as a child, mocked or, perhaps worst of all, ignored.[5] Recent research by the Alzheimer's Society found that many people with dementia only experience two minutes' social interaction in six hours![6]

HOW THEN CAN WE APPROACH THE PASTORAL CARE OF PEOPLE WITH DEMENTIA?

Since 5 per cent of people over the age of 65 suffer from dementia and 20 per cent of those over 80, and churches have ageing populations, it is inevitable that all clergy will be called upon to minister to people with dementia. Many are frightened of dementia, feel lacking in confidence to approach people with the disease and wonder whether a visit is worthwhile when the person may well have forgotten you've been shortly afterwards. However, visiting and being alongside them will help counter their many negative experiences with other people and will mean much to their family. If you wait to visit until you think you have all the skills and competence, you may never begin.

When approaching a person with dementia we need to remember that they remain people up to the point of death. They are held unconditionally within the love of God and even if they don't remember him, he remembers them. Somewhere within the confusion is the spirit of the person we knew and loved and, although you and your visit may be quickly forgotten, the good feelings generated will remain. There is ample evidence that people continue to respond to feelings long after they no longer seem to understand.

There is a lot of experience now which shows that given skill, patience and commitment it is possible to communicate in a meaningful way with people with dementia and those of us without the disability must believe that it is indeed possible. Some useful tips for improving communication are:

- Don't rush your visit.
- Introduce yourself by name and relationship every time.
- Key into the other person's feelings.
- Sit at the same level.
- Endeavour to establish eye contact.
- Speak slowly and simply but don't patronize.
- Allow time for the person to reply – don't be afraid of silence or pauses.
- Only ask one question at a time.
- Use touch where appropriate.

Many people with dementia have an amazing capacity to recall long-ago ritual and hymns and prayers. If you are able to use familiar prayers and Bible readings on your visit, you will often find the person joining in, which gives them a wonderful sense of still belonging to the Christian community. If possible, and if it is welcome, take Communion to those who have been accustomed to receiving it. Again, the familiar ritual and the repetition of familiar words brings the person back for a time and is a cue into their spirituality.[7]

HOW CAN THE CHURCH AS A WHOLE RESPOND TO THE NEEDS OF PEOPLE WITH DEMENTIA?

Meeting spiritual needs is not simply a matter of providing opportunities for religious observance, although that may be an important element in the Church's care of people with dementia.[8] A person's spirituality is linked to their sense of identity and the need for this linkage is nowhere more urgent than in those with dementia, whose personhood is so often denied in current practice. People with dementia are already likely to be a disadvantaged group – often old, certainly vulnerable and frequently confused. To ignore their spiritual needs increases still further that social exclusion.

The Church can begin by continuing to welcome people with dementia and their carers to worship for as long as possible. We are often indulgent to children who act inappropriately in church but disapproving of older people who do the same. After the service we can talk to them just like we would to any other member of the congregation. Conversation is like gold dust for people with dementia.

We need also to be very aware of their family and carers and offer both practical and emotional support. Sometimes it is helpful to stay with the person with dementia on occasions to allow the carer a period of respite either to go out on their own, to attend an event outside the home – or even just to have a peaceful sleep.

A very much appreciated ministry is to those who are living in care homes, 70 per cent of whom are suffering from a degree of dementia. We've already looked at the question of visiting and of the importance of familiar worship. The panel on page 99 gives some tips for leading worship in care homes.[9]

If at all possible, schedule time to remain and talk to people afterwards, so you can get to know people as individuals. When people are unable to join the group, visiting them, by invitation, in their own rooms may also be much appreciated. One-to-one time, attention, human contact and conversation may be as important a ministry as offering worship.

CONCLUSION

People with dementia often respond positively to music. After a musician with an accordion had played for a group in a care home, one of the residents said: 'You have touched the strings at the very centre of my heart.' We have the capacity to do this for people with dementia if we can only stifle our anxieties, lose some of our self-consciousness, and let love accomplish its amazing transformations.

Malcolm Goldsmith's book *In a Strange Land: People with Dementia and the Local Church* (see note 4) enlarges on many of the topics covered in this chapter. To conclude with some words from this significant book:

- An important first step is to establish a good relationship with the manager of the home, making it clear that you would be coming in to serve them – not with your own agenda!
- It is helpful to identify a specific member of staff so that you can liaise with them on an ongoing basis.
- A phone call just before the planned service will ensure that the home is ready for you, as circumstances can change on the day.
- Allow yourself time to arrange the room if life seems busy for the staff.
- Check whether there are any significant events like birthdays, anniversaries or deaths.
- If possible bring some members of your congregation to the service, which will normalize the occasion.
- Begin by reminding the congregation who you are.
- Use appropriate symbols and familiar rituals during the service. In general using visual aids helps concentration.
- Discover the residents' own favourite hymns or religious music and readings and include these.
- Provide large print versions of any written material, as many residents will have problems of visual impairment.
- Speak slowly and pronounce your words clearly as many will also have hearing problems. Avoid raising your voice too much or using a condescending tone.
- Be brief! Some residents' attention span will have become limited and 15 to 25 minutes is usually long enough.
- Be aware that people living with a degree of dementia may exhibit unpredictable behaviour and responses.
- Don't worry if there are verbal interruptions or if residents leave the room for the toilet or for other appointments. Sometimes these are unavoidable and showing understanding is important in developing good relationships.

We need to shift the attention from us to God . . . it is not what we do, it is not what we believe which is important, it is what God does! What God does is that he remembers us and the fact that he remembers us means that we are of immense worth. Our spiritual life does not depend on our remembering, it does not even depend on our believing, it depends on God's love and mercy alone.

FOR FURTHER REFLECTION

Exercise 1

What memories do I have which cause me pleasure when I reflect on them? What memories cause pain? Can I resolve any of the latter while I am still able to reflect and put things right?

Exercise 2

What do I know about provision for people with dementia in my area? Have I ever visited a specialist dementia care home?

Exercise 3

Participants at a Leveson Centre seminar revealed that they often fail to visit people with dementia because they feel frightened and don't know how to approach them. Do I avoid them and is it because I am frightened?

Exercise 4

Within the confusion is the spirit of the person you knew and loved. What would you want the staff to know about you if you were a resident in a care home for people with dementia? Could you start making a life-story book or memory box now? (See Appendix 2.)

Exercise 5

Being rather than doing is particularly important for people with dementia. Consider what you would do if you had an hour a week just to be. Would you listen to music, enjoy nature, stroke the cat or what? Could this be seen as your spiritual need?

CHAPTER NINE

Older people: intimacy, relationships and sexuality

LISTENING TO EXPERIENCE

Losing interest

In a recent conversation about a strong bond of affection which had developed between two people over 80 in a neighbouring congregation I was surprised to learn of other people's reactions. These reactions ranged from amusement to significant distaste. As the conversation developed it was clear that many people assumed that older people lost interest in making new relationships, and sex.

Nancy

Here where I live in Temple Balsall the site embraces a Templars' hall, a church, and a primary school as well as housing and care for older people. Every Thursday morning from my window I watch the 170 children walk from their school past our flats, down to church for their weekly service. I love hearing them talk and watching the excitement on their faces.

The children have a close link with the older residents here and often come to see us. A small group of children came to interview me about my experiences of the war. I am also glad every Christmastime to go into school to watch the Nativity play. Being part of a community that includes children is terribly important and gives us all a great deal of stimulation and encouragement. I hope, in our turn, we can be helpful and encouraging to those young lives.

Margaret and Michael

We both retired to this sheltered accommodation complex with our respective partners nearly 15 years ago and have been very happy to be part of the community here. Sadly, both of us lost our partners and we got to know each other as we attempted to support one another during our loss. As time passed we realized that we had much stronger bonds of physical affection for one another and at the age of 84 and 78 we've embarked on a very exciting new commitment. We greatly enjoy having sexual activity and feel that our newfound love and passion for one another has brought us a tremendous improvement in the quality of our lives.

Bill

I am very fortunate to have been able to live so long – I am now entering my eighty-sixth year. I have been blessed with a good family and have three children and seven grandchildren. Sadly my first wife died in her fifties but I married again and took on a further two children from her first marriage.

The children from my marriage and the children from my second wife's marriage have never really got on and that has been a cause of some difficulty and discomfort. We've done our best to get people together at family parties, but they seem resistant to wanting to connect with one another. However, the grandchildren do get on well together and I really enjoy seeing them. I have been able to support them financially in small ways and I always enjoy hearing about their new friends and adventures. I've learned a great deal from my grandchildren and they also are kind enough to want to hear me reflect on various matters.

Anne

I am a 79-year-old lady living alone. My husband died some 20 years ago and unfortunately we were not able to have a family. I live in the suburb of a large city in a house that has been my home since we married in our early twenties. I have experienced the place change around me but have always appreciated the diversity of neighbours and the ways in which any community adapts to the challenges and difficulties of any given time.

I keep reasonable health, though I am conscious that my body is slowing up and my mind is not as sharp as it once was. I try to keep as active as possible and I really enjoy the range of different groups that I belong to. The first thing that I would want to say is how important my church is. It struggles to keep the doors open and we're an older congregation but it's a place of real community and friendship and support. I do what I can to make sure that new people are welcomed and I help with the coffee after church on a Sunday. Our vicar is very busy and rarely has time to visit but I think it's important that we support her in the very demanding tasks that she has to hold together.

I go to a keep-fit club on Tuesdays, a painting class on Thursdays and I have two monthly lunch clubs which are really interesting. We have a speaker and it's good to have a nice hot meal with old friends. I still try to keep up with my WI colleagues, but that has been rather difficult of late due to some of the strong women falling out with one another!

I worry about the future and sometimes wonder if I shouldn't go and live in a sheltered accommodation set-up. To be honest, I don't really want to live too closely to a whole lot of other older people – I enjoy my independence and my routine and the networks and groups to which I belong. As human beings we have a fundamental need to belong. There are many facets of belonging: relationships with family, friends, groups and community. This discussion about sexuality and intimacy needs to be put into a broader understanding of the network of relationships of which the older person is a part.

The subject is important because it has been demonstrated that older people are more able to cope with some of the challenges of ageing if they are part of a network of close and sustaining relationships. In one of the first major studies of people over 75 years of age in Britain, Abrahams asked respondents to give their own description of what makes for a satisfying old age.[1] The biggest single group of replies concerned having good neighbours and good friends. This was rated above good health or enough money. While subsequent studies reveal that as people live longer, their health 'status' has become more important, a supportive social network continues to be a very significant part of a sense of well-being. A network of family friends and acquaintances can sustain older people and give their lives meaning. A distinction can be made between primary and secondary affiliations based on the intensity and importance of relationships. For some older people their connection with a faith community enables them to have a strong sense of sharing and belonging.

Any pastoral understanding of this area for older people should be aware of how difficult it can be for an older person to maintain relationships within their generation. Friends and family die or move away and keeping in touch can become more problematic. It is not uncommon to find ageing spouses or siblings living in relative isolation and struggling to maintain themselves with few supports.

In this respect friendships can be as important to well-being as the family. They often provide the critical elements of life satisfaction: commitment and affection without judgement, personality characteristics that are compatible because they are chosen, availability without demands and caring without obligation. Friends may share a lifelong perspective or may bring a new dimension into a person's life.

Here is a summary of why people value friendship that emerges from the work of the Foundation of Lady Katherine Leveson.[2]

- Friendship acts as a buffer against social loss.
- Friendship can provide socialization in old age.
- Friendship enables people to share activities and mutual interest.
- Friendship helps to preserve a sense of worth and value.

Couples in later life have needs and expectations that change from those of their earlier years. Sometimes couples married for 40 years or more describe a happy marriage as related to congruence of perception. This does not mean that couples always agree, but rather that they know what to expect of each other. Of course, not all who stay together are necessarily happy. There are many strains that are put on couples in the last phase of their lives. These include health, finances, relationship with children, matching needs for activity or disengagement and ability to support each other through crises.

When considering the pastoral needs of an older person it is also important to bear in mind the special needs that older spouses have in caring for partners. This can cause a significant strain. The sibling relationships of a partner are not always easy to accommodate. These relationships may be fraught with lingering resentments dating from childhood and competition for parental approval. They can be close and supportive but in the family, like all relationships, there can be times of strain and conflict.

GRANDPARENTHOOD

It is widely acknowledged that becoming a grandparent is a very significant experience within the network of relationships in a family. The experience offers the opportunity for personal development, family cohesion and intergenerational support in middle and later life.

Most grandparents demonstrate a combination of these attributes:

- They play a central role in the upbringing of their grandchildren.
- They are a source of advice and wisdom.
- They promote a sense of family history and continuity.
- They are able to relive the past through their grandchildren.
- Grandchildren enjoy being indulged by their grandparents.
- They are a source of practical help, usually readily given.

Grandchildren can bring a new lease of life to older people. There is a significant amount of energy and creativity in this particular intergenerational connection.

GROUPS AND NETWORKS

Although family and friends seem to be the most effective in acute and emergency situations, others are needed for long-term support, enjoyment and variety to augment the primary relationships. The development and maintenance of peer groups is important for older people. The great advantage of group affiliations for older people is in the diffusion of relationship intensity and constancy over much time. There are a range of groups and networks which deepen a sense of belonging. They are usually recreational or 'service'-orientated and perhaps somewhat superficial, and they are constrained by specific needs or goals. It is important that we understand a person in the context of these groups which are supportive to older people in the local community. The groups may be formal or informal but they provide an important sense of social support and relationship.

Figure 9.1 sets out the importance of social support groups for the older person and the whole range of ways in which older people can feel themselves to be connected with both community and society. It is important to consider these issues because aloneness and loneliness can be a very significant pastoral challenge to older people. In the UK a large percentage of older people, mainly older women, live alone. This reflects the affluence of our times, the likelihood of widowhood for women, the involvement of families willing to assist older people in maintaining their independence, and the cultural value of individual independence that is highly treasured in our society. We must also bear in mind the sheer cost of care.

While many people have a strong need to be alone it's important to understand the difference between loneliness and being alone: it depends how easy it is for the person concerned to move from aloneness to loneliness. For pastoral care in assessing the difference, the following points will need to be borne in mind.

- Loneliness is an affective state of longing, emptiness and feeling bereft.
- To be alone is to be solitary, apart from others and undisturbed.
- Lonely people may be alone or surrounded by others.
- People who are alone may be lonely or satisfied.
- Loneliness can be viewed as a condition of human life that sustains, extends and deepens humanity.
- Self-growth can come from a person's ability to recognize and cope with loneliness.
- Factors of loneliness and aloneness change as a person moves and grows older.
- Loneliness accompanies self-alienation and self-rejection.
- Loneliness is evidence of the capacity or desire for love. The degree of attachment is directly correlated with self-loss when detachment occurs.

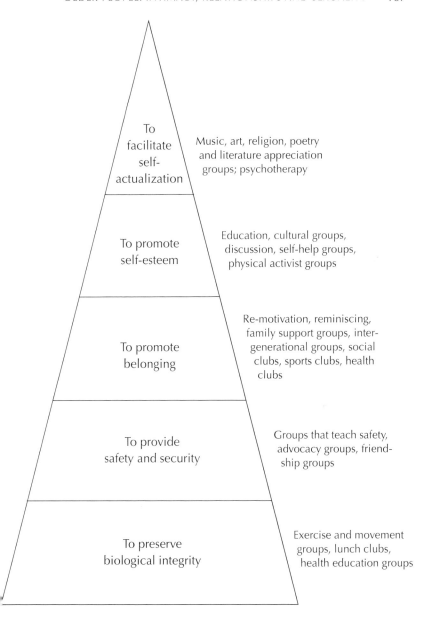

To
facilitate
self-
actualization

Music, art, religion, poetry
and literature appreciation
groups; psychotherapy

To promote
self-esteem

Education, cultural groups,
discussion, self-help groups,
physical activist groups

To promote
belonging

Re-motivation, reminiscing,
family support groups, intergenerational groups, social
clubs, sports clubs, health
clubs

To provide
safety and security

Groups that teach safety,
advocacy groups, friend-
ship groups

To preserve
biological integrity

Exercise and movement
groups, lunch clubs,
health education groups

**Figure 9.1   Maslow's hierarchical needs met in groups with
older people**

In summary, we have seen that the majority of older people have sustaining social networks, though an increasing number of very old people are at risk of social isolation. We've also noted that families are usually supportive to their older members and very often take on a range of caring roles. In particular, friends and peer groups provide mutual support and self-esteem for older people. In our pastoral understanding of the older person, it is important to differentiate between loneliness and a person's wish to be alone.

INTIMACY AND SEXUALITY

It is in the context of belonging and relationships that we now address complex questions of intimacy and sexuality. Sexuality is a fundamental aspect of being human that continues through life. One of the main points in the remainder of this chapter is that the need for contact with other human beings, closeness or intimacy does not automatically diminish when individuals reach a certain age.

Figure 9.2 (p. 114) offers a broad understanding of sexuality. The term itself has many dimensions and meanings. There is no single understanding of the concept.

Perhaps it would be helpful to offer a composite definition: 'Sexuality is a quality of being human, all that we are, encompassing the most intimate feelings and deepest longings of the heart to find meaningful relationships.'

If it is partly true that sex and sexuality is a taboo subject among the current senior generations, then addressing it in relation to older people is bound to be problematic. It is important to contextualize sexuality within relationship and intimacy. Sexual activity is only one way of communicating and getting to know someone else. Sexuality, intimacy and relationships are about promoting health and well-being: celebrating pleasure, excitement, vigour and self-affirmation; chiefly expressing love.

A sexual relationship is perhaps the most widely recognized form of intimacy. This relationship may be impersonal and involve no exchange of confidences or personal information, but it always involves physical intimacy – some physical experience of another person. As we have noted, this physicality is often a subject of both anxiety and distaste, but also paradoxically a source of fascination as individuals and communities become prurient in their curiosity about what people do with their bodies as expressions of sexuality. Most older people of the present time have lived through a huge change in attitudes to physical intimacy. There are very few who can discuss their feelings and experience openly. There will be many who feel that sex and sexuality is not a subject for public discussion and that this area of life should remain both personal and private.

The whole idea of sexually active older people fundamentally challenges the stereotypes most of their juniors have of them. If so, the invisibility of older people's sexual lives mirrors their common invisibility in many other areas, and when their sexuality does become visible they can be subject to a whole range of negative reactions. But why might we want to deny older people such a life-affirming experience? Why should older people be marginalized from these aspects of life? Persons, at all stages of their lives, need to be supported, to grow, change and develop, and to relate to others.

The social and political dimensions of a discussion of older people and sexuality should be seen in the context of changes in physical functioning which affect the way some older people experience their sexuality. The physical side of sexual activity is not purely governed by levels of hormones or levels of fitness. As the development of the drug Viagra has shown, it is possible to restore some sexual functioning – though this is only part of a very complex picture. For some, the physical dimension of sexuality is not the most important part – the ability to relate, feel, connect and engage, making possible the expression of affection, are often more significant elements. Other important aspects of sexuality are the emotional dimensions of intimacy, closeness and caring. These elements can lead to a wide variety of different sorts of relationships that older people may have with friends, peers and family.

There is a World Health Organization definition that describes sexuality as 'the integration of the somatic, emotional, intellectual and social aspects of sexual being, in ways that are positive, enriching and that enhance personality, community and love'.[3] This notion properly expands the concept of sexuality beyond narrow definitions of sexual intercourse to encompass sexuality, self-esteem, self-image and intimacy.

We should also affirm an understanding of the connections between sexuality and well-being in that it offers opportunities for intimacy and closeness. In other words, sexuality provides individuals with the opportunity to express affection, admiration and affirmation of one's body and its functioning. This wider conceptualization of sexuality relaxes its character as confined to sexual activity: it becomes more a part of everyday life. As it becomes integral to life experience, it also becomes integral to a sense of well-being. Some writers have argued that sexual health care is an essential component of overall 'wellness' during one's developmental life span and they offer the following challenge: 'All individuals, especially those who are ageing and those who have been chronically ill, need to express their sexuality in alternative ways in order to maintain and enhance their quality of life.'[4]

Many older people feel that their sexuality is neither encouraged nor acknowledged by others. Listening to the voices of older people, agencies have discovered that society fails to recognize the importance of sexuality to the well-being of older people. Further, society can impose barriers, which result in the sexuality of older adults being devalued.[5] Our images of the sexuality of older people are therefore important, in the way that they shape and are shaped by our attitudes to sexuality in later life, and the ways in which we support, discourage or ignore it.

It is difficult to imagine the kind of church forum within which these issues might be discussed either by older or younger people. Those involved in researching how older people look for support point out that older clients, understandably, in the light of what has been said above about popular attitudes, do not often confide in professionals about their sexual needs or difficulties. This leads to an invisibility or conspiracy of silence where everyone ignores what, for other age groups, is regarded as a legitimate and important part of life.

It is important for churches and others to confront what is going on in this process of denial. Part of it is based upon a strong unease or distaste that many have at the idea of older people having sex. Some have argued that this distaste is linked to the connection between sexuality and attractiveness – the idea that sex is only for beautiful people.

So, it is important to acknowledge the difficulties here and to encourage some sensitivity on the part of those who are charged with pastoral care. Sexuality is an important part of everybody's life, including older people, and those distastes or blockages which might prevent listening and engagement need to be acknowledged and dealt with. Within the field of social gerontology that is radically committed to listening to older people and their experience, there are many indications that views, attitudes and images may be changing. An older person today will have lived much of their life after the sexual revolution of the 1960s and the birth of the permissive society, where contraception became more available and the rules about sex outside marriage were widely seen as relaxed. They will also have lived in a society that bombards us with sexual images and discussions, from advertising with suggestive and sometimes quite explicit images to media items about the intimate sexual lives of the famous.

It may be true that many older people do not approve or feel comfortable about this but nevertheless it will have shaped some of their attitudes and perspectives. So some up-to-date older people will be the first generation to have viewed sexuality more from a companionate than a reproductive point of view. It follows that it is doubtful whether they will necessarily choose to hide or disguise their sexual interests or needs. They can be expected to challenge the existing representations and forge new ones.

Kingsberg[6] gives some examples of ways in which images are changing for women. Cultural stereotypes of middle-aged women as grey-haired, frail and asexual have given way to images of them as strong, active and sexual. Also there are corresponding images of sexually active older men beginning to break the former stereotypes. These positive images, however, are of people who are fit, attractive and not very old. Perhaps the real breakthrough will come when role models of positive sexuality in older people incorporate very old people who have physical limitations and who are not beautiful in the conventional understanding of the word.

We must accept that, as those gerontologists who research the lives of older people indicate, many older people simply get on with their sex lives. Results of most research in this area show that most older adults with partners continue to have sex, although it gradually gets less frequent over time. Some researchers have argued that those people who have stayed sexually active live longer and that they sustain sexual activity despite discouraging attitudes and contexts. However, there are some limitations on sexual activity, perhaps most significantly illness and lack of opportunity. People who have physical impairments may find sexual activity difficult because of a lack of flexibility, stamina or sensitivity. People who have lost their partners, through death or divorce, may feel frustrated because the opportunities for sexual activity with a partner have gone, and finding a new partner may be difficult. There are limitations placed on an older person by the inevitable physical changes that old age brings, but these do not mean that sexuality becomes any less important for an older person and frustration may well become an insuperable problem.

It may be useful here to remind ourselves of some of the changes in sexual functioning that can occur as people get older. Changes in blood supply, muscle function and connective tissue may make arousal more difficult. In men there may be a loss of libido, as testosterone declines. In women there is a decline in oestrogen and testosterone production after menopause which also may lead to a lowering of libido. In addition to these inevitable life-cycle changes, there may also be some disease-related changes in sexual function. Disease processes that are more frequent and common in older people can make sexual activity more difficult. Arthritis and prostate problems are obvious cases and diabetes and thyroid problems are other examples of how illness and disease carry the risk of having effects on sexual activity.

Social gerontologists emphasize the psychological aspect of ageing. While there may be some age-related changes, the greatest impact that ageing has is on the confidence and self-perception of the older person, in this as perhaps in other areas. Uncertainty and anxiety about sexual capacity, whether related to health problems, medical treatment or growing older, may both hinder sexual activity and make older people less likely to engage in it.

Some of this anxiety may be connected to feelings and attitudes that people have acquired through their lives; some of it may be a response to wider societal views. It is important to realize that sexual activity is not just physical, but psychological and emotional, bound up with feelings about the self and others. Pastoral care needs to work with some of these questions and challenges to self-image and attend to strategies of support that can build up self-esteem.

It may be worth finishing this chapter by allowing older people to give voice to their views and perspectives. This is done with a view to wanting to shape and inform our perspective as we engage, listen and learn from older people.

Here are some of their voices:

- It's about being close, it makes you feel alive.
- It is difficult for me to talk about this subject because I was brought up with the belief that sex was for men, and women had a duty to do it.
- The only good thing I got out of sex is my daughter!
- I can't talk about sex without thinking about my strong Christian upbringing, that taught me that sex was only about having children.
- Sex outside of marriage, if you got caught, brought great disgrace and fear.
- If you have genuine love for someone and you enjoy their company for any length of time, that's what love is, it is not necessarily to do with the bodily function.
- Sex is as important as intimacy – they must go side by side.
- Sex must be related with relationships, feelings, experience. To talk about sex is good – better to have the opportunity to talk to others.

CONCLUSIONS

Figure 9.2 summarizes the interrelationship of dimensions of sexuality viewed, as we have done, within the context of belonging and relationships.

Interrelationship of dimensions of sexuality

Intimacy, relationship and sexuality are fundamental aspects of being human. Sexuality can be a powerful, complex and potentially difficult aspect of life. We have noted that there is a tendency in Western society to suggest that the expression of sexuality or desire for intimacy in older people is inappropriate. We must be aware that some older people can internalize these stereotypes and can be socially controlled by other people's expectations. Pastoral care must open itself up to a wider appreciation of these issues of belonging, relationship, intimacy and sexuality for older people.

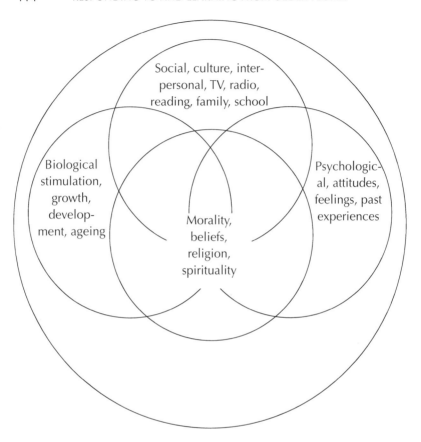

Figure 9.2   Sexuality

FOR FURTHER REFLECTION

Exercise 1

Make a point of studying images of older people in the media (newspapers, radio or television). How do they present older people's relationships and sexuality?

Exercise 2

Think about an older person whom you know quite well. In the light of this chapter reflect on this person's needs for belonging and relationship.

Exercise 3

How would you go about enabling a constructive discussion about the expression of sexuality in your own faith congregation or family?

Exercise 4

Talk with an older adult with whom you have developed a close and trusting relationship. What does sexuality and intimacy mean for them? Has it changed over the years? Were there any events or situations which have had an impact on their thoughts, feelings or behaviour? How have they coped with difficult periods of their relationships? Have there been particularly good times? How important do they consider sexuality and intimacy as an aspect of life?

CHAPTER TEN

Sharing our story: pastoral engagement with older widows

LISTENING TO EXPERIENCE

Jean

Jean is 72 years of age and has been widowed for seven years. She has three children and eight grandchildren. Jean left school at the age of 14 and has had numerous manual jobs, both part-time and full-time. When she was 18 she met and married Albert who was in the Merchant Navy. She was pregnant when she got married. Her father was opposed to the marriage (her mother died when she was still at school) and offered her little support as a young mother. Primarily for financial reasons, Jean juggled work and home commitments throughout her married life. She also acknowledges that she has always enjoyed meeting other people, and work outside the home offered her such opportunities. She worked in a factory, with her children in nursery, and subsequently undertook shop or bar work to fit in with family commitments. Money has always been tight and she and Albert lived in rented accommodation, initially provided by the council and latterly by a housing association. For most of their married life, Jean and Albert coped with his ill health and increasing disability. Despite that, and within the confines of family life, they were both very sociable.

In retirement they had made new friends who, along with the family, helped Jean when Albert died. Jean is now an active member of the local senior citizens' centre where she serves on several committees. She joined the centre six months after Albert's death. With her friend Phyllis, she has been instrumental in starting up dancing afternoons – dancing was her passion before she married, but she gave it up during her married life.

She has numerous friends, of whom Phyllis is special. Jean now lives in a one-bedroomed flat in the next housing association block to where she lived with Albert. She regularly attends a Methodist church and feels her religion is an important part of her life. She is in regular contact with her children and grand-children but fiercely maintains her independence (with the knowledge that any one of them is on the end of a phone should she need help). She is very content with her life.

Sylvia

Sylvia is 73 years of age and was widowed when she was 59, after 39 years of marriage. She now lives with another partner but has decided that they will not marry. Her childhood years were diffi-cult. Her father had his own kennels and was frequently away from home, meeting up with other dog breeders and owners. Sylvia was expected to work in the kennels when she came home from school and she had little opportunity to make friends. She passed her scholarship examinations but was unable to continue with her education because of the cost.

Sylvia started work as an office junior and became pregnant when she was 17. She refused to have her daughter adopted and three years later met John, whom she married. They subse-quently had another child and Sylvia gave up paid work. When Sylvia's father died, her mother moved in to live with her and John. She lived with them for the next 30 years. Sylvia returned to work when the children were older and her mother helped in the house. John was ill for a number of years before he died and so too was Sylvia's mother; Sylvia was their principal carer. Even-tually, Sylvia's mother was admitted to residential care and four weeks later John died. Sylvia has never had any close female friends; she and John used to go out dancing when he was well, but latterly they had spent most of their time at home.

She felt very alone when her husband died and started drinking heavily. She joined a bereavement club and then decided to go back to the dancing club she and John used to go to. It was here that she met James, her new partner. Sylvia's daughter does not approve of the relationship and they are now estranged; this saddens Sylvia greatly. She has always felt that family members should support each other, just as she and her mother did, and cannot understand her daughter's hostility. Her relationship with her son and his family is close and they have welcomed James. Sylvia still has a few friends of her own, although she and James have had a very active social life, and she does occasionally worry about what she would do if anything happened to him. Most of the time she lives life to the full and continues to enjoy her new relationship.

Dorothy

Dorothy is 71 years of age and she's been widowed for five years. Her childhood was not particularly happy and she spent some time living with her grandma. She did not enjoy school and left when she was 14 years of age. She had a number of jobs but could not settle to anything in particular. She met her husband, Roy, when she was 16, but very soon afterwards they both enlisted in the forces. She enjoyed forces life and feels that she would have made it her career had she not had to leave on medical grounds.

She was married in 1956, and after initially living with the family, moved into a new council house. She has three sons. She juggled work and home life in order to supplement the family income, but always put the children first. She was determined to be a good mother, but also acknowledges that she was, and still is, a very possessive one. It saddens her that her sons, now, have little time for her, nor do they understand how she feels. Her interests were centred on the house, sewing and baking. There was little time for socializing, because either she or Roy worked in the evening. In later years she felt they did very little together and regrets this. She became a school dinner lady, a job she did for 25 years, and was very upset when she had to retire.

After an accident at work, Roy had to retire and was ill for a long time before he died. These were difficult times and Dorothy still feels guilty about the times when she lost patience with him. She always refused to discuss the possibility of one of them dying, even when Roy made out his will, and she was surprised when he died. Dorothy has found widowhood difficult, especially birthdays and anniversaries, but she has always tried to keep busy. She has some close friends, who are either single or widows, and she works part-time. She's also a volunteer at the primary school where she was a dinner lady. She tries to look forward and has devised strategies, such as planning holidays and organizing her week, in order to ward off her sadness. She feels she's always been insecure and this is exaggerated now that she is on her own.

Faranza

Faranza is 63 years old and she's been widowed for two years. Two of her sons and their wives and children live with her in her house. Faranza was born in Pakistan. She left school at the age of 12 when her mother died and went to live with her sister-in-law and took over the care of the family. She was married at 17, having met her husband formally at her in-laws' house. She has six children, three of whom were born in Pakistan and three in England.

She still lives in the same house that she moved to in 1969. Her other sons and daughters and their families all live nearby and visit regularly. Faranza particularly enjoys the visits from her grandchildren and the support she gets from her children. She has some close friends from Pakistan whom she meets at the mosque; they have all been friends since they came to England with young children. Although Faranza's husband was not in good health, he was not really ill, so it was a great surprise to her when he died of a heart attack. At that time, four of Faranza's children were still unmarried so she had a lot of responsibility. As a Muslim, she always tried to put her trust in Allah, and she believes her faith has helped her to cope. She feels she manages well now that she's got used to having all the responsibility which she would have shared with her husband. She spends most of the time at home with her daughters-in-law, who sometimes take her shopping, or she goes to the mosque. Her religion is very import-ant to her; she says prayers five times a day and recites the Koran.

She feels her life is very different now, not because she is a widow, but because she is getting older and her children are grown up. Her life is centred on her children; she has never worked outside of the family home. Now her family look after her; for example, her daughters-in-law do all the cooking. She has pain in her leg when she walks and her diabetes sometimes gives her problems. She lives her life from day to day, trusting in Allah to get her through any difficulties. Her world is her family.[1]

This chapter deals specifically with the experience of widowhood. We should be reminded that marriage, rather than widowerhood, is the norm for most men. However, over half the women who are beyond their sixty-fifth birthday are widowed – which reaches four-fifths of those who are over 85. We note too that older widows tend not to remarry. In our consideration of widows and widow-hood we must ask whether it is inevitably lonely and unhappy. As we learn to value age, what can we learn from listening to older women? What mythology surrounds widowhood and how do women cope with this particular experience? In order to dig deeply into the narrative, more extensive experience has been shared at the beginning of this chapter. The reader might want to spend some time looking at one or two of the stories and to note what it is that strikes them about the experience of widowhood.[2]

The question of our identity is a complex one and it is shaped by many aspects of life, notably the impact of marriage and the marital relationship, age, gender and our view of the world. Those of us involved in pastoral care will acknowledge that later-life widowhood is a time of vulnerability and requires sensitive lis-tening and engagement.

The social context within which we shape our attitudes to the widow is important. Often widows are viewed as lonely, depend-ent or even depressed. Indeed, in nursery tales the old widow is often portrayed as a hag, harridan or even a witch! We should acknowledge that there are often inappropriate jokes about older women in relation to the network of relationships they have with daughters and sons-in-law. These stereotypes affect our individu-al and collective attitudes.

In the significant amount of literature on bereavement, there is a consensus that the death of a spouse is one of the most stressful of all role transitions. Bereavement is likely to impact on the physical and mental health of the widow as well as causing a major disruption to her sense of self. Following death and the process of bereavement, what is the potential for growth and change in the move from wife to widow? Part of the difficulty in this area is that in our society, there is no formal ritual, there is no prescriptive or accepted framework which presents grief and grieving as an appropriate, normal or proper process. Who is to say what is a healthy or unhealthy response to death?[3]

In the writer's own pastoral experience, the process of adapting to the death of a spouse is a long and hugely painful one – and despite the common acknowledgement that you are keeping busy or the claim that you're 'getting on with life', there is a danger in relation to avoiding emotion or the sadness of the bereavement.

There are very few places or opportunities where older widows might express their deepest anxieties, fears or emotions. In other words, how much human fragility and vulnerability are we as a society prepared to embrace and allow others to express? Indeed, other factors need to be taken into consideration – for example, where a person lives, what kind of community they are part of, employment outside of the home, voluntary work, the ability to drive and, significantly, the presence of children. All these might be considered as important dimensions of the process of adapting to change in life.

We should also recognize that successive generations will age differently depending upon how their society shapes their culture and values. For example, today's older widows, marrying in the 1930s or 1940s, have experienced longer marriages which were largely unlikely to be terminated by divorce. They learned from childhood that they were expected to marry, to be a good wife and mother and to put the needs of others first. Indeed, they were even encouraged to think of themselves as belonging firmly in the home. In such a patriarchal society women were judged in relation to men – many of them had little more than elementary education and went on to train for specifically female occupations. We should not therefore underestimate the radical changes in society during the 1950s, 1960s and 1970s.[4]

One of the challenges that women have to face is the discovery of the answer to the fundamental question: 'Who am I if I am no longer a wife?' Of course, this is predicated, ideally at least, on the sense of satisfaction, fulfilment and happiness experienced within the marriage. Sometimes, however, widows are faced with the reality that the death of a husband brings, perhaps guiltily, relief, and they often reflect on how much they have had to put up with.

The range of experience at the beginning of this chapter demonstrates that different women will experience widowhood in different ways. Some autobiographical research has suggested that widows struggle profoundly with their identity. There is, it is argued, a crisis of identity, which shows up the widow's capacity to struggle with change. Sometimes, widows talk about a transformed identity: although they would not have chosen to be widows, they like the new women they have become better than the ones they were when they were wives. Some women talk

about being more at peace, more serious, braver and more confident, responsible for self, more sociable, more tolerant and more
integrated.

This process of becoming a widow is a complex one and involves
a number of questions and opportunities. Older widows speak
about the importance of this period as a time to recover; to take
stock; to re-establish or restructure friendships and relationships. Others describe it as a time for discovering a new and different lifestyle – a time for personal growth and change; a time
for reasoned consideration of life and the possibilities of the
future.

There follows a brief description of some of the theories which
attempt to describe or conceptualize widowhood. The first
describes widowhood as pathology. From this perspective widowhood is located within the literature and understanding of grief
and suffering. Widowhood is a time of difficulty and stress as the
individual adjusts to life without a loved one. While it may be
important not to underestimate the challenge and difficulty of
bereavement, to locate widowhood simply within a pathological
model does not help us understand how older widows experience
the rest of their lives – nor does it offer us insight into the ways
they make sense of their lives.[5]

When considering widowhood, phrases like 'she's lost without
him' and 'she doesn't know what to do with herself now that he's
gone' are quite common in both family and professional discourse.
This sees widowhood as a loss of role and such an event will surely
precipitate an older woman's disengagement from society.

We should acknowledge, however, that widowhood is a major
milestone in the life course of women which most women manage
effectively. Within this perspective, widowhood is theorized as
part of the life course and becomes accepted and integrated into
life rather than being viewed as an illness or a 'condition'.

We note from the accounts chronicled above that widows
choose a range of ways of expressing their experience. There is a
measure of loneliness and despair, as these women give voice to
their loss of confidence and articulate that something is missing.
There is a sense of the enormity of the experience which is difficult to grasp, which makes them different, and can lead to an isolation where there is little pleasure from life and the future feels
bleak. While this loneliness and despair are acknowledged, there

is also a deep sense of the necessity to get on with life and to manage the transition and change. Widows often give voice to a calm acceptance of the inevitable and can reach a point where they are able to celebrate good memories and realize that there are few regrets. In the process of coping or getting on with life, there is also an inevitable loneliness and concern about finance and health. Women are very often good at keeping busy and keeping some of these anxieties at bay.[6]

For some women what emerges from the experience is a new self-awareness and a new freedom where there can be an opportunity for relationships and new interests and openings. Some of the women look forward positively to life and what it might be able to offer to them.

In this lived experience and narrative, a range of 'senses' of self are expressed. Faranza and Jean might best be described as having high self-esteem. Their stories demonstrate self-confidence and a strong value base. They are secure and independent and ready to learn from experience. Contrast this with Dorothy and Sylvia who feel powerless and lonely. They express a lack of self-confidence and some feeling that they have failed to live up to expectations. They are constantly seeking others' approval; in other words, they struggle to have much sense of individuality.

Of course, within the context of our understanding of self-esteem, we note that it is something that fluctuates in life's experience. All of us have regrets – times when we say to ourselves and others, 'What might I have been?' In reflecting on the self, perhaps these women wonder whether they might have been someone else and entertain a range of scenarios which led them to choose one path over and above another.

For some of the women that we have listened to in this chapter there is, as we have already noted, a very strong sense that the social context of their lived experience has been powerful and shaping. Some of these women belong to a generation that has experienced the war and has not experienced much comfort and security. These women have lived through significant social, cultural and sexual change. This 'belonging to a generation' has also been shaped by gender: in other words, the relative lack of access to education, the importance of becoming a wife and mother and living within the cultural belief that a woman's place is in the home.[7]

As we listen more closely to older widows' lives, pastoral care must attempt to validate the richness and diversity of their experience. In the listening and reflection, pastoral care must try to make sense of what the lived experience is all about. In this exploration there is potential for growth as concerns are addressed and negativity given voice to. One of the lessons to be learned from the people we have listened to is the importance of being reflective about our own biographies.

CHAPTER ELEVEN

Men and age: images, questions and reconstructions

LISTENING TO EXPERIENCE

Robert

I am 67 years old and I am in the third year of my retirement. I have been divorced for nearly 20 years but have managed to keep good relationships with both of my children and their partners. Since my divorce much of my life and energy has been taken up with my work, which was rich, varied and totally absorbing. I certainly achieved some measure of success in my working life which was rewarded with responsibility and status. My work demanded much of me and I was enormously fulfilled through its long hours and the significant number of people with whom I worked and had connection with.

In my early sixties I experienced a change of leader at the head of my organization and was unsuccessful in a number of applications for more senior appointments. I decided, therefore, to retire a little earlier than I had expected. I am financially secure and have a comfortable regular income. I have been fortunate enough to invest wisely, especially in a good pension plan.

I do not regard myself as old – I keep fit and have a great deal of energy and interest in people. I haven't found retirement easy and I feel the loss of purposeful activity very acutely indeed. In some ways I regret giving up my job and while I have enjoyed leisure I still feel I have something to offer to others.

Jonathon

Sometimes I envy the calm conviction of personal worth enjoyed by the very young (if they are fortunate enough to have had truly loving parents) and look at some of my grandchildren who are experiencing adolescence and see how they have to embrace dreadful uncertainties. Of course, the self-doubt can linger well into adult life and as I look back on my middle years I see them as almost a constant struggle to come to terms with my sense of self and the doubts I had about who I might become.

Well, I am 71 and I suppose I am in the sunlit uplands and losing shame about almost everything. Yes, there are a few shadows ahead; illness, incapacity, bereavement, my own mortality, but I have trained myself to refuse to think about these matters until I must. I am going through my world with the confidence I would have killed to have had at 17 or 27 or even 37, come to that.

In my seventies I regard it as perhaps an age of indiscretion. I can and I do say what I like, when I like, flirt with whomsoever I choose, and generally enjoy behaving disgracefully. Disgracefully, according to my younger self, that is.

This period of time has been a tremendous opportunity for discovery and rediscovery. I think it took me until the age of 60 before I really achieved any sense of wisdom. I had discovered that the world would not wobble on its axis if I didn't work all the hours there were, that it is permissible to take life a little easy from time to time, that work, enjoyable though it has always been, is not the be-all-and-end-all of life. There is great satisfaction to be found in discovering words spoken centuries ago that can mean something for us today. The ones I have found were spoken by Oliver Cromwell when he was having great problems persuading Members of Parliament to act as he wished them to. They kept on arguing with him and at length he burst out: 'I beseech you, in the bowels of Christ, consider it possible that you may be mistaken!' It is something I have said to myself many times, as well as to other people. It's remarkably creative and effective. Why don't you try it?

So, 70 – a bit battered by time, I cannot deny. I slipped and fell heavily on my knees in the dining-car of a train in China (at least that sounds a little glamorous!). The long-term effect of that, as is too often the case in older people, is that one injury has a domino effect and leads to all sorts of other ills, this time the need for a knee replacement. That didn't work and it had to be renewed, followed by the other knee, which, fed up with doing the work of two for a year or more, decided to give up the ghost and demanded its own replacement. I may have lost a great deal of my mobility but, as I say, there are compensations. These struggles with my health have taught me to know the truth and value of a piece of ancient wisdom that my grandmother was always quoting to me. She said it was an old Chinese proverb, a description I never believed, and was so maddened by it when she never stopped trotting it out that I wanted to bash her over her head! It was to be used in bad times and good times, she told me, wonderful times and dreadful times, and it would always help: 'This too will pass.' It works amazingly well because it puts matters into a manageable context.

The final lesson I want to share is that age is almost irrelevant when it comes to one's inner life. Inside this 70-plus old frame, I am an indeterminate thirty to forty-ish creature, slender as the morning and lovely as the dawn. And it's the pleasure that there is in indulging one's inner self that never goes away and can provide satisfaction even when your view of yourself in a mirror fills you with amazed horror. For my part, I am glad to be old and – to quote a cliché again – it sure beats the hell out of the alternative!

Roger

Personally, I did not notice much change in myself until I was 75. From that age on, I found my memory deteriorating and my senses becoming less acute. My hearing isn't as good as it was and sometimes I fail to see something I am looking at when it is staring me in the face.

There is a saying that when you are old you either widen or wizen. I have done both. Physically, I have wizened; I have lost two stones in weight. I can no longer run up stairs as I used to. I find travel very tiring. Psychologically I have widened. I am much more interested in people as human beings and can imagine them at every age from childhood onwards when I see them.

I have lost all my interest in power and position and no longer worry about making money. I still enjoy my work but do only what I want to do.

I am now much more sensitive to colours, shapes and sounds. My eye will automatically compose a clump of flowers or a corner of a landscape into a picture. I enjoy music even more than I used to because I get a greater pleasure out of the sound of different instruments. I have become exceptionally sensitive to sunlight; it immediately moves me to pleasure. I use my increased leisure to look at paintings and sculpture, to enjoy opera and drama. I love my wife, my children and my grandchildren more than ever and spend much more time with them. To use Freud's expressions – I have lost interest in my ego, much preferring my super-ego, while my 'id' continues to wane.

At a Leveson Centre conference, when I presented a session on this subject, a number of people asked whether the gender differentiation between men, women and age is appropriate. It is not the purpose or scope of this book to deal with how the experience of ageing is different for men and women; indeed, some of the issues discussed in Chapter 10 are shared by men and women alike. But rather it is the purpose of Chapters 10 and 11 to encourage those involved in working with older people to understand some of the questions and experiences that shape age and ageing.

At this point the reader might look at the three case studies above and highlight what strikes you about each story.

We should acknowledge the complexity of our understanding of self. While we may hold the belief that we know ourselves, how might this help us to find our *sense of self*? What are the disconnections between what we see and how we view ourselves? In other words, what is it about our lives that we might want to change? What are the things about the shape of our narrative that we would alter if we were given the opportunity? There is an inevitable partiality and subjectivity about the image we construct and the biographies we write. These narratives are always an act of perception and construction. This becomes even more complicated (and interesting) when there is some measure of disconnection between what we see and how others see us. The art, therefore, of expressing our experience and understanding of our lives is rich work for those involved in pastoral care.[1]

Robert, Jonathon and Roger (pp. 125–8) all reflect on their ages and their ageing bodies. The predominant factor within this reflection is medicalization. There is an inevitable emphasis on how our bodies work or do not work. It is not surprising that individuals feel easily disempowered when age restricts or diminishes. How might each of our individuals be helped to humanize the inevitable changes that ageing brings? How are they to embrace the power of their own fear in a world whose values are so dominated by those of production and consumption? For example, in Robert's case, what is the meaning of 'purposeful activity'? How much of our sense of self is invested in the work role? What is it about our lives that gives us a sense of stability and security?

In all of the case studies above there is some measure, which may be more difficult for men than women, of embracing human weakness. For all three biographies there is a measure of social decline and some deep ambivalence about the concept and nature of retirement. In this context, while much attention has been given to the pastoral needs of older women, there seems to be a need for men to be helped to consider these challenges of identity and their fulfilment. This may be more difficult if older men are separated from other generations, or indeed if younger generations fail to begin to prepare for the loss and changes which begin in middle age and continue through to old age and death. There is a fundamental social question about the political economy of older men and how far that economy is life-enhancing.[2] Does the rest of society understand them?

Particular attention should be given at this point to the issue of retirement. A number of reflections follow. It is surprising that it is often only at the retirement party that the retiree is made aware of their importance or significance. We live or work within contexts where, too often, we fail to encourage, give praise or express our gratitude for people and their gift to us.

The early stages of retirement can often be a 'honeymoon period' when new freedoms are enjoyed – freedoms of time, travel and new ventures. However, this may be followed by a more difficult stage which can be marked by disengagement, even despair and depression. Some of these existential questions are expressed in Jonathon's story.[3]

It is one of the tasks of pastoral care to offer some support to enable an individual to develop a new stage of self-construction and meaning.[4]

What all of our case studies share is the intense meaning that is projected into work. This is a potential danger that all those over-preoccupied with work as the only source of self-worth should be warned about.

It should be acknowledged that work *is* the basis of much of one's sense of worth and, indeed, for many decades of life. It is the arena where we make friends. Work is a source of prestige and recognition. Work is the source of experience, creativity and self-expression. For some, work gives an opportunity to serve others and it may also be a way of passing time. It is therefore not surprising that many men, in particular, find it difficult to move away from the work mode into a different role or way of living.[5]

We should acknowledge here that men's experience of age is complex. It is dominated by images of disengagement, changing roles, redundancy and retirement. There is a political need for men to explore what the meaning of social power is for them. It should be recognized that men *do* experience ageism. From the perspective of this book, further work needs to be done on the particular spiritual challenges for pastoral care of men.

CHAPTER TWELVE

Lifelong learning and older people

LISTENING TO EXPERIENCE

Doris

I am 88 and ever since I retired at 60 have spent two afternoons a week helping out at my local Age Concern shop. I think that one or two of my fellow volunteers believe I should give up, but I am not going to give in to their negative views of old age. I am not a very bright person and don't like reading. I never take a newspaper and have never had a television set. I love people and I am always at my happiest when I am meeting people. My link in the shop brings me into contact with all kinds of people. Some of them come in here for company! I love listening to people's stories and hope I can be of some use especially when things are hard or difficult. I don't think that people take enough interest in one another. That's what keeps me alive and going! I think people are quite extraordinary in their courage and wisdom.

The Discoverers

We are a small church group that meet together each month for an outing. We are all shapes, sizes and colours but the thing we have in common is that we are all getting on a bit in age. The format for our group is simple. We meet for a short service in church. The minister leads us if she can make it and then we borrow the old scout bus for a trip. We visit a park or garden; a house or sometimes a shopping centre. We start with lunch (that's important for us all) and try and call off for a cup of tea somewhere after the visit.

We all enjoy it. We try and support and encourage one another. We love visiting new places and meeting new people. You are never too old to discover something new.

Rachel

I have worked all of my life in social work which has been very stimulating as well as demanding. I ran my department for some years but I spent most of my time working with people and enabling them to respond to challenges and problems. I have spent most of my working life as a hospital social worker.

When I retired it was the liberation from paper, forms and computers that I most appreciated. I decided to move house and to let go of many of my books. I kept 30 or 40 of my favourite ones as faithful companions. I decided to embark upon something completely new and different: drawing and painting.

I joined a life drawing class and enrolled on a couple of painting holidays. I also decided to try and learn more about the history of art with a local college, but I have found some of this rather academic.

I have discovered so much about myself and the world around me. I am using different parts of my personality and experience. I have got in touch with a different dimension of life and it has been transforming.

Maxwell

I decided to go back to church when I was 70! No one much noticed me and, in some ways, that rather suited me. I wanted to take a few steps back and reflect on the shape of my life and what it has all meant to me and those I have tried to love. Is church helpful? In some ways it certainly is – I am intrigued by the Bible and the shape of the Christian message. The priest does his best to bring it alive and make connections, but I wish I could have opportunity to have some dialogue. I would like the church to answer *my* questions rather than *their* questions. I believe that some older people do become more questioning and reflective, and learning for me should be about discovering and rediscovering meaning and purpose on our journey. I should like to share some of these discoveries with others.

Much of our understanding and appreciation of the issues related to older people and learning have been shaped by the pioneering work of the National Institute of Adult Continuing Education (NIACE) and through the research of Dr Alex Withnall in the University of Warwick. The Leveson Centre itself has become a focus for the inclusion of older people at every level of our social and economic life and has consistently argued for the positive benefits of education in later life. In particular, the work of the Foundation of Lady Katherine Leveson (which embraces the Leveson Centre) has attracted a wide number of groups who wish to learn more about history and spirituality and reflect on some of the problems and possibilities of growing older.[1]

I have been particularly interested in what the University of the Third Age movement has achieved and the enthusiasm its members have for learning. I would best describe U3A members as spiritual adventurers who with discernment choose, and discover, as all consumers do, what best helps them to grow and make sense of life and live creatively.[2] The metaphor of journey is prevalent in many fields of study. People are attracted by looking at other people's journeys through their biographical reflections. For many the Christian message is grasped through story – its story intermingling with our own: in other words, we get to know God biographically. This journey has its continuities and discontinuities, its ups and downs, with which we cope, often with the help of significant others. From this perspective ageing is an existential condition for personal growth. As we have seen in Chapter 4, older people's spiritual needs tend to change and increase at certain stages of their life journey and for some this can lead to a deeper belief and faith. This is well put by Harry Moody, a pioneer educator in this area working in the USA, when he reflects on the life tasks that assist this growth and movement:

- Self-determined wisdom.
- Self-transcendence.
- The discovery of meaning in ageing.
- The acceptance of the totality of life.
- Revival of spirituality.
- Preparation for death.

Source: Six dimensions of spiritual well-being, Harry Moody[3]

The educational and learning elements of the journey and the possibilities associated with growth are outlined by a number of writers.

The learning journey

Four issues for older people to resolve

- Self-sufficiency vs. vulnerability.
- Wisdom vs. provisional understanding.
- Relationship vs. isolation.
- Hope vs. fear.

Four tasks of the later spiritual journey

- To transcend difficulty, disability, loss.
- To search for final meanings.
- To find intimacy with God.
- To have hope.

Source: Elizabeth MacKinlay[4]

It is certain, from a pastoral perspective, that this work is best done in formal or informal conversation. Some of the issues raised might be very specialized and require additional attention or support. The challenge to pastoral care is whether we have the time and preparedness to assist older people with this range of learning tasks that can assist growth. Albert Jewell, who has dedicated much of the latter part of his ministry to this area, is very clear about the responsibility of faith communities in helping older people to reflect on the nature of their encounter with God. He believes that as they do so they can come to terms with their experience, particularly losses and difficulties, and through this work develop a positive awareness of reconciliation and closure. Of course, from this perspective, age is both important and unimportant for all, at whatever stage of our journey we might be. We have a lifelong spiritual task to live; to love; to learn and to leave a legacy.

The mission challenge for faith communities is whether enough pastoral time and expertise can be released to engage in these spiritual learning tasks. There is some indication that the churches, even in the face of steady and relentless decline, have both the imagination and the energy to make this fostering of spiritual growth, especially among older people, a priority.

However, this challenge is not only to the churches but also to society as well. In a groundbreaking piece of work NIACE demonstrated the exclusion of older people from learning, based on a number of negative stereotypes, images and assumptions.[5]

NIACE have certainly been successful in putting lifelong learning onto the government agenda, with a number of agencies acknowledging that older people in retirement have learning needs and can see that education has health, social, individual and economic benefits.[6]

Employers are becoming more conscious of the opportunities that older people offer to their businesses in terms of experience and competence. In addition to the less obvious economic benefits, it is argued that learning programmes for both younger and older adults serve many good purposes. Also there are additional factors associated with being old which should be considered as part of nurturing an inclusive society. We should acknowledge the value of older people's experience, to be offered to younger generations, whether as sources of memory, knowledge and reminiscence, or as serving as mentors or researchers.[7] Older people often have unique insights into the way things were, which can bear on historical understanding of place, community or some current issue. Promoting learning also gives older people a voice. It can be helpful to include and empower them directly in care planning and in education for older age. In any bureaucracy it is easy to overlook the customer or client as the focus of the work. Often professionals feel more comfortable doing something *for* older people rather than doing something *with* them. We should acknowledge their continuing contributions to the community, as well as those made when younger, via work, taxes and 'the war effort', when there were (and still are) few state benefits available in return. As we've already seen, a commitment to reflection and learning, carried out with sensitivity and care, can enable older people to embrace some of the frailties and disabilities of increasing age. Finally, if older people are given a voice then we might go some way to tackling ageism in society generally, as well as ageism in education provision and employment.

In planning for older people's learning, whether in church or some other agency, teaching needs to take these needs into account. For most older people, learning is for now and not to be stored up for the future; yet learning is not necessarily about the past, but will embrace the present and the future. So a commitment and investment in education for older people can enhance employability, and develop the voice of older people. It can enable them to take stock and live well; empower them in decision-making processes; allow them the opportunity to meet a wider range of people and thereby minimize their isolation. It also gives benefits to us all in developing greater understanding and sensitivity in older people. Pastoral care and carers need always to *listen and to learn from their listening* as they are opened up to new ideas and new perspectives.

It is worth giving some space to convey the findings of research for it provides some very useful further understanding of the nature of our society in which older people find themselves living and which so powerfully shapes their lives.[8]

Background false assumptions

- Older people are all the same.
- Older people have nothing of value to say.
- It is not worthwhile encouraging older people to engage in learning.

We are reminded of how easily we think of older people as belonging to one identifiable group. We have already noted that every individual ages differently and growing older can be seen as a complex interaction of biological, psychological, historical and social processes. So when we grow older we become more different rather than more alike and need to be treated with individuality and respect. We have noted that the force of ageism – probably the most damaging aspect of ageism, defined here as stereotypical beliefs and attitudes because of people's chronological age – is that it involves making sweeping generalizations about individuals based on their physical appearance. As people grow older they accumulate a wealth of experience, not just knowledge and skills, but memories, impressions, wisdom and the capacity for life review, as well as the ability to be creative – which many people retain well into later life. There is now a wealth of evidence that suggests that when older people are encouraged to express their views and discuss their experiences – and to recognize that these are important and will be listened to – their confidence in their abilities improves and they are often motivated to undertake things that they would not have previously considered.

Further, there is increasing evidence that recognition of older people as potential learners can confer benefits on society. To deny the potential of older people as learners is to restrict their opportunities to remain active and involved members of their communities and of society as a whole.

MISCONCEPTIONS ABOUT COGNITIVE FACTORS

- Older people have less brain capacity.
- Older people's brain power has diminished.
- Older people are too slow to learn anything.
- Older people forget things.[9]

Chapter 8 has already dealt with some of these factors in relation to memory and indicated that while there is some slowing up in cognitive function, the presence of growing numbers of older people living happy, independent lives in the community is ample proof that physiological deterioration of the brain and loss of capacity are certainly not inevitable. Older people are able to use their brains and retain their capacity for skill development and productive activity in much the same way as younger people. There is some evidence, for example, that engaging in activities that keep the brain active, such as chess, word games and cross-words, has beneficial results in the same way that exercising a muscle or joint helps keep us all mobile. It follows that older people are our most untapped human resource, possessing a range of experience, skills and talent that do not necessarily lessen with age. A man in his nineties who is still working as a supply teacher was recently profiled in the media, with colleagues and children alike testifying to his skills and the range of valuable experience he brings to the job. One of the reasons that we should grasp the opportunity for learning among older people is to develop the use of skills acquired in earlier life which can not only benefit others but also give the older adults a greater sense of purpose and so enhance their confidence and self-esteem.

MISCONCEPTIONS ABOUT PHYSICAL FACTORS

- Older people have mobility problems.
- Older people have poorer eyesight.
- Older people are deaf.

These physical factors may sound very obvious but again all work together in fuelling our negative images of ageing.

MISCONCEPTIONS ABOUT DISPOSITIONAL AND ATTITUDINAL FACTORS

- Older people live in the past and don't like change.
- Older people are not interested in today's world.
- Older people are frightened to go out.
- Older people do not travel.

At a time when we are witnessing change on an unprecedented scale in many aspects of our lives, it is perhaps not surprising that people often, no matter what their age, try to deny the reality of an uncomfortable present by seeking refuge in the past. Older people are more likely to live alone, and some researchers suggest that recalling past times when things were believed to be better helps them focus on the values of family and the community which they perceive to be lacking in present-day society and in their lives. This is reflected in the popularity of articles about the past in magazines aimed at older people.

It is possible to acknowledge this factor without then asserting that this means older people are not interested in the present. For many, the ability to read, write and carry on a conversation is maintained throughout later life. Older people's engagement with their family and neighbours keeps them in touch with the world around them. Work on intergenerational relationships reveals that many older people are keen not just to share their own memories or offer their skills, but also to learn from younger people. Perhaps the challenge is not whether older people live in the past or in the present, but how we can all live together to appreciate how elements of the past can help us all to live in the present.

Older people often have a lively interest in what is going on around them and many would like to play a more active part in their local communities. In the local geographical area in Solihull many voluntary organizations depend upon older people for their continuing survival. Older people work in the local hospital in the WRVS shop; some residents in Temple Balsall work in Age Concern shops; they support the Marie Curie hospice, the WI and many other similar organizations. Indeed, if an age limit was set by the churches for those holding voluntary office (PCCs, church elders, churchwardens, stewards, treasurers) of, say, 65 then vast numbers of our churches would cease to be able to function properly!

Issues surrounding isolation, transport and community are very significant for older people. Older people live in a diverse range of settings and types of accommodation, and older women in particular are likely to be living alone. The idea of 'home' can be understood from a range of perspectives, but for most older people it will evoke positive feelings of comfort, independence and a sense of being in control. So attitudes to home change and for some old people venturing out of the house can be a stressful and tiring experience. However, in spite of these problems, there is considerable evidence that maintenance of a sense of identity, of belonging and purpose, in later life can involve not just home but extends to feeling part of a neighbourhood and a local community.

The increased popularity of holidays for older people counters any misconceptions about their apparent reluctance to go out, which certainly does not prevent many older people, whatever their personal circumstances, from making retirement a period when they focus on extending their horizons by travelling farther afield when circumstances allow.

MISCONCEPTIONS ABOUT ATTITUDES TO LEARNING

* Older people are not interested in learning.
* Older people are not interested in learning anything new.

- Older people are not interested in information communications technology.
- Older people are not interested in environmental issues.
- Older people only want to learn with older people.

Older adults experience a number of practical barriers to learning opportunities which include lack of transport and unwillingness to go out at night. Some cannot go far for health reasons, but also the costs of the provision of education can present an obstacle to many. The absence of large numbers of older people from adult education courses does not necessarily mean that they are not interested in learning. There is evidence that they, like learners of any age, move in and out of formally organized learning activities according to their personal circumstances and needs. Personality and background play a part in the choice that people exercise in deciding what they want to learn and how they prefer to learn it. Again, as has been implicit throughout this chapter, there are a number of opportunities for churches to set up opportunities for drawing in older people to learn new things.

Unfortunately there are still many older people who do not have access to the computer or the Internet but this is changing, especially as the baby-boomers are reaching older age. It is apparent that there is an increasing demand for IT skills among a growing number of older people and there is much lobbying going on to provide the resources for older people to have such training and access to facilities.

Finally, environmental issues have been attracting increasing interest from all sectors of society and people of all ages over the last three decades, as the realization of the impact that our activities can have on the environment has grown. A number of older people have become involved in pressure groups such as Greenpeace and Friends of the Earth. A number of churches have developed opportunities for their members to access fair trade goods. Older people's interest in these issues makes the environment a rich agenda for later-life learning.[10]

The work in this area demonstrates the importance of a commitment to providing opportunities for lifelong learning for all people, but especially older people. One of the aspects of this work which can enrich pastoral care is the apprehension of wisdom which can be the outcome of spiritual well-being, successful ageing and effective learning. Closer attention to older people and their lived experience demonstrates that wisdom is indeed age-related and can accumulate and develop over time. Time and experience are the raw materials to shape wisdom, and older people have these two things in abundance. Wisdom is, of course, different from knowledge; different in content, process, outcome and purpose because it is grounded in everyday life. From this perspective, wisdom can be a kind of 'ordinary theology' as it is accessible to all as they reflect on their life in the light of faith and God.

Wisdom is also accessible through narrative and biography; always individual and unique and almost impossible to measure. Wisdom can be mistaken for foolishness: for it is sometimes neither conventional nor rational. Wisdom is life-stage-related and can emerge as a result of resolving conflicts or engaging in a range of tasks. Many older people bring to the task of learning a desire to come to terms with their past with all its diversity and richness. Wisdom can be related to continuity as it embraces changes, moves on and lets go, and seeks to quarry inner resources. Wisdom, from this point of view, needs to be put into a broader perspective and is related to the quality of life, wholeness, health and living a good life. It is important that we respect elders and their wisdom as it can give cultural and social meaning to younger generations. They are guardians and transmitters of truth and purpose.[11]

CHAPTER THIRTEEN

Retirement

LISTENING TO EXPERIENCE

Alan

I am 72 and have absolutely no intention of retiring. I haven't any time for any of this modern nonsense of work–life balance. I thrive on the demands and stress of work. I think my wife wouldn't let me retire – she doesn't want me around the house and enjoys spending the money that comes from my business which I have built up over the last 50 years. My two sons are keen to take over but they will have to wait. I believe I have experience, including the experience that comes from making many mistakes, and this experience can guide the business through the many demands of the modern, unpredictable marketplace.

I am afraid that I am very impatient with my retired friends – all that golf and pointless foreign travel. Work is all I need and I am thankful for the chances that life has given me and for my ability to seize the opportunities of the moment.

Marjorie

My husband died three years ago after a long illness. While I miss him, we had plenty of opportunity to say goodbye and put things in good order. I live in a large house in the suburbs of Birmingham and I have a great passion for our garden and growing plants from seed. I have run the plant stall at the church summer fair for the last 28 years and appeared on television talking about my green fingers!

Well, it is time to be sensible. The house and garden are far too big and I need to move to something smaller and more economical.

I have decided to move to a small retirement community, to a two-bedroomed bungalow. It is going to be quite a job sorting out all these years' accumulated clutter, but it has to be done. I enjoy the challenge of a task.

The advantages of such a community (about 120 people) are very clear. I will have to pay a maintenance charge and they will look after all my needs. No more problems with roof tiles, plumbers or grass-cutting. There will be new people to get to know and lots of different sorts of activities to join in. I am, of course, fortunate enough to be able to afford this kind of accommodation. The most important thing, for me, is that I shall be living in a place where, if I need extra support, I shall be able to access it. There is a residential and nursing unit on the site which is a tremendous source of extra security. I am pretty stubborn but know when it is sensible to ask for help.

Alison, Jon, Martha, Roger, Kate and Marcia
We have all been friends for some time and got to know each other through a variety of ways, mainly over our shared interest in art and music. We are in our sixties and those of us with children are relatively free of responsibility. However, three of us have older relatives who are becoming increasingly dependent upon us. That is a concern.

After a great deal of thought we have decided to sell all of our houses and pool our resources in a common pot. We plan to move into a large house together in our retirement and run a small co-operative community. We are having great fun thinking through the aspects of how this will work. There are issues of both internal and external space. We also have to attend to the complex financial dimensions of the project and even have a plan when conflict happens. For us it is the perfect solution – a community of shared interest where we make decisions about what we need. We will 'buy in' a range of services as and when we need them, including care support. We want to work together to maintain and develop healthy ageing and to improve our quality of life. We also want, in our retirement, to offer something back to our community. Some of us will retain part-time paid work and others are planning to embark upon new avenues of growth and learning.

John

I retired 20 years ago to what some of my friends regard as a life of idleness! I cannot tell you how liberated I felt from the burdens of work and responsibility. I sleep well, enjoy some gentle exercise, take an active interest in current affairs and read very widely. I cook and enjoy entertaining friends. I drink and smoke on a regular basis. I am not especially introspective – I take each day as it comes and do my best to enjoy what these remaining days offer.

Barbara

While I was looking forward to retirement my plans to move to the south coast were changed by the premature death of my father. He was the main carer for my mother who has Alzheimer's disease. I stepped into his shoes and sold my house to move into the family home. I do my best to remain cheerful and positive but, as you can imagine, it isn't very easy. I have a great deal of support from social services and friends but the care is relentless in its demands. I do get opportunities for some space when my mother goes into respite care but sometimes find myself resentful that these 'golden retirement' years have been taken away from me by circumstances.

FURTHER REFLECTIONS ON RETIREMENT

These five case studies demonstrate clearly that it is impossible to generalize about older people and the diversity of perspectives that they bring. Here is a summary of a range of different reactions to retirement.

Rewards

- The sense of freedom which is absolutely wonderful.
- Being useful to my children and grandchildren and having the time to reconnect with them.
- Not having the burden of holding things together in my job.
- Being able to write letters and emails.
- Being free from some of the hassles of life.
- Being able to sleep whenever I want.
- Having the freedom to read new things and to discover new things.
- Being able to say the things that I want to!

Trials

- I never wanted to give up work and feel lost without it.
- Downsizing into a smaller home was tough.
- Saying goodbye to people I cared about.
- Unsure about why I should get out of bed in the morning!
- I wasn't quite sure that I was of worth any longer.
- Dealing with my ageing body and things slowing down.
- Concerned about having to spend my time entirely with older people.

Surprises

- Finding how tired I was when I stopped moving and sat still!
- Discovering all kinds of connections when I sat still and contemplated.
- Taking delight in small everyday things.
- A new sense of achievement at what my working life had done.
- Finding that I didn't have the slightest desire to go back to my work and role.
- Finding that I had more money than I expected to do the things I wanted to.

FACTORS AFFECTING RESPONSES TO RETIREMENT

The above responses, taken together with the case studies, illustrate a wide variety of reactions to retirement. This variation stems, in part at least, from differences in spirituality, in personal psychology, in life experience (and especially work experience) prior to retirement, in health, in family circumstances and other social networks and, not least, in the financial provision that it has been possible to make. Not only do these differences exist between different individuals but circumstances will change, and so will their relative significance, for the same person as he or she proceeds further into old age. It is important, therefore, in terms of pastoral care of those approaching retirement or those struggling to adjust to it, not to suppose or to suggest that there is a blueprint for a happy retirement which can simply be applied to every case. Sensitivity to the factors which may determine the nature of the retirement experience is essential. A good way of approaching retirement issues is to look at some of these factors in more detail, beginning with the more practical aspects.

FINANCIAL FACTORS

All who go into retirement from full-time paid work will wish their standard of living to be maintained or at least kept at a level fairly close to that which they enjoyed while working. Some may find to their surprise that this is not as difficult as they had feared, particularly in the case of couples where both have occupational pensions as well as state pensions, but for others the new financial restraints may come as a rude awakening. Although, as businesses and advertisers have begun to realize, there are older people with money to spend (consider the rapid growth in cruising as a holiday activity), there are also many older people for whom poverty is a real issue.[1] Age Concern says that 1.8 million pensioners live in poverty, that 68 per cent of pensioner households depend on state pensions and benefits for more than half their income[2] and that around 7 million people are not saving enough for their retirement[3] (see <http://www.ageconcern.org.uk>). They also point out that there is an 'advice gap' whereby some people have too much income to be getting advice from welfare agencies but too little to be of interest to the financial services sector.[4]

For those who are able to arrange it, having an adequate pension (company or private) and sound investment advice are two important factors in arriving at a financially worry-free retirement that will be maintained for many years to come. This ideal situation is more likely to be achieved if the planning starts at an early stage in life and is ongoing. It is for this reason that planning plays an important part in retirement education. The issues to be addressed might include some or all of the following:

- Adequate pension provision.
- Insurances.
- Ongoing investment security and strategy.
- Decisions on buying or renting property.
- Mortgage implications.
- Understanding of current taxation including capital gains tax.

- Inheritance tax planning and covenants.
- Sources for sound financial advice.
- Rights on change of employment (for example, pension transfers).

Finally, it is worth saying before leaving this section that the ability to live happily within a certain level of income is not simply a matter of how big the figures are. It depends in part on having realistic expectations and the ability to come to terms with what is possible. There are people living on low incomes who perceive themselves to be rich and those living on incomes two or three times the size who bemoan their poverty. While it would not be true to say that it is 'all in the mind', perceptions of wealth and poverty do not correlate precisely to levels of income.

FAMILY AND SOCIAL CIRCUMSTANCES

As the case studies and subsequent comments illustrate, retired people display a vast range of different family and social circumstances. Retired people may be single or partnered, men or women. Those who are partnered may or may not have children or grandchildren. They may also have one or more parents still alive, needing varying degrees of attention; and they may or may not have brothers or sisters who can share the task. Other members of the family may live round the corner or across the world. The only certainty is that what it means to be a member of a family in retirement is likely to differ in some degree from what it meant when working. And, like every other aspect of retirement, this may be good or bad.

On the one hand, many retired people welcome the opportunity to see more of their families in retirement, especially grandparents who delight in seeing their grandchildren growing up. On the other hand, it is much harder in retirement to refuse any request that families may make and a third of grandparents provide the equivalent of three days a week childcare.[5] One wonders how many of these made a positive choice to spend their retirement so heavily committed and consequently so restricted in pursuing the other possibilities which retirement might be thought to open up. Thus it can be that managing one's relationships with one's family becomes quite a major issue.

The factors that relate to families can also be relevant to other social networks. If you are fortunate enough to have many friends, retirement is an opportunity to spend more time with them, but if they are widely scattered around the country there may come a point where the amount of travel involved becomes a burden. Even if they live locally there is an issue about how much time you wish to spend in social activity and how much time you want to devote to more solitary pursuits like tending the garden or reading. Again these are matters which may require active management.

There is a further consideration in this. Many retired people take up activities which 'get them out of the house' and these may require varying degrees of commitment. If you join a choir or a musical group the other members will depend to some extent on your presence so it becomes a commitment. Likewise working one or two days a week in a charity shop or going to hear children read at the local primary school will involve agreeing to be there at set times. This may be exactly what some people need to provide structure to their lives and avoid that feeling of 'what do I have to get up for today?' On the other hand, it impinges on that freedom which many retired people consider to be the prime benefit of retirement. Here again psychological and temperamental differences are significant as some are capable of living with very little structure and others cannot do without it.

HEALTH ISSUES

Health – or lack of it – can obviously have a profound influence on a person's retirement prospects. For most people this may not be a major issue in the early years of retirement, though it obviously will be for those forced to retire through ill health. Even in relatively early retirement, however, minor signs of physical decline may be in evidence, such as the need to take more frequent and longer rests when engaging in strenuous physical activity. As the years advance such limitations are liable to increase until one enters what David Wainwright has called 'the zone of perpetual maintenance'.[6]

Beyond the obvious advice about making healthy lifestyle choices and taking care not to fall, there is not a lot that anyone can do to forestall the diseases of old age, but again attitudes can be immensely important. I have written extensively elsewhere about attitudes to illness in a Leveson Paper.[7]

LIFE AND WORK BEFORE RETIREMENT

The shape of retirement is bound to be heavily influenced by the nature of a person's life, and especially their work, prior to retirement, particularly in the first years when the contrast is most stark. This, of course, can cut both ways. Sadly, it seems that many people today can hardly wait to retire because of the pressure they are under at work yet they may still be surprised at how much they miss going out to work, and the social contact that it provides. Conversely there are those who find it hard to imagine life without work but find the transition surprisingly easy once it happens. And of course it is possible for the same person to have ambivalent attitudes: on the one hand, 'Thank goodness I don't have to go to work any more' and on the other hand, 'Help! How am I going to fill my time?'

Which of these feelings is predominant is bound to depend to some extent on the part that work has played in a person's life previously. Those who have 'sold their souls to the company' will obviously be in a different position from those who have regarded their work as a nine-to-five occupation to pay the bills and whose 'real' life has always centred on their leisure interests.

There will also be clear differences between those, mainly in professional positions, who can continue doing some freelance work following their retirement or may use work-related skills in a voluntary capacity, and those whose work has to stop totally because it cannot be done outside a specialized environment, for example, a car production line or a laboratory. There will be further differences in the extent to which work is missed because of the 'perks' it offered, ranging from indefinable elements such as social status and sense of self-worth to very practical issues such as access to a photocopier.

What many find is that the distinction between work and retirement is less sharp than they had imagined because certain aspects of retirement assume the characteristics of work. The only child who, in retirement, has to care for a parent with dementia will have less freedom than they ever had in their working life and their 'working hours' will be far longer. This is perhaps an extreme example but in every retirement situation there are those things that have to be done as well as those things we can choose to do. Nevertheless for most people retirement will bring an increase in choice and control, though that can in itself be problematic when there are too many choices and it becomes a major task to manage all the available options.

PERSONAL PSYCHOLOGY

It seems obvious that various aspects of personality will have a huge effect on the kind of retirement a person leads and how readily they will cope with different aspects of it, so it is surprising that these issues do not feature more prominently in the literature on ageing. A number of psychological profiling tools have been developed over the years and some of these are regularly used by human resources departments both in screening candidates applying for jobs and in mounting staff development programmes. It is undeniable that one's personality type, whatever the tools one uses to define it, or the terms one uses to describe it, is highly influential in the way one relates to other people and in the way one approaches a task. It is therefore inevitable that it will be a significant influence in how people choose to shape their retirement.

At a most obvious level the widely recognized distinction between introverts and extraverts will come into play. Those who depend on being with others to bring them alive will surely seek out the company of others and will want to engage in a range of social activities while those who are more self-sufficient may be happy to 'do their own thing'. This is not, of course, an absolute distinction but a matter of balance. Introverts are not necessarily averse to company nor extraverts incapable of sitting quietly by themselves for a while but their differences in personality will be a factor in shaping their choices.

Other kinds of personality trait may be equally influential, for example, the distinction already mentioned between those who need everything to be 'cut and dried' and those who are happy to 'go with the flow'. Certain aspects of ageing can be particularly trying for those who like to be in control and have been accustomed to being in control throughout their lives. How does such a person cope when they contract an illness which means that they cannot tell from one day to the next what they might be capable of doing? How do they learn to 'go with the flow' when all their instincts favour having a plan?

Personality factors may be particularly important in decisions about accommodation when it becomes increasingly difficult for a single person or a surviving partner to remain in the house they have lived in for many years. Many surveys have shown that one of the losses people living on their own feel most keenly is the loss of community. In many ways it would seem that the obvious solution for this would be a move to a residential home, especially as one of the well-known personality profiling tools claims that extraverts outnumber introverts three to one. But what of the 25 per cent who show varying degrees of introversion and especially the smaller percentage who are highly introverted? Even if all care homes were as good as the best, such a person might find living in residential care very difficult to bear and it might be more appropriate in such a case to try to continue to support him or her in their own home, however difficult this may be.

Given that personality differences seem not to be widely discussed as an issue in retirement it may be important to pay particular attention to this aspect.

SPIRITUALITY

The ultimate question – in more ways than one – for those embarking upon or struggling to cope with retirement is, 'Who am I?' In this respect retirement has surprising parallels with adolescence. Just as adolescents go through a period of angst trying to discover who they are and what their lives are all about, so the same questions rear up again 40 or 50 years later and, if anything, in an even more acute form. Whereas the adolescent may reach some sort of answer by defining themselves in terms of the career they intend to pursue (I'm a budding doctor, car mechanic, policeman) that option is no longer open to the retired person. They can no longer define themselves by what they do; they are compelled to ask themselves who they are.

This question carries with it a cluster of others. Who am I? Is there a 'me' that is not defined by my work? Is it necessary to have a 'purpose' in retirement or is it all right to be completely aimless? What might such a purpose be? Is self-development a sufficient purpose or is that just another name for self-indulgence and, if it is, is that all right? And where might any greater purpose (call it God or what you will) come into any of this?

It is not for those in pastoral roles to tell people that they need to be addressing these questions but to be aware that they may be asking them, even if not in precisely this form, and to be prepared to explore possible answers with them.

THE PASTORAL TASK

In the light of all that has been said above, pastoral care should be sensitive to the range of possible responses to the experience of retirement and offer the opportunity for people to reflect on its emotional and spiritual dimensions. People come to the experience from a variety of perspectives: some cannot wait; others are simply very, very tired; some find it almost impossible to live without the status and role that their work has given to them. Careful listening can help a person to resolve life changes and to be self-reflective about the advantages and disadvantages of their particular situation. Helping resolve such things is often a matter of working out the relationship between circumstances rather than focusing upon a single factor, be this personal or situational.

There is no blueprint for retirement and anyone in a position of pastoral care who thinks there is may well do more harm than good. There is no substitute for listening to the experiences of the individual and engaging with them wherever they are.

CHAPTER FOURTEEN

Older people:
illness, healing and death

The human encounter with illness is a rich and complex one. This is due, in part, to the fact that illnesses are not the discrete or precisely defined entities that one might suppose. We have struggled to understand the causes of illness and argued about what makes for health. The answers to both those questions depend on such a wide range of factors that the encounter with illness presents us with a major challenge: we have to struggle to understand and connect with this ambiguous and paradoxical reality. Our meeting with illness is always open-ended because there is no language or agency that can fully comprehend or control this dimension of our human story.

This chapter will attempt to take an overview of some of the questions and challenges that illness presents to us all, but especially to older people. In addition, the pastor needs to think theologically about the encounter and look at ways in which our grasp of illness can reshape appropriate pastoral responses.

Recognizing the grace of God is a lifetime's work. It is shaped by the story of our lives and deepened by our soul's commitments. Illness is part of our human condition and it is God's purpose for us that we should see the 'good' and 'bad' parts of our lives as of a piece – equally part of the design, both necessary for the picture as a whole. We cannot choose who we are and few of us escape illness. Indeed, older people can expect to experience illness at some time during the third or fourth stage of their life. We all become ill at some point and in this sense illness is a natural process – it is a biological response to something going wrong. While illness can often be painful and sometimes tragic, it is also an inevitable and natural part of our human existence.

We all know that people cope with illness in many different

ways. Some disregard it and maintain an admirable level of activity in the midst of it. Others can be submerged even by relatively minor ailments. These different attitudes depend not on age but, in part, on our temperament and on our expectation of normality, perhaps on our attitude to faith in God.

Illness reminds us of personal limitations. It also faces us with the challenging reality that there are limits to human knowledge. While medical knowledge has expanded and continues to do so, it is foolish to assume that all illness can be cured. Perhaps the modern expansion of medicine since the 1950s has given us the expectation of 'limited immortality', as we harbour a sense that nothing should go wrong with our bodies that cannot be rectified, even in old age. Medical science is not all-knowing and there continue to be gaps in our knowledge and in the capacity to cure and to heal. Put a different way, it is impossible to live for ever!

But illness, when it occurs at any stage of our lives, can cause us anxiety and unpleasant emotion because it threatens our well-being and the steady tempo of life, and the older we get the more we may resent disruptions in the order of our existence. We are told that fear is aroused by a sense of local threat, from which the victim feels an impulse to flee, whereas anxiety is typically aroused by a known or else unintelligible stimulus. Illness often seems mysterious to the one who suffers it, even if it is well understood scientifically. The pastor must engage with this fear and anxiety.

Faced with illness or the threat of illness, whether in ourselves or others, we may feel anxious about our very being. We sense the possibility of meaninglessness and perhaps a sense of guilt that can foreshadow death. Illness can separate us from our loved ones: it can cause anxiety in those who depend upon us for whatever reason. Anxiety is aroused by threats to survival and also by the risks to our sense of personal identity as accorded to us by family and community. Anxiety in the face of illness is a natural and honest emotion that is an essential part of our human condition. It can never be eliminated, but it is not impossible to turn it to creative use. Part of what this volume is attempting to do is to alert and sensitize the pastor to the range of anxieties that shape a person's world.

This part of our vocation as Christians is to share 'one another's burdens' (Galatians 6.2). Deliberate and compassionate sharing of the burden means a careful sensitivity to the realities of illness in all its complex rawness and unresolvedness. How often does the doctor or the priest, for all his or her technical excellence, fail to be truly personal (let alone vulnerable) in responding to the anxiety of those encountering illness?

We have noticed a surprising, perhaps even perplexing quality in those who grow old and live with the fragilities of growing old. Many older people show amazing courage and fortitude in their adversity and manage to assert some measure of control over their dependence. Perhaps here there is a dimension of Christian ethics: what we may see as a 'cross-related' moral and spiritual emphasis. We know the prominence of Jesus' passivity in the Passion story as told in the Gospel of Mark. These factors, when identified as having Christian significance, ultimately go back to the Christ-centred character of Christianity. The theological truth is that the passivity and pain and sheer raw vulnerability of the cross, as a human experience, speak to the human condition notably as we embrace illness. We need to ask what kind of language might help older people to articulate this passivity and vulnerability, as sharing in what may look like a community of suffering.

I remember the hospital chapel in Birmingham. The focus of this simple room was a plain wooden cross, which spoke powerfully to people who found their way there. It helped them to describe and make sense of what was happening to them. From the pastor's perspective, this theological dimension to the encounter with age, frailty and sometimes illness feels fundamental to a containing of human existence in the light of the experience of pain, loss and anxiety. In this sense, Christianity is a religion whose meaning makes it wholly appropriate to be our guide in the search for wholeness through all aspects of the journey of our life.

A part of the responsibility of our ministry among older people is to offer some encouragement to one another in the honest articulation of some of the unease that is experienced in age, but particularly in illness. There is a kind of terror, a weariness and intensity about human experience to be felt as a result of illness. Some people have described themselves, as they reflect on their illness, as being only partially alive. Put in another way, their illness has given them the opportunity to live more deeply, to see new things, to discover a dimension to their living that had remained, to that time, hidden or untouched. There is a theological agenda here, if it is true that the purpose of our religion is the creation of new life and the regeneration of energy in the light of faith in Christ. Then there is, or can be, both a theological experience of redemption and an emotional experience of healing. Perhaps some would not wish to give this any theological significance, but it seems that the inherent reality of the cross is being re-enacted as a person comes to a new awareness of what is important, what is worth living for and dying for. Anxiety, therefore, may be a friend rather than an enemy in that the inequalities of suffering may grasp people and allow them to live more fully and deeply. It is a rediscovery of the self in the light of something that lies beneath and beyond human comprehension. It is a kind of meeting with God.

From a theological point of view any discussion of the creative anxiety of the cross can usefully include the contribution of Paul Tillich, in his book *The Courage to Be*.[1] He sees certain types of anxiety as inescapable. To avoid them is to lose one's humanity. Courage to take this inescapable anxiety upon oneself assumes three main forms: the courage to be part of a larger whole; the courage to stand alone; and the courage to accept the fact that humankind is carried by the creative power in which every creature participates. Tillich argues that the neurotic person is the one who is more highly sensitive to the threat of self-destruction, of non-being. This person retires to a castle and defends it by all means of psychological resistance, both from reality and from any help that is offered. The neurotic handling of anxiety becomes evident as the inability to take one's existential anxiety upon oneself. But from the Christian perspective anxiety is not to be borne alone. It serves to make meeting with God even more imperative. The impending necessity of such a cross, by way of illness, thrusts humankind into the very presence of God. Our dependence upon the providence of God and our finite weakness, manifest in the anxiety of creatureliness, are made plain. The pressure of the sense of estrangement in grief, the awareness of sin and the need for liberation from it – all these may come to a kind of crescendo of sheer terror, pain, loss and anxiety in the face of illness, which might be described as a kind of holy dread – provided it is perceived in the light of God. This is where existence is changed, as it takes on a different shape in the light of illness.

Waiting, watching and hoping: these are key realities for those who experience illness and for others who stand on the margins and observe it. All healthcare professionals and, indeed, patients, need to understand that situations are not treated with as much sensitivity as they might be. Recognizing people's dignity means listening to them with all of the energy we can muster. The best kind of pastoral care takes place when those involved are truly engaged in the situation. It means employing human skills and empathy, listening, and putting sensitivity into practice by recognizing and responding to a range of needs. This means that the individual's wishes and choices, their view of the world and understanding of it, are taken into consideration. Emotions, such as anxiety, fear, delight, confusion and pain, need to be encompassed and embraced. People often have an amazing inner strength and beliefs and attitudes that can be used creatively and positively.

The Gospels tell us that Jesus identifies himself in a particular way with the poor, the sick and the imprisoned. Jesus gives emphasis to the truth that it is his followers' hands that are used for his work of healing. So Jesus is at one with both the healed and the healer, the victim and the carer. John V. Taylor's concept of the Holy Spirit as the 'go-between God', who is knowable in the relationships between people, is of vital importance here. The heart of this doctrine tells us that in all the relationships which an individual has with those who are trying to help in the illness, the Holy Spirit is present and active.[2]

The Spirit is particularly at work in our waiting, watching and hoping. This theme is particularly illuminated theologically by the words of Jesus in the Garden of Gethsemane: 'Watch with me.' The word 'watch' says many things on different levels, all of importance to us: there is both a kind of vigilance and a kind of guarding. The relatives and friends know their vulnerability and distress. They are close to those they love; and begin to understand what kind of pain the person experiences.[3]

We know that people need warmth and friendship in illness as well as technical care. They need support and companionship. We who watch need to be aware of what it feels like to be ill: to be painfully separated from the person that you were, to be separated from loves and responsibilities. Our care has to learn to feel 'with' people, without being able to feel like them. Such attitudes give substance to the sense of relationships in which the role of the Spirit of God is experienced as reality. This coming close to people transforms their lives.

There is a still deeper level at which the words 'watch with me' are significant. Our learning of skills and techniques and our attempt to heal are not the whole of the matter. However much we can ease distress, however much we can help people to find a new meaning in what is happening, there will always be the place where we have to stop and accept that we are really helpless. 'Watch with me' means, at the heart, just being there.

There can be no hope unless all concerned recognize that this part of the person's experience is very hard. The problems and difficulties need to be faced honestly: the anxiety, the depression, the weakness, the dependence, and the isolation from other people's lives and activity. Only the acceptance of the facts of loss and darkness and the possibility of death in all their negativity makes for the creative hope of resurrection, of new birth, of light beyond the darkness.

The Christological dimension, pointing us to models in the life of Jesus, adds another aspect to our shared approach. Christ may be seen as present in symbols and sacraments of all kinds. We may have in mind the giving of a cup of cold water (Mark 9.41) and the washing of the disciples' feet (John 13.1–15). Comparable acts of relatives and friends will speak silently to the person about love. In the relationships between the patient and loved ones, in speech and act, there is a basis of trust and respect in which something very important is happening.

There are, of course, all kinds of questions and issues raised, above all those of Why and How. Dennis Potter, the playwright, has spoken about the freedom of the human being as something that is given. At the time of an interview with Melvyn Bragg, he was disabled by a painful and rare form of arthritic disease. He said:

I have the sense that the world is made every day, second by second, minute by minute, and we, living in this world, give back some of that initial gift minute by minute, second by second; that even the most trivial choice can have awesome consequences; we choose to live in relation to other people in a continual tension of choice; that choice has its origin in a loving creation, and that loving creation is continually in battle and tension with, and in obvious opposition to, the misery, cruelty and crudity of an imperfect world that we have to endure and live in and do battle with.

(Dennis Potter, *Seeing the Blossom:
Two Interviews and a Lecture*, p. 5)[4]

A TRADITION TO DRAW UPON

At this point I want to attempt to offer the beginnings of a dialogue between the traditions and framework that shape our theories about health, disease and healing, and some of the human experiences that refract a number of hopes and fears in relation to healing. From a Christian perspective we are convinced that all of us involved in health and healing need to do more than look at the malfunctioning part of any person: we need to view it from the outset as part of a total person, and that person as part of a community and environment. The person is to be viewed in an eschatological sense in that the reality of death (the 'end') is affirmed. Within the dialogue I am especially concerned to encourage interconnections and uncover, where they exist, sources of integration and the areas where interpretation and connection seem impossible. The hope of Christian healing is problematic and deserves care and caution.

If we feel acute physical pain, then it is more likely that we shall ring 999 and call for medical assistance than ask our parish priest for prayer and anointing. There is, of course, a long history of the priest's involvement in dying and death. From the fifth century until relatively recently, most Europeans called the priest if they were thought to be dying; no doubt the agenda was the desire for a good and holy death, and the fear of damnation was often stronger than the hope of healing. Nothing shows this more plainly than the fact that, in the Catholic framework, anointing has long been chiefly part of the 'last rites' rather than a means of healing. The modern person, in Europe and North America at least, experiences illness as a threat to their health and full life, which can be dealt with wholly or partially by medicine administered by a scientifically trained medical profession. We value life and want to preserve it against the threat of disease. Modern medicine has distanced us from a good deal of pain and early or 'predictable' death. We take this situation for granted as our expectations have been raised over the past two generations. My grandmother's experience of health was very different from mine today.

When we read about New Testament times and the practice of some Christian traditions today, we are reminded that illness may be dealt with by charismatics speaking words of power. Further, these acts of healing are sometimes effective without drugs or surgery. Sometimes, 'fate' is seen as the dominant factor: what will be, will be. On the whole, most Christians in the modern West put their trust in science and think that the New Testament stories are suspect or simply irrelevant, reflecting the ways of long ago. Other Christians put their trust in both; they pray with confidence for healing and blame failure on faithlessness. Anyway, friends and family take over and go for the most likely aid – in the sphere of medicine.

Some New Testament scholars interpret the gospel stories as pointing, even for their writers and first hearers, to inner attitudes, for example, not being anxious or accepting ultimate dependence on God; or else allegories for accepting the call to faith (the blind receive sight). In doing this, they bypass the stories as history and as expressing a non-scientific mythological (and obsolete?) world view. These approaches are useful in so far as they affirm both medicine and faith as valued responses to illness. But they can seem feeble or evasive alongside the apparent convictions in the Gospels and those of modern believers who share them.

There are choices to be made in the way we construct our shared framework of meaning and values in relation to healing, and in our ways of acting from within it in order to promote it. Specifically, what models of God and of pastoral care undergird the practice of Christian healing?

In the Scriptures there is no philosophical notion of natural law that claims to understand how the universe operates necessarily along uniform lines. A miracle is described and understood as an event in which God acts in a special way in order to disclose or accomplish his purposes or demonstrate his power; the idea of such interventions is ready to hand where scientific knowledge is so meagre. While a consultant and his junior doctors assent to a scientific framework that understands how the body functions, some doctors appreciate that there are events and occurrences that are beyond present human understanding or explanation.

There seems to be a limit, itself the result of a kind of pragmatism, to the lengths some doctors will go as they try to explain what they have experienced. Put another way, mystery has not been banished from our world, even though it is more marginal than it was for our ancestors. There are some dimensions of human life where it is impossible fully to comprehend the meaning and purpose of what happened and why it happened.

Yet our perspectives on those gospel healings should not be governed only by issues of historicity, that is, did they actually happen? We ought also to have the creative space to explore the inner meanings of the stories, as has already been hinted. Put another way, our concern should be 'what is written about' rather than just 'what is written'. Take the text of the New Testament: what perspectives on healing does it give for us today? The healing events in the New Testament are set out as proof of Jesus' role in the purpose of God, of which we are today a continuing part. Healing is an indication of the presence of the kingdom of God in which wholeness and spiritual advance take place under God's rule and a new governance is born. For Christians, we still live under that rule, living in and for that kingdom of love. These matters are more fundamental and comprehensive than the question of the historicity of those stories – as indeed of the character or genuineness of their modern parallels. There is, in any case, always some source of explanation within this world, for these are physical happenings, even if that explanation eludes us. Faith in God remains broader than such questions and is essentially unaffected by our response to them. It must also learn to thrive in the predominant absence of such happenings.

The challenge of how we might become the agents of healing for God in illness remains. Jesus' method in healing was to evoke latent attitudes of faith and to link these with the healing power of God. Sometimes in the stories the faith of others is invoked to heal, so faith in the sufferer is not seen as wholly essential: we might say that healing is a shared enterprise! Jesus therefore provides an opportunity for faith and divine power to coalesce in creating a new order. Healing in the New Testament is an extraordinary event performed as a sign to the community of faith concerning God's purpose for his people. That is why it was written down for the community to read – as it has done from that day until now. They saw no difficulty in working on what we should regard as different levels of meaning at one and the same time.

It is important for us to remind ourselves what the predominant theoretical picture of the world order in relation to healing is. It runs as follows. Nature works according to mechanical laws and everything can be explained by logic and reason, working on the evidence. This world view sees God (if it includes him at all) as a rather remote monarch: a transcendent being who orders everything from above without any direct involvement. Indeed, part of the theological tradition of the churches assents to this mechanistic world view in which everything that happens is causal. This theoretical picture is, however, often combined with mixed and confused responses when we turn to people's actual perceptions and responses to their sufferings. So, the doctors may feel that there are times when medical knowledge is a paradoxical mixture of certainty and doubt that cannot explain or understand all experience. They may feel with and for a patient in their pain and fear, but cannot allow themselves to act on it or show it. The medicalization of health is often followed through for the patient's safety, and clear boundaries and ordered control are offered. Whether it comes from the doctor or from the patient, perhaps the plea for 'salvation' – for life amidst the threat and certainty of death – is, in small part, a response to the intuitive feeling that there is more to health than the physical and that there are other powerful forces at work in living and healing. We need to be reminded that we should never demean God and reduce him to puppet-management. There is inscrutability and ultimate mystery behind all our understanding of God and of ourselves in the world.

This debate is as urgent as ever and we are all caught up with it as we encounter illness. There is an ongoing tension between the sacred and the secular. From the person's perspective, however, the two may well belong together: for many believe that there is a God at work in their lives and their world, and that mystery remains. It looks probable that we shall have to live with the specialization of function which modern medicine has bred. But there should be some opportunity to bridge the gaps and redeem the failures that emerge when doctors fail to treat the emotions or spiritual capacities and environmental contexts of persons – and when pastoral care is tempted to have little to do with the life of the body and its processes.

The question of divine action is the heart of the problem. Can we now see God as breaking into the sequence of cause and effect, of which we think we are aware and which seems to be the way things do and have to work? There are some theologians, for example, John Polkinghorne, who have attempted to cast doubt on the prevailing popular scientific assumptions from the point of view of modern physics.[5] Other theologians, like Austin Farrer and Maurice Wiles, seem less interested than the scientist in 'finding room for miracle' or explaining strange occurrences; rather they are seeking to see divine presence in 'what is'. Farrer said: 'God makes things make themselves' (see *A Science of God?*), giving full space for the independence of the created universe at all its levels.[6]

Much of the above concerns one aspect of the wider issue of changing ways of seeing Christian belief in the light of changing cultural assumptions, highlighted here in the matter of New Testament ideas of healing compared with modern medicine. Pastoral theologians have yet to face these issues straightforwardly and in the context of an understanding of cultural change as a whole. It simply is the case that the prevailing myth (way of picturing or telling the story) about disease and healing changes from one period to another; and while remnants of old myths are around (or are revived, as by 'healers' of a religious kind), they are superseded for practical purposes by other myths. The Christian world at present is deeply torn between those who seek to grapple with modernity as itself God-given and those who hold on to versions (often modified or distorted) of old (especially biblical) myth. Often the latter group do not fully pay the price: it would mean alienation from the greater part of Western culture and intellectual life. Of course this second group is, world wide, much more powerful in Christianity as a whole. But those who are of that persuasion are usually blithely unaware that their lives are totally based on a myth which in their religion they deny. For example, the use of modern technology (they use the Internet, fly hither and thither), including medicine for the most part. Without realizing it, they really do live in a curiously schizoid state culturally. For some, the problem could be dealt with by pitching the use made of the modern myth at a lower level. That is, you can say: I use modern technology and modern medicine simply because they work in this way and that; and I do not go further, that is, I don't bother myself about possible theoretical or total pictures (myths) which lie behind them. I just do this or that piece of surgery or car repairing or computer constructing and still believe fervently in angels and demons and God intervening in my child's examination chances or my disease. How do we bridge the deep gulf between those who can bear to go on like that and those who think that it will not do if integrity is to be preserved?[7]

The question of prayer comes in again in this context, this time the prayer of petition or intercession. The tradition here is more complicated and interesting. It is true that intercessory prayer has overwhelmingly been modelled on the idea of a suppliant approaching a king or lord who has benefits to bestow or withhold. That model fitted very well through the greater part of the Christian period, given the way the universe was seen to be run under God's direct governance and, of course, connected with the way social and political life worked: lords – officially at least – had total power to dispose, and success consisted in getting their ear, while to lose their ear spelt disaster. Of course this might be modified by checks and balances (laws and parliaments) but it remained the underlying assumption about social relationships. So of course prayer to God followed: and there could be no more of a problem about failure to get answers to prayer than there would be if an earthly ruler refused to comply with one's petitions. You could complain, but there was no intellectual problem – it was his to give or not to give. Once divine action ceases to be seen as direct, in the old way, a problem arises: how can the picture work at all? What point can there be in asking for this and that? And if the system of the universe withholds goods and doles out evils, what a terrible system! So, though we go on using it in every liturgy, 'asking prayer', in this crude form and verbalized in the form of simply asking, is always unsatisfactory if viewed in this way. As alignment of the self with God or as placing one's affairs in the wider light of God, of 'the depth of things', prayer in relation to some person or situation, makes much more sense. We may note that at the start of Christian prayer, in Matthew's version of the Lord's Prayer, asking for needs to be fulfilled is specifically ruled out as the point of it (Matthew 6.8, 25–34). So, for Matthew, the meaning of the Lord's Prayer cannot be to seek the meeting of one's needs, but rather to desire earnestly the splendour of God's presence (kingdom). 'Thy will be done' is the key. The fulfilment of God's purpose is its sole and entire content. Even the 'daily bread' is not what it seems: it is the 'bread' of the kingdom that 'feeds' us for God. This aspect of spirituality demands further thought and reflection from the pastoral theologians; for prayer is one area where theory and practice meet.[8]

WHAT THEN IS HEALING?

We should now ask how we might define or understand healing. We should be aware once again that culture will play a significant part in shaping the ways in which we understand the process by which healing is defined.

The *Oxford English Dictionary* defines 'healing' as having no fewer than four aspects:

1 To make whole or sound; to cure.
2 To restore to soundness.
3 To save, purify, cleanse, repair or amend.
4 To become whole or sound: to recover from sickness or a wound.

All four of these overlapping definitions are applicable in all cultures, but cultural differences affect the way the processes are perceived and felt. For example, in a religious culture reconciliation to God and neighbour will be a major aspect of healing: so may the whole apparatus of 'a good death'. In a secular culture, these aspects may be subordinated or absent and the stress will be largely on physical and psychological recovery.

In the light of this preliminary outline I propose the following broad definition of healing in relation to our understanding of illness: it is the process of being restored not only to physical normality, but also to emotional well-being, sound mental functioning and spiritual wholeness. Healing, from the Christian point of view, is always linked with spiritual advance. God is part of this process and healing or wholeness are pastoral metaphors for what religion speaks of as salvation, which itself concerns the whole person. Therefore, what healing is or means will always be an area of controversy because of the complexity and diversity of views on the nature of God and providence. In addition, it will always be impossible fully to understand the paradoxes and complexities of the human person in its totality.

How should we think of God's part in healing? Perhaps there are times when God can be said to be at work in the process of making whole through a variety of agents and in ways that are both obvious and mysterious. Even if God is not seen as acting directly to heal, a religious person may still feel that 'the God dimension' is important, even absolutely paramount: that I, he or she holds to the presence of 'ultimacy' or 'death' in the situation and, indeed, in the process of healing – in its total effects for both self and others.

Above all, when considering the subject of healing it will be important to understand that the theoretical popular 'fiction' of medicine, as a world of activities and techniques, is one that is held by people who are themselves, by assumption, usually 'healthy'. It exists 'out there'. It is far removed from the perceptions of the self as patient or even as vulnerable and fragile, always potentially a patient. In that role, much more mixed responses come into play. At this point even medical persons have no immunity!

These responses are wildly out of kilter with the strong, controlling and healthy scientific picture. But disease and healing should never be viewed only objectively or examined and treated on a scientific basis alone. Suffering and pain are always felt at a number of ambiguous and complex levels. The pastor's task is to try and bring his or her engagement with these perceptions of mixed and vulnerable attitudes to the attention of the medical establishment and institutions. The healing may come from the God who in the process of pain and uncertainty promotes growth and wholeness through a change of perspective. Perhaps the key recognition is that 'health', as commonly seen in this world, is not God's greatest gift to his creatures or the sum of all good.

THE LAST ENEMY?

When we reflect on illness it is difficult to remain unaffected by the depth of feeling that facing human fragility gives rise to. In part, we fear the very threat of death itself as the end of all that we know and see. An important aspect of the challenge of facing illness is to integrate this experience of loss so that it can be part of our living and loving. But how can we achieve this integration?

Ernest Becker sees the whole of human life as an enactment of our inability to face our own mortality. We repress the sense of death. This repression means the exclusion from our consciousness of any feeling or idea of death, the open acknowledgement of which would be unbearably threatening or painful. Our repression is not within the conscious control of the person and, indeed, has destabilizing effects on the personality. It would follow then that as long as the sense of death is repressed we are, in many respects, in flight from reality, from our true self, and from the possibility of living a first-hand, authentic life of our own. It is a paradox that while the denial of death is endemic in humanity, that denial turns out to be profoundly anti-life.[9]

There is much about modern medicine that colludes with this denial of human fragility and death. What is intriguing is the way in which many doctors describe death, which surely reflects their attitude to it. It is a subject of fascination and interest as the doctor attempts to understand the steps and processes whereby the body ceases to live. It can, of course, happen by a variety of means: heart attacks and strokes; the effects of ageing; murder, accidents and suicides; cancer. While it is clear that dying is often a messy business, the details of death become crucially important for doctors. They need to understand how the heart ceases to work, how the body deteriorates with age, how cancer kills.

The effect of this insistence on grim detail is complex for those who work in a medicalized environment. At one level it frightens. There is the prospect of death one day for themselves, of pain and degradation and of being in the power of strangers. At another level, though, the effect of knowledge is more nearly that of liberation. It is as if a deep collusive silence has been broken, and there is no longer any need to pretend. Often hateful, the facts lie before you; and in acknowledging them, you free yourself to look more squarely at the benefits life holds in store. This candour has contributed significantly to the culture where images of death are used unremittingly as a vehicle of entertainment, and in which death in the flesh is played down. It is also a culture in which attitudes are bizarrely quirky. Most of it serves to put fragility, mortality and loss into a corner.

The role of a Christian understanding of death, within a culture that struggles to integrate death and loss into life, remains ambiguous and strange. It is important not to overgeneralize; for even with such a fact as death, personal and cultural modes of perception inescapably help to create the reality of what is perceived. Though death must be part of the human condition always, it is not absurd to conceive of 'modern death' as very different from experiences of death even in the recent past, let alone those of the nineteenth century or medieval times or Japanese death or death in many parts of the less-developed world. In many different traditional cultures, death is commonplace; public, terrible, ceremonial and often beautiful. TV pictures of funerals in other parts of the world often strike us as wild or even frightening. The whole gamut of emotions is involved, evoked by all the various varieties of dying. Traditional death is a significant plunge into the awful unknown, paradoxically a creative act.

For many facing illness there is a kind of crisis of selfhood: 'What am I? What do I signify? Am I of value – if so, to whom? To my family, to posterity, to God?' The religious dimension obviously adds to the options and sharpens the focus. This is where the concept of a good death needs to be revived, for it has validity – and a meaning that might help us to integrate death into life. An egalitarian and individualistic urban culture deprives the ordinary private person of any social or public representative role, and therefore of any clear intrinsic general importance. It is easy to see how loss and death themselves disappear from view and how, in our kind of society, the act of death is no longer creative or even much noticed. We no longer give 'respect' to the passing cortège, no longer ring the passing bell.

In the Christian churches we are at a curious and paradoxical state of belief about death. The notion of heaven as a valid objective for personal striving is rarely presented in sermons, and the notion of hell is often dismissed as barbarous. Do we believe in the resurrection of the dead or punishment beyond death? In short, what is death?

If death is conceived as total extinction for everyone (as it is by a considerable proportion of the population), it may seem at first to enhance the importance of life above all else, but in reality it does, in fact, often have the reverse effect. The concept of total extinction may or may not be true, but it removes from life the clearest basis of all ultimate significance, all obligations, and all final accountability. If death is extinction for everyone, it has no lasting significance: in so far as death loses significance so does life – or so many may feel. Hence the trivialization of both life and death in much of ordinary culture and the nihilism of most contemporary art. The effects throughout our culture are enormous. Modern angst and modern concepts of death depend upon, perhaps arise out of, freedom, individuality and prosperity. We feel that freedom, individuality and prosperity are intrinsically good – and are open to personal control and management provided we stay within the law. They are undoubtedly imperilled by the nihilism and irrationality which accompany them.

In order to preserve the good things which we value in this life, the most important achievements then that we can hope for in religion, and in fact also in social and political terms, would be the development or re-creation of generally acceptable belief in some kind of other life, a personal survival beyond death if only we could believe in it. May it not be that our future is simply unimaginable, so that our speculating is simply fatuous? God is beyond our imagining, and so are his ultimate gifts – we simply do not know what may be in store and if we did, faith for its own sake would become debased. But first in our engagements with illness we need to develop an art of letting go, of death and dying. Such an art would need to take proper account of our dignity, our relationships and our achievements. We all have a 'place in history'. It needs recognition as we celebrate our life and reflect on it at all crisis times. And it is all in and under God.

THOSE WHO STAND BY

The role of those who stand alongside people who engage with loss is an important and crucial one. There is much evidence to suggest a crippling level of role uncertainty for many Christian professionals within this situation. Often the role has been marginalized unless one has worked to become a professional among professionals. Techniques and skills informed by social sciences are of vital importance, but they are not in themselves Christian skills and there is nothing in their fundamental character which makes the one practising them recognizable as one proclaiming the gospel or as plumbing the depths. Christianity has developed a 'know-how' in these matters. But in fact we may hold that what makes the carer a good carer is not what they may or may not believe, but their level of competence as a professional and their qualities as a human being. Perhaps the role is one of friendship, of self-disclosure, of sharing questions and feelings; of a dying person speaking to a dying person, attempting to integrate this experience of dying, from whatever perspective, into loving and living. The Christian carer must offer these qualities at the very least.

In this human encounter with illness in its various facets, there are many common strands which bear further reflection: coming clean and facing facts honestly; making the encounter with suffering, pain and loss more constructive; drawing close to people and, above all, confronting the reality and finality of our mortality, and being able to be weak and vulnerable. There is one key thread, which is easy to miss in our death-denying society. We are perhaps conditioned to avoid confronting fear, to avoid the wilderness, the desert places in our own hearts and world. We live under what some have called the tyranny of certainty; where apparent strength, confidence, life and security dominate our emotional and ecclesiastical lives. In the quest for healing and wholeness, we seek those things which reassure us, rather than those which confront our doubts and fears.

The individuals whose stories are shared with us ask us to think about how further significance is part of our lives and, above all, where our security and strengths are. Fearful Christians build fearful Christian communities, where uncertainty, contradiction, paradox and ambiguity are masked by false security, apparent strengths and a façade of certainty. The integration of living our experience of dying means facing our own and each other's vulnerability. In some senses, when we are vulnerable there can be healing and growth as we accept our need of others and when we let go of our independence and of our drive to assert. The gospel, in this and other contexts, demands that we are drawn out of the tyranny of certainty – to be powerful through our giving and to be vulnerable through our receiving, as we hold together the paradoxes and contradictions between life and death, faith and fear, hope and despair, loving and hating, alienation and relationship, fragmentation and connectedness.

THE PLACE OF FAITH

Perhaps the role of our Christian faith and commitment is more problematical? Is it possible to become so accustomed to the starkness of the imagery and meaning of Christian symbols that they lose the power to challenge and confront us? Too often our religion opts for purity, clarity and distance. At the heart of faith is the death of Jesus and the power to create new life, to form both life and death; but it is in essence a mystery, inviting ever-deeper penetration. The meaning of mystery is not a truth so great that we are not required to have any understanding of it, but a truth so deep that our understandings will be insufficient to understand the whole. Peter Harvey speaks of the gospel message as offering a certain promise only of uncertainty, of continuing loss and change. He reminds us that comprehending mystery is the process of recognizing not *what* we do not know, but *that* we do not know. The integration of our experience of loss is engaging with the struggle to manage the profound paradoxes and ambiguities as a condition of our living.[10]

Perhaps there is too much about human experience, including the encounter with illness, that makes it difficult to believe in a God who unfolds to us a picture of our world as a friendly and meaningful place. The world, for many, is a process in which one feels alienated, engulfed and lost. But it is into that process that God comes and speaks to us. The only liturgy that God gave us is the liturgy in which death is celebrated.[11]

The gospel offers us an alternative to our repression of loss and death. We are shown in a particular death a capacity for offered suffering and are invited to live in its light. This is what we have to offer others as we attempt to live out this truth in our lives. So it is that we should want to resist anything that denies death, for when it is denied it casts a shadow over all our projects; it threatens our whole life's course with a lack of meaning. God's promise and invitation is available in and through loss: there has to be surrender, even the risking of intimacy with God. We need, therefore, to become less strong, less confident, less and less defended, less and less identified with our own ideas of God, and more attentive to the promptings of the Spirit and to other people's experience.

Perhaps this is what those who share their experience of illness and loss have to teach us: that we have to accept our loss and death in the unfolding of the capacity to live our own lives in all their pain and complexity.

FOR FURTHER REFLECTION (ALONE OR IN A GROUP)

Exercise 1

Read this passage:

> What happens can never be anticipated. What happens escapes anything you can ever say about it. What happens cannot be undone. It can never be anything other than it is. We tell stories as if to refuse this truth, as if to say that we make our fate, rather than simply endure it. But in truth we make nothing. We live, and we cannot shape life. It is much too great for that: there is nothing that cannot somehow be said. Yet there at last in her presence, in the unending unfolding of that silence, which still goes on, which I still expect to be broken by another drawing of breath, I knew that all my words could only be in vain, and that all I feared and all that I had anticipated could only be lived – without their help or hers.   (Michael Ignatieff, *Scar Tissue*, p. 172)[12]

Michael Ignatieff explores the world of illness with the power and force of a novelist's skill. At the heart of *Scar Tissue* is a son's account of his mother's voyage into a world of neurological disease, losing her memory and then her very identity, only to gain at the very end a strange serenity. The son in the novel, who is obsessed with his mother's transformation, sets out on his own quest for self-discovery.

- What can we say of illness and how do the intellectual and the emotional belong together?
- Should we regard illness as meaningful in any kind of way?
- In the end, whatever is said, perhaps we will never be able either to anticipate what happens or to explain it?

Exercise 2

Read this passage:

> Below my window in Ross, when I'm working in Ross, for
> example, there at this season, the blossom is out in full now
> . . . it's a plum tree, it looks like apple blossom but it's white,
> and looking at it, instead of saying, 'Oh that's nice blossom' . . .
> last week looking at it through the window when I'm writing,
> I *see* it is the whitest, frothiest, blossomest blossom that
> there ever could be, and I can see it. Things are both more
> trivial than they ever were, and more important than they
> ever were, and the difference between the trivial and the
> important doesn't seem to matter. But the nowness of every-
> thing is absolutely wondrous, and if people could *see* that, you
> know. There's no way of telling you, you have to experience it,
> but the glory of it, if you like, the comfort of it, the reassur-
> ance . . . The fact is, if you see the present tense, boy do you
> see it! And boy can you celebrate it.
>
> (Dennis Potter, *Seeing the Blossom:*
> *Two Interviews and a Lecture,* p. 5)[13]

The piece from Dennis Potter's interview with Melvyn Bragg a
few months before he died is a moving and powerful statement
about one person's experience of the transformation of perspective through terminal disease. It is a testimony of how death
changes seeing and knowing in life. It is also a reflection of the
paradoxical nature of the relationship between the quantity and
the quality of our lives and living.

- Imagine yourself with only a few days to live – where are you?
  Who is with you? What do you see?

Exercise 3

Read this passage:

> Illness. Not the beginning of the end but the beginning of
> THE beginning. To be honest I did not FEEL this very
> strongly until about six months ago. Nevertheless, I lived

every day since my diagnosis to die fullest knowing physical exertion would speed the progress of the illness. To sit back, however, would only have robbed me of moments with my family and friends. Thus I continue. Only now I sense if I had become a stoic or a fighter, I would probably have gone by now. Rather I face each day with a prayer. I try to be completely open to whatever Christ brings.

(Michael Ignatieff, *Scar Tissue*, p. 130)

Somehow these two perspectives need to be held together. Illness is both meaningful and meaningless. The voices of illness can say many things to us as we face the ambiguity of disease and its message to society and the individual's relationships within it. Meaning is often ambiguous and the words work in different ways. Perhaps the body speaks a particular kind of language through the functioning of its organs, and even expresses something of the essence or the soul of humanity. So illness is connected with the whole variety of aspects of life. Illness is both alienation and communication, and it is the source of many and conflicting values. Yet we must continue to ask whether every event has a cause and in what way our inner and outer worlds are linked.

FOR THOSE WHO LISTEN AND CARE

But amidst all this there is an essential loneliness or unspokenness about illness. The pastoral attempt at solidarity with the sick is not always respectful of the immense and proper solitude of those who find themselves ill. Illness takes them into a foreign country; and it tests the already limited ability of humans to put themselves in each other's skins, to empathize with them through shared memories of the same condition.

Above all, in the encounter with illness what is required is honesty and attention: honesty in the engagement with experience and attention to the sheer diversity of voices and influences which shape that experience. In the introduction to Dennis Potter's interview in *Seeing the Blossom*, Melvyn Bragg shares his anxiety in anticipating his encounter with Potter, and in doing so offers the following advice which is a powerful paradigm for modern Christian pastoral care:

The main problem as far as I was concerned was to avoid mawkishness, sentimentality and any whisper of the wrong sort of intrusiveness. Or any sort of intrusiveness. The main purpose that I had was to give him as much space and time and energy as possible for as long as possible.   (p. xi)

Bragg succeeds in so far as he allows Potter to articulate his experience and what shapes it, with richness, profundity and meaning. So may we:

- Pray never to lose the human simplicity in illness and death: it is the simplicity of Christ.

- Learn to see that there is no life without sadness; no sadness, without glory.

PART THREE

The future of ageing

CHAPTER FIFTEEN

Ageing and social policy

The pastoral care of older people has been put into the broadest possible context in this volume. This chapter is different in tone from most of the book. It is designed to outline the current situation in order to map out the social policy agenda with regard to the care of older people in this country.

Social care is one of the major areas of public service. At any one time, up to 1.7 million of the most vulnerable people in our society are relying on the social care workforce for support.[1] Social services departments are major players in the fight against social exclusion since they work with people who are very vulnerable through age, infirmity, disability, mental health problems, addiction or homelessness. We may all of us at some time need the help of social services for family or friends – and probably eventually for ourselves.

Social care for older people covers a wide range of services, which may be provided by local authorities, the private and voluntary sectors or a mixture of more than one of these. Under the heading of social care for older people come domiciliary care, day centre activities, care homes, volunteering and community development. It also covers services such as providing personal and intimate care for people with disabilities, support for people with alcohol and drug misuse problems, and care at the end of life.

In considering ageing and social policy it is important that we remember that older people are still citizens who, within their communities, are affected by universal commercial and public services as well as primary and secondary health and social care services. Older people do not primarily define themselves in terms of the service they receive, but still have ambitions and aspirations and a variety of roles and contributions to make within their continuing capacity and commitment. For social policy therefore a perspective is needed which sees older people more roundly, in a wider context that is not restrictively defined only in terms of needs and services.

HISTORICAL PERSPECTIVE

The advent of hip and knee replacements, complex heart surgery and successful treatments for cancer as well as an improvement in general health have meant a significant increase in life expectancy over the past 50 years which was certainly not envisaged in 1948 when the welfare state came into being. At retirement in 2002, a woman could expect to live a further 19 years and a man another 15,[2] but sadly not all the extra years are healthy years and as a result demands on health and social services have increased enormously.

The 1980s saw a phenomenal rise in the number of care homes in the country, fuelled by the ready availability of income support (without assessment of need). Following the Griffiths Report in 1988[3] the UK government passed the 1990 NHS and Community Care Act which meant that from 1993 access to care homes was limited by assessment and means testing.

From that point the public policy environment in which the concerns of older people are set changed greatly. There was an expectation that market forces should apply to providers and that individuals should have choice in the services they received. Local authorities increasingly became enablers rather than providers of services. Older people began to expect and demand more and this is likely to increase still further as the grateful post-war generation is replaced by the consumer-orientated baby-boomers.

1997 AND A LABOUR GOVERNMENT

The new Labour government was faced with a triple whammy of poor government funding for social services, an ageing population and rising costs. Within a short time they had set up a Royal Commission into the funding of long-term care and over the next ten years a stream of reports, health and social care legislation, and Green and White Papers has poured out of government offices. But it is difficult to conclude that life is better for older people in 2008 than in 1997 – or 1987.

It is impossible to cover all the reports and legislation that have been produced in the past ten years but we can look at some of the key themes and issues in social policy and refer to some of the ways in which the government and others are trying to tackle them. The depressing thing is that so often there is a large gulf between government rhetoric in policy documents and practice on the ground. This makes it impossible for the rhetoric to become reality.

KEY THEMES IN SOCIAL POLICY

Encouraging a much closer working relationship between the health sector and the social care sector and generally more joined-up thinking

For too long social care has been seen as the poor relation of the National Health Service. True, the NHS Plan in 2000[4] included significant plans for social care as well as health, but we have a Department of *Health* and it was only recently that a Director General of Social Care was appointed with similar status to health counterparts. There has always been a dichotomy between fully funded NHS services and means-tested social care. Endless debate takes place around responsibilities for personal care of older people at home and in care homes – is it a social or health service? There is frequent cost-shunting between the two arms, nowhere more noticeable than in the case of hospital discharge where the NHS is allowed to fine social services if they fail to organize the discharge of patients when notified that they are ready.

The government rhetoric of working together, less central control and more local responses, partnerships and joined-up thinking can be seen in practice in some areas and a very encouraging recent development is the signing of a concordat, *Putting People First.*[5] This sets out a 'shared vision' for social services in a series of steps to achieve a situation in which individual citizens are at the heart of a personalized system. For the first time the concordat brings together the commitment of six government departments, the Local Government Association, the Association of Directors of Adult Social Services, the NHS, representatives of the independent sector (private and voluntary) and the Commission for Social Care Inspections.

Giving users and carers more independence, choice, dignity and control

This vision of individual citizens at the heart of a personalized system has been a constant theme of Labour policy. The *National Service Framework (NSF) for Older People*[6] had person-centred care as its second standard while the white paper *Our Health, Our Care, Our Say*[7] promised to give people more choice and control over their care services. The introduction of direct payments and, more recently, individualized budgets is intended to allow older people to choose the kind of care they wish to have delivered to them and to choose who the provider might be. We would all support a greater element of choice, but these new initiatives must be underpinned by systems of information, advocacy and support for vulnerable older people. In this context the government's introduction of mandatory Criminal Records Bureau (CRB) checks for all those working with older people and the existence of a Protection of Vulnerable Adults (POVA) register were very welcome.

The In Control partnership[8] of government, local authorities, independent organizations, families and individuals has been set up with a mission to change the organization of social care through a transformation into a system of self-directed support so that people who need support can take control of their own lives and fulfil their role as full citizens.

Fair access to care

Anyone who is involved with older people in seeking access to services appreciates that this is an area in which the so-called postcode lottery is operating. The *Fair Access to Care* (FACS) guidance[9] attempted to remove the uncertainty by instructing local authorities to assess people into four categories: critical, substantial, moderate and low. However, there is a massive inconsistency between local authorities, many of whom deny help to those whose needs are not substantial or critical. Thus they provide only a safety net for the most ill and the poorest in society and run counter to government policy to develop preventative services. In January 2008 the government accepted that this was the case and announced an independent inquiry. There is still an urgent need for a system of allocation of care that is simpler, fairer, transparent, sustainable, consistent and flexible.

Development of preventative services

We have just seen how lack of funding has resulted in some local authorities refusing to offer low-level services to older people. Such services would not only help to delay admission to care homes, but may well prevent the development of higher-level needs. The government constantly speaks of the importance of preventative services, emphasized through the NSF. The need for intermediate care (Standard 3), drew attention to the importance of falls prevention (Standard 6) and reduction of strokes (Standard 5), but the government consistently fails to support these initiatives through adequate funding.

Debate on funding of long-term care

The issue of funding is key to all social policy and nowhere more so than in the provision of long-term care. Sadly the Royal Commission recommendation in *With Respect to Old Age*,[10] that all personal care in care homes should be paid for from general taxation, was accepted only in part by the government which introduced so-called free nursing care (but not personal care), preferring to spend money on intermediate care, a rehabilitative service designed to keep people out of residential care. More recently the Wanless Report, commissioned by the King's Fund, *Securing Good Care for Older People: Taking a Long-term View*[11] has suggested restricting means-testing for personal care and putting into place a free package of basic care topped up by personal contributions matched by the state. The continuing debate focuses on the balance between personal responsibility for the funding of long-term care and the duty of the state to provide.

In autumn 2007 as part of the Comprehensive Spending Review, the government announced a Green Paper to reform the way that older people pay for long-term personal care, recognizing the need for a 'radical rethink' aiming to ensure that state funding is spent effectively and the growing numbers of older people have sufficient choice. This Green Paper could be a Beveridge Report for the twenty-first century, encouraging a national debate on the respective roles of state and individual. Sadly there is significant reluctance, even among Christian people, to engage in this reflection and conversation and certainly to pay more tax to improve services for older people.

Focusing on performance and quality in care

While in the Thatcher and Major years there was developing concern about performance and standards, it was in the Blair years that action was taken. The new Care Standards Act 2000 brought into being a National Care Standards Commission (later Commission for Care Standards Inspection, CCSI) which inspects all types of care home against new national minimum standards contained in *Care Homes for Older People: National Minimum Standards.*[12] CCSI is now to be merged with the Healthcare Commission and the Mental Health Act Commission to form the Care Quality Commission – responsible for quality and performance across the board.

As we have seen before, the problem is generally financial. Most care homes are more than willing to raise their environmental, caring and staffing standards but the money needs to come from residents' fees, and the financial support for those unable to fund themselves has not yet risen appropriately.

The government has in addition introduced the idea of star ratings for homes in relation to their compliance with standards and regulations. The use of the words 'excellent', 'good' and 'adequate' is contentious. Who wants their relative to live in a home that is only 'adequate'? Undoubtedly the standards in care homes have risen in recent years and some poor providers have been driven out. The *My Home Life* initiative[13] is another partnership of organizations which is attempting to improve quality of life and care for residents.

Concern for carers

The value of unpaid support that carers provide has now reached £87 billion a year according to a new report by Carers UK – more than the annual total spent on the NHS, which stood at £82 billion in the year 2006–2007, and more than four times the amount spent on social care services for adults and children by local authorities each year – £19.3 billion in the year 2005–2006.[14]

This is some indication of the extent to which our economy relies on the care provided by family and friends. If only a small number were to give up caring – perhaps through ill health or lack of support – the economic impact could be disastrous. With an increasingly ageing population, it shows the urgent need for better recognition and support for carers. Many remain isolated and unsupported, with thousands living in poverty and unable to take up paid work or have a normal social life.

The government has improved benefits for carers, allocated more money to local authorities to provide breaks, and taken measures to support working carers. Under the *New Deal for Carers*,[15] the government announced a revision of the National Strategy for Carers.[16]

This is an area where individual church congregations can have a significant role. Many carers cease attending worship or other activities for lack of a person who will sit with their relative. Surely this is a service many churches could offer.

Improvement of life for people with dementia

As we saw in Chapter 8, older people with dementia and their carers have very special needs. Few people realize that dementia costs the country more than heart, stroke and cancer combined. At last, after much lobbying, the government has recognized the importance of this and has announced a consultation on a national dementia strategy, due to be published in autumn 2008.

The promotion of health and active life in older age

This is Standard 8 of the National Service Framework and, in many ways, helping and supporting older people to continue to live healthy and active lives is the aspiration of all other social policy in this area. There is a growing body of evidence to suggest that the modification of risk factors for disease can result in longer life, sustained levels of functional activity and improved well-being. In addition, improvements in this area can help to counter the social exclusion of many older people and thus have benefits for the individual and society. A range of measures has begun to tackle these issues, such as the winter heating allowance, healthy eating campaigns and the Keep Warm, Keep Well initiative, together with a fresh look at pensions provision in the Turner Report.[17]

The first ever cross-government strategy, *Opportunity Age: Meeting the Challenges of Ageing in the 21st Century*,[18] looked specifically at the issues facing society as people live longer healthier lives. It addresses extending people's working lives, supporting active ageing in the community, and giving people more choice and independence, especially shedding the stereotypes that surround older people.

In its final report in 2006, the Social Exclusion Unit published *A Sure Start to Later Life: Ending Inequalities for Older People*.[19] This details government plans to mitigate the exclusion, poverty and isolation experienced by older people based on the successful Sure Start model for children and families. The aim is to develop a single accessible gateway to wide-ranging services in the community.

CONCLUSION

Despite all the work outlined above, there are still groups of people, using social care services or seeking support, who give significant cause for concern. These include people who are not using services and who find it difficult to access support and good information about what is available; carers, unpaid relatives and friends who are bearing the costs of tight eligibility criteria for services; people who have little or no choice or control over the services they use; people who are using services that are simply not good enough; and people whose specialist needs are not being met.

Clearly there are other factors in play as well as social policy. Older people live in a community context. High levels of depression in older people who use social care services may be linked to a narrowing of friendship networks, to bereavement and loss of close family and friends, but also to some loss of capacity and physical and intellectual functioning. Opportunities for older people to remain socially active and engaged within their communities, with valued roles and status and with social and intellectual stimulation, may contribute to tackling depression more than the array of help from social services. As we have seen, it may also encourage continued physical activity, delaying or minimizing the onset of physical deterioration or ill health.

Other initiatives which may enhance the life experience and opportunities for everyone within a community include: tackling nuisance, crime and the fear of crime; increasing the availability of and access to transport, leisure and retail services; and providing safe and attractive environments with reasonable and appropriate housing (see the Department for Communities and Local Government *National Strategy for Housing in an Ageing Society*).

The difficulties faced by older people should not be underestimated. Some social commentators have argued that during the early part of the twenty-first century government has failed to engage with the economic and social challenges of the growing number of older people. Some of these issues have been highlighted by campaigning groups such as Help the Aged. In its *Spotlight Report*[20] we are reminded of our failure to care. Persistent poverty still exists among older people: 11 per cent of older people in the UK are living in severe poverty and 21 per cent live below the median line of earnings. This translates to an average weekly disposable income for single pensioners of £138. This poverty, together with other factors, leads many older people to express their feeling that their quality of life continues to get worse. Thirteen per cent of older people informed the researchers that they are often or always lonely, that they live in fear of crime and that their access to shops is limited through inadequate social services. These are merely some of the indicators that social care for older people is inadequate.

We have seen at various points in this book that it is not just a matter of inadequate or misdirected resources. It is also a question of attitudes where ageism is a persistent reality for many older people. Chronological age may influence but does not define or determine people and their needs. However, we need to move away from older people who are viewed as dependent, despondent recipients of services to developing services which are responsive to individuals' needs and wherever possible enhance their dignity.

There is also a challenge to leave behind the legacy of the Poor Law. That legacy appears in those of our current policies which are still focused on determining who is *not* entitled to assistance; on a continuing dependence on segregation in care homes which for many still have reminders of the workhouse; and on continued territorial differences between local authorities in access and standards of service for older people.

As pastoral carers we need to be advocates for the development of an ageing agenda in Church and society and to have an understanding of the issues which concern the older members of our congregations. Whatever future directions are taken we should acknowledge that this is a complex area that is likely to be a subject for significant debate and disagreement in future decades.

CHAPTER SIXTEEN

A theology of ageing

In the Leveson Centre we, along with others, have come to view older people as the Church's 'natural spiritual constituency'.[1] Research and experience both suggest that those who reach their fifties and beyond become more spiritual; more reflective about their life and its shape and direction; more aware of the meaning of life in the light of old age, perhaps influenced particularly by an awareness of mortality.[2]

The purpose of this chapter is to draw together some of the wide-ranging issues and questions that have been raised by this book and to put some of my own personal experience into theological perspective. There can be no definitive answers. Each of these chapters, in their broad scope and range, has attempted to provide a stimulus or springboard for those participating in the pastoral care of older people to consider what theological questions are important about age and growing older. We might also want to consider how our faith is able to be a resource for helping us age well. Pastoral care should always be seeking to expand imagination and deepen understanding. It can never be content with closed answers. We should also continually articulate both the gaps and connections between ourselves and those we endeavour to serve through our listening and care.

We should be intrigued about the place of faith. As practical theologians, we should be concerned to know more about how faith shapes us as human beings. Does my faith help me to understand the world around me? Does faith contribute to my aspiration to age well or 'successfully'?

These questions should be deliberately asked in a personal way as we struggle to connect the 'head' with the 'heart'. As we have acknowledged, those involved in the pastoral care of older people need to ask themselves about their own relationship with age, because that is a critical factor in the generation of imaginative pastoral care. Ian McEwan expressed this process of imagining in this way: 'Imagining what it is like to be someone other than yourself is the core of our humanity. It is the essence of compassion and the beginning of morality'; and 'imagination is the basis of all sympathy, empathy and compassion. Other people are as alive as you are. Cruelty is a failure of the imagination.'[3]

One of the many elements of reflecting on how we value old age lies in how we choose to conceptualize the life journey. Is it, for example, helpful to see life as a progression of effort, moving 'uphill', with old age as a gentle movement 'downhill'? Which part of our life requires significant effort? When are we at our peak? At what point in our lives is it possible for us to have a 'view' that enables us to put experience into a broader perspective? The thought of decline (or going downhill) denies the possibility of our living being at all stages rich with growth, love and opportunity. There may be gains and losses at all stages of our life. We need to be in touch with these realities.

Perhaps age is partly a matter of attitude. Some people live as if age simply does not matter – they refuse to think about it. For some people the best attitude to ageing is to resist it (or even deny it); some people are determined not to allow life to get the better of them. Balance and perspective, openness and flexibility seem to be key virtues in enabling individuals and communities to find balance and embrace change. Our lives are always a complex mixture of harmony and dissonance. Michael Mayne expresses it in this way: 'Perhaps it is only as we grow old that we can discern the cantus firmus (the firm ground, the absolute rather than the relative) of which we can say "this has been mine and mine alone . . . This is ground base."'[4]

One of the aims of pastoral care should be to help people understand the richness and complexity of their lives. Through this understanding, new depth can emerge with the possibility of perspective and celebration. Gratitude and humility are further virtues to be nurtured through reflection.

We have already acknowledged that old age can bring with it significant diminishment. There are social diminishments, such as the challenge of retirement from a job or role where many have depended upon skills, to one in which you are no longer in charge and may become increasingly dependent upon others. There are two common reactions to old people that are hard to negotiate: being patronized and being overlooked or not being noticed. Finding it difficult to come to terms with change (not least for churchgoers) and learning to receive help and not being in control are all important areas of life to negotiate.

There are other changes and losses. Perhaps the most significant is the loss of friends and contemporaries and often the loss of a life partner. This can bring a grief and loneliness to old age that is hard to bear. For some, these pains lead to a sense of loss of God and the fundamental questioning of any rational and loving purpose to the world.

The losses need to be counterbalanced and redressed by the not inconsiderable gains. Perhaps the bus passes, free television licences and other advantages given to senior citizens are some of the pluses, but there are not so easily listed – rather more subtle – gains. The big events that have shaped our life, the realities both of darkness and light, become burned into the grain of who we are. If we are wise, we shall have learned from them and gained new understanding of what it is to be human. Inevitably, there will be regrets and curiosity about the path not travelled – 'Where might I be now if I'd done this rather than that?' And you see how your life has often turned on some seemingly trivial moment, a word said, a meeting, a saying 'yes' rather than 'no' or (more likely) 'no' rather than 'yes'. We regret some of the things we did, and at the same time regret even more the things we haven't had the courage to tackle. 'We live forward – we understand backward' (William James), or, 'The light which experience gives is a lantern on the stern, which shines only on the waters behind us' (Coleridge).

There is a profound difference between those who view their lives simply in terms of Shakespeare's seven ages – from infancy to second childishness – and those who see their lives as an inner journey, a journey of the spirit as we travel home to God. At first our journey is from dependence to a proper independence, the search for identity, meaning and self-worth, and coming to terms with ourselves, growing in knowledge and experience. The second kind of journey, from independence to dependence, is different. The autumn of our lives is also a time for learning a new dependence on God.

But it can be a time too for learning new skills, things we have not had time for, learning to see not just the inevitable endings but also the potential beginnings. Loving one another doesn't get much easier with age, but perhaps seizing the day does. For with an increasingly limited time ahead, we might think of those places we shall never see, and those things that we shall never do, and perhaps we might even come to see that it doesn't matter – that what alone matters is that we begin to come to terms with what we have made of our life in the only moment that counts, which is the moment that is now.

There is another quality of old age that can be pure gain, and not just for ourselves: wisdom. Once people were called 'elders' because in a long life they had harvested wisdom – which is very different from that gathering of information with which our culture is so obsessed. Wisdom is not what you know about; it is what you know, deep inside you, the essence of your inner life. Wisdom is the art of holding together the old and the new, of balancing the known with the unknown, the pain and the joy; it is a way of linking the whole of your life together in a needful integrity. Growing ought to mean just that – growing as we age. Growing in a sense of wonder at the familiar and in curiosity about the new, just plain curiosity about life. Growing in wisdom, patience and a contentment to move more and more from 'doing' into that equally rewarding and much more important stage, the state of 'being' – so that we may discern what matters and what doesn't. It will mean detachment and learning to let go, and it may indeed mean replacing a life of independence with one of increasing dependence on others. We cannot prepare ourselves for birth – we can for death.

But we may utter generalizations about ageing and, like most other generalizations, they are often useless. Some people seem middle-aged in the cradle and there are those in their nineties whose relish for life is as vivid as it was in their twenties. Perhaps it's true to say that whatever age (or birth age) we are, it feels like all ages wrapped into one. There is always a bit of us that still feels ten years old, or 21, for there is within each of us this recognizable and changing core. Each day is a miracle in itself with all the mystery and wonder contained within the patterns of the natural world. No two days are ever quite the same. There is always some possibility contained within the fabric of each day.

Neurologists tell us that they understand about a tenth of what there is to know about the human brain, and are still baffled by the riddle of human consciousness; yet one of the most rewarding gifts of age can be to revisit the place where our vanished days are gathered – whose name is memory. For many people, of course, memories can be largely painful and unrewarding – for some agonizingly so. But for most of us, unless we have dementia, it is the good memories of people which dominate, and those life-shaping events which remain as vivid as ever.

'Perhaps being old', wrote Philip Larkin, 'is having lighted rooms inside your head, and people in them, acting.' Time gives us the opportunity to think and reflect and remember. Old age ought to be the time when we can visit that place in order better to understand and integrate our lives, a time of harvest.[5]

Everything we have ever seen and every person with whom we have spent time have somehow been translated in our brains into images and feelings – and we can immediately conjure a host of them from that most strange yet intimate centre that is 'me'. And at the level of my unconscious all my experiences exist timelessly, for what we call time is merely the way we turn the flow of the successive moments into some kind of manageable order. When I seek to tell my own unique story, it is by linking together memory and imagination. For then I can gather lost moments and experiences, overcome the gap between the past and the present, bring them together and hold them as one. This is how we gain a hold on truths which seem to us timeless, and which speak of human experiences that are universal. We are born, we grow, we are moulded and changed by life. Some of us adapt to change and others resist it at all costs. Some greet change with resignation and others relish the prospect of a challenge. Some are energized by life and others retreat into boredom. Some long for their youth and find it hard to 'age'. Pictures of ourselves in our twenties or thirties may seem almost unrecognizable. And yet we can recognize a consistency in the responses and the behaviour of our friends and loved ones – as they may do in us. I am unmistakably 'me'. My body is ageing, but I am not just my body. It may be that our brain takes longer to come up with facts, but I am not just my body plus my brain. I am much more than the sum of my parts. And, yes, that child who stares out from the yellowing photograph album is really me, and I still carry him with me.

We each have our own story to tell which is like and unlike everybody else's story. We each need to discern it and marvel at how, in retrospect, it begins to make sense and we can see how everything – the bad times when God seems to have deserted us as well as the good – was grist to the mill; and how, a bit battered, we have not only come through but (hopefully, though not always) learned lessons that make us more rounded people; and how all in the end is part of the harvest of our lives. For those who are granted the grace of a reasonably healthy old age, one of its gifts is the chance to explore the shape of one's life and its inner journey – all the relationships, all the experiences of beauty and sorrow, love and loss, all that we know to have been authentic and all that has formed and changed us, and made us what we are.

As we grow older, memories play a larger part in our lives. There is not much we can do to change the general shape of our story. There may be fewer things that we can expect to achieve. However, every person has something to offer and share. It is part of the pastoral task to discover the giftedness which is within each individual and help them to express that. Remembering is important and we should try to remember in the right spirit.

The temptation in old age is to say, 'I am what I was.' But that's only half the truth; until the day I die, I am what I am. And when I come to die, I shall no longer have a past. I shall be remembered as a complete being, formed by my relationships, by all that has happened to me, and by all that I have made of it. It is very likely that those tasked with our funeral or memorial services will attend to this celebration of our lives and what we have shared and given. Perhaps they will also have the courage to be gentle with our weaknesses and shortcomings. The light and darkness, successes and failures, are part of the same picture. For even now there is a consistency and harmony about our lives – whether good or bad or indifferent, happy or unhappy, with spells of both, it hangs together. So often we tell the story and retell it to ourselves, in a way that suits us and not the truth. In the end, we have an enormous tendency to push the shadow side of our lives away and never to allow ourselves to look at the whole picture in the full truth of the light. For it is just as important to remember the bad things, and to remember them honestly and accurately, to face the rich truth about ourselves and others. If we do not, then perhaps we shall never know or be able to give happiness.

This uniqueness that is me is what I have been, is what I have to offer to my Creator, who knows me infinitely better than I know myself, and who graciously welcomes me home, not in spite of what I have been, but because of what I am.

But what of the unfinished business, specific and named unrighted wrongs, the negative memories that come back to haunt us in dreams or in the wakeful hours of the night? Central to achieving a gracious, contented old age is how we acknowledge the great healing power of forgiveness. There may be in our lives all kinds of unsatisfactory loose ends – disappointments, family rows, anger, guilt, even bitterness – that need to surface and perhaps be resolved. No one can go through a human life and not make mistakes, do selfish and regrettable things. But we can learn from these memories; we can learn about our own need for forgiveness. We can admit our faults and express our regret. We may not succeed in putting everything right, but if we refuse to remember things as they really were, then we do not live creatively and truthfully with our lives and our memories as they are. And at such times we may need, above all, someone to sit beside us and listen to us, as in however stumbling a way we tell our stories. As those who accompany our journey listen to us they can help us do for others what in later life we can be best at: that is, passing on help and encouragement and wisdom.

But we shouldn't wait until our deaths for this resolution. For the chief task, perhaps, of the last period of life is a spiritual one: it is that of integration. Integration in the life of a nation, a community, a family or an individual, is the art of bringing together what is scattered and diverse and forming a satisfying whole: its opposite is segregation, division and alienation. In personal terms, integration brings contentment and peace of mind, whereas the failure to integrate leads to discontent, depression, confusion and even despair. But we are complex creatures, and our minds function at a surface level but also at a profoundly deep one as well. The surface mind, the home of the ego, is the 'me' that wants to be in control and fears the unknown, and needs the mask we all forge (consciously or unconsciously) with which to face the world. In childhood most of us learn to protect our vulnerability and bury deep all our unresolved baggage. This deep level is where we continue to store away unwanted thoughts and emotions, old hurts and painful memories. We may have carried a burden of hidden resentment or of guilt. And one of the gifts of age is that we have opportunity to lay these potentially damaging ghosts to rest. We may need help, but we can learn to address and settle our negative feelings, our wounds and our anger – facing negativity where it exists, the poison of resentment, and to know ourselves forgiven, to accept that forgiveness and in turn to forgive ourselves.

Helen Luke, a Jungian analyst, writes about the journey into simplicity, which is an important theme for her in old age. She writes that it is as if, as we grow old, we have to learn a new language. These are the gifts reserved for old age and they have been discussed above. They are, first, the willingness to accept that which the ego fights against: the gradual loss of energy, the diminishment of hearing or sight, the enforced move from active to passive.[6] We all have to learn to receive as well as give.

We need to bring our nostalgia under control. The world of our youth has been cruelly pushed into the past and its familiar touchstones – the songs, the clothes, the manners – are now considered 'old-fashioned'. We know how fashion changes! We are not the first generation to feel that the change from then to now is largely for the worse – though perhaps it has never happened quite so fast. Perhaps there is no period so remote as the recent past. We may privately deplore the losses, but we must have the grace to celebrate the undoubted gains. We hope that those who listen to us will be patient and take some delight in the story shared more than once! There is often something new to be heard. And if younger people won't listen to us, that doesn't prevent us listening to and maybe learning from them.

But it is the final gift that is perhaps the hardest to accept. We can either continue, as we age, to cling to our past achievements, a desire to dominate and control, or learn gracefully to let go and discover a new freedom and a new unity with the created world in all its beauty and its creatures in all their variety. We can begin to piece together the story of our lives, to look clear-eyed at the suffering and the sorrow hidden in our memories; to come to terms with our sins, our mistakes, our failure to love as we might have done, and our desire (often unrecognized until now) to control and manipulate others.

It may be that because our thoughts about life become simpler and deeper as we age (we have fewer choices), we may be given the grace to understand that we have only one overriding choice: to cling to our past achievements, growing resentful and lamenting what is lost; or to accept our natural loss of energy and growing weariness, feeding off our own good memories of the past and laying to rest our bad ones. We can choose to reflect daily with thankfulness and wonder on this amazing gift of life.

Suddenly old age can feel like lowering our sails as we drift into harbour. In certain monastic communities it has long been the practice to lie in your coffin as a way of meditating on your own mortality. A little extreme we may think, but reflecting on our own death and leaving clear instructions of the form we would wish our funeral to take can be an important expression of love. Looking at death and reflecting upon it can also help us to deepen our sense of life and its meaning.[7]

We can, of course, draw life in a number of different ways – imagining its shape, both its inner as well as its outer journey. We can see it simply as a straight line from birth to death, emerging from darkness and going back into darkness. Or we may picture it as a circle. There is the natural cycle of the seasons, echoing the rhythm of our lives: the growth and vigour of spring; the richness and maturity of summer; the gradual diminishment of autumn, a time of harvest and the falling of the leaves; the bleak, but often beautiful landscape of the winter, when the shape of the trees becomes so much clearer. The autumn and winter of our lives are the times when we begin to come full circle. Perhaps best of all, we can add the dimension of height (and by implication depth) when we see our lives as a slowly ascending spiral. For a spiral suggests a life where each new circle – each new year or decade – still contains within it the make-up of the old, the feeling of familiarity; the octogenarian still aware of what it felt like to be the child, the lover, the parent he or she once was, and still displaying the same recognizable characteristics, but wiser now, shaped by life's knocks and able to say, 'I have been here before and learnt a thing or two.'

Towards the end of his life, Malcolm Muggeridge described life as being a sea voyage nearing its destination. He wrote this:

When I embarked I worried about having a cabin with a porthole, whether I should be asked to sit at the captain's table, who are the most attractive passengers. All such

considerations become pointless when I shall soon be dis-
embarking. The world that I shall soon be leaving seems
ever more beautiful. Those I love I can love even more, since
I have nothing to ask of them but their love; the passion to
accumulate possessions, the need to be noticed and to be
important, is too evidently absurd to be any longer enter-
tained.[8]

Perhaps that is a lesson for us all – the recognition of what is
truly important in our lives and to be freed from all the para-
phernalia of life. Looking back we can begin to understand our
own unique story and see that the very best of things are to be
found in human friendship and love, a reflection of that love
which God has for us in Jesus Christ. When we become more
loving as we grow older then the world itself becomes a better
place and we can see its promise in those around us. Above all we
glimpse the beating heart at the centre of it all – God.[9]

CHAPTER SEVENTEEN

Successful ageing

There is a difference between living and being alive.

Growing older is about adding life to years rather than just adding years to our lives.

At this point the reader will note that no case studies have been provided as part of our engagement with the commitment to listening to experience. Rather it might be fruitful for the reader to imagine him or herself as the case study at the beginning of this chapter. Whatever your stage of life, imagine what shape old age might take for you. How would you define successful ageing? What steps might you like to take in order to enable age and the ageing process to be as fruitful and creative as is possible or desirable? This book has taken a brief overview of some of the pastoral questions and issues that face older people – but which are, in the end, challenges, issues and questions for none other than us.

Looking back over the earlier chapters and attending to other people's experiences serves to reinforce the effect and experience of modernity on the life course. The engagement with ageing and the ageing process have been transformed as a consequence of an increasing acceptance of a life and a world which are both complex and diverse. There is a great deal more fluidity in the life course and much less predictability than we may be led to suppose about the fixed life stages outlined by many theorists.[1]

It becomes, therefore, more difficult to get a wider perspective – as true and adequate a picture of reality as we possibly can. Heterogeneity rather than homogeneity is perhaps the new reality: our views of the person and the possibility of ageing are surrounded by an awareness of a great plasticity in our understanding of the person and of human behaviour. Postmodern lifestyles, for young and old alike, involve a dynamic mix of uncertainty, ambiguity and diversity. The pastoral care of any individual, but especially those individuals who are growing older, needs to consider the necessity for us all to be flexibly adapting to a constantly changing world. This has led some theorists to argue that any serious commentary on 'successful ageing' must address the plasticity and adaptability of human nature, which includes the ability to adapt positively even under the most adverse of life's conditions and circumstances.

At a number of points in this book we have noted that the later life stages test older people (for example, Chapter 10 about the inevitability of most of us having to deal with loss, change and illness to a greater or lesser degree). Part of the privilege of pastoral care is to see the amazing untapped resilience and reserves that people have for coping with altered life circumstances. Very often, older people demonstrate the most inspiring of spirits in the way in which they continue to recognize and adapt to life in a climate of constant movement and loss. The secret of 'successful ageing' may be in part the result of our ability to draw upon those strengths and attitudes that will allow us to stay connected with life. Religion and spirituality often play an important part in the nurturing of inner resources which enable individuals to adapt, connect and recreate the shape of their inner lives.

DEFINING SUCCESSFUL AGEING

The concept of 'successful ageing' is a rich one and its initial entry into the field of social gerontology can be found in gerontological literature over 30 years ago.[2] The term is appealing because it implies that ageing can for the most part be a positive and rewarding experience. There is, inevitably, a range of perspectives identified with the concept. It is worth noting that the concept of 'successful ageing' is often related to the concept of middle age or the 'mid course' of life, in that 'successful ageing' is identified as, in effect, the continuation of the activities, interests and involvements that have been developed in that phase of a person's life. Some gerontologists have offered an opposite view, seeing older people as progressively disengaging from life, this being an important part of normal 'ageing'.[3]

While this volume has discussed some of the age-related changes sometimes associated with the ageing process (Chapter 5), we should note that growing old need not mean an inevitable trend towards disease, disability and impending death – though this is the pattern of age for some people. Chapters 12 (Lifelong learning and older people) and 13 (Retirement) discuss how age might be a continued time of development and new experiences.

'Successful ageing' has often been defined in the following way:

1 The absence of disease and disability.
2 The maintenance of intellectual and physical functions.
3 Engagement in meaningful activities.[4]

Such a viewpoint is consistent with the World Health Organization's definition of health as a state of well-being rather than merely the absence of disease.[5]

This concept should certainly embrace a wider social perspective. Studies of ageing tell us that good health, healthy interpersonal relationships and personality characteristics such as self-efficacy are significant predicators of continuing functional independence and indicators of 'successful ageing'. A person's ability to shape the quality of life is a significant dimension to 'successful ageing' and has an inevitable materialistic, financial and class base.

One of the weaknesses of much of the gerontological research in this area lies in the absence of input from older people. It is becoming increasingly important that research should be based on the diverse experiences and perspectives of older people themselves so that harmful or false stereotypes can be avoided.

'SUCCESS' AND YOUR JOURNEY?

When considering what valuing age might look like for us, one of the questions that all individuals ask at some time is, 'What will the future bring?' This is a question which occupies individuals who approach the stage of life known as old age. Sometimes this stage can be precipitated on an individual basis by a major life crisis, and one's philosophy of life might be in need of examination in the light of the circumstances. We should remember that over the life course all human beings change in the definition of themselves and the world, their modes of

response and adaptation, and in aspects of their basic orientation and value judgements. Religion and its importance for an
individual can change and be shaped by a number of external
and internal factors.

So older age, if nothing else, will provide an opportune time to
explore the undiscovered self. This might be problematic or traumatic work as some of the cherished hopes and aspirations have
to be reformed in the light of experience. It is also a time when
individuals may need someone to accompany them on this pastoral journey. There is some negotiation to take place with self
and others on the ageing pilgrimage. In other words, some of the
geography of old age might be anticipated through the processes
of planning and a balanced level of reflection. Fears and anxieties
need to be faced and choices to be made about what the direction
of the journey might look like. Emergent trends in Western societies show that for increasing numbers of older people there is
plenty of opportunity for personal growth and development.

People are complex, adaptive organisms and there is no reason
to think that they can be easily explained. Part of this social call to
'successful ageing' is to engage in more explicit conversation and
debate about the meanings that older people attach to their lived
experiences, including notions about ageing well and 'successful
ageing'. Why let ageing happen to us? Is there a possibility of
empowered reshaping of what this pilgrimage might look like?

Antonovsky indicates that well-being is not an outcome as
much as a dynamic predicator of an individual's ability to cope
and adapt to the changes and assaults of life. All of us should be
more interested in health and well-being but the key variable to
be understood is the sense of coherence, whose three major components – comprehensibility, meaning and manageability –
are dynamically interrelated as people deal with the inevitable
challenges of existence. From this perspective Antonovsky sees
health as a personal resource to be used against those forces that
constantly affect our personal existence.[6] One might conclude
that consumerism, individualism and materialism are significant
forces in postmodernity that tell against the individual's capacity
to have the space and spiritual depth which enable him or her to
make life worth living. Many people experience superficial completeness or well-being but have a deep and prevailing sense that
life is not worth living. Success and material wealth can also

bring gloom and emptiness. From a Christian perspective we might affirm the power of the human spirit, created and nurtured by God, which can propel the individual forward in full recognition that the ultimate task is to affirm one's position in relation to life and the world. This sense of perspective can bring depth and nurture, hope and meaning.

Social planners would be well advised to understand that the aged of tomorrow will make very different lifestyle choices compared with the aged of today. Looking across the generations it seems unlikely that my generation will tolerate some of the choices presently provided for the older generation. People reaching middle age and beyond are now beginning to understand and appreciate the potential contribution of the lifestyle factor to personal health and well-being. In essence, lifestyle is a descriptive term for the unique pattern of living adopted by an individual in terms of his or her interaction with the self and the social world, with implications for a dynamic relationship between personal values, beliefs and strategies for coping with life and change. The spiritual task here is to ask, 'How might we live more meaningful lives?' Many older people are experiencing an awakened life – an understanding that freedom is the absence of unnecessary restrictions on how life should be lived. The third age will increasingly be seen as a stage for adding new dimensions to the lived experience – the seeking of enhanced flexibilities in lifestyle choices.

The process by which an individual connects with and associates with the nature of meaning is a complex one, influenced by a person's previous history, and involving culture, language and lived experiences. It is well to remember that the life journey involves the self-interpreting person in a series of real-world context changes, formed by such matters as education, marriage, divorce, relationships, work, unemployment, retirement and illness. Indeed, as people age they are progressively involved in a matrix of constant change and loss. The quest for personal well-being during old age is virtually impossible if one's life is contaminated by a continuing sense of apathy, inertia and meaninglessness. Any reference to well-being and old age must also be cognizant of the view that loneliness is an important consideration in old age which needs further examination if we are to understand the subtleties of why it occurs and how it can be ameliorated.

Some writers advocate that well-being is reflected in part by those individuals who are willing to be open to new ideas, risks and opportunities. This perspective is extended by introducing the concept of the individual who might embrace continual renewal and growth by seeking new adventures, meanings and motivations. Equally important is the need to understand that the person's experience of ageing takes place in a social context, thereby exposing the individual to a dynamic range of interacting social forces. A single older person may experience age in a very different way from a married older person given the importance, for good or ill, of the network of the immediate and extended family.[7]

We should draw attention to the fact that many of our thoughts and feelings about age are socially constructed and result in a range of stereotypes about what it means to be old. There can often be a tension between how we ourselves feel and how society sees us.

We should not underestimate the spiritual and existential search for meaning that age can bring. The following questions: Who have I been? Who am I now? Who will I be? What will become of me? are very significant. These questions will no doubt generate a range of reflections resulting in meanings and interpretations that have a significant influence on the health and well-being of the older person. Life review, story-telling and story-sharing can offer a real potential for facilitating a definition of the self and exploring this in the light of the concept of 'successful ageing'. Existential issues that come to mind in this conversation and sharing are death, freedom, hopelessness, meaninglessness, responsibility, discipline, despair, obsolescence and loneliness.

In all of this reflection, all of the pastoral accompanying, mistakes will be made, errors of omission and commission will occur, and undoubtedly they will continue to occur. Life, however, must and will go on – we have to decide how much energy we wish to apply to the pilgrimage or excursion. Of course some people waste much of their time on regret, guilt and ruminations of the worst kind. Some people talk of killing time, when they fail to see that in the end time will quietly kill us all.

The pursuit of 'successful ageing' must always be seen as work in progress. There are many pathways to its achievement. With this in mind I want to end this book by offering my own thoughts about what makes for 'successful ageing'.

1 *Be flexible* As we have discussed above, the modern world is an amazing mix of uncertainty and ambiguity – and flexibility helps us to adapt to the changes in the world around us and the changes within us. This flexibility or adaptability can help us to respond positively even in the most adverse of conditions and circumstances. We might be surprised what inner resources are there waiting to be used when the time comes.

2 *Be ready to define yourself beyond work or the work role* Too much of our identity is imprisoned in the status or importance or control that our work and our work role bring. If we invest too much in work, it can reveal all the cracks and problems that we hide away from once it is removed.

3 *Discover your inner self* Older age, if nothing else, will provide a time to explore our undiscovered self. This might constitute a challenge, but ageing can be a pilgrimage and an opportunity to look inside at what we really believe to be true, what bothers us, and how we might make a difference in this particular stage of our lives.

4 *Learn something new* Learning new tricks keeps us alive – it broadens our sense of comprehensibility and meaning. So let's go on a Spanish course, learn about the classification of trees or revisit those endless rows of books on our shelves which are waiting to be digested. There are also new people to be interested in whose lives can change ours and who may be changed by knowing us.

5 *Take the opportunity to be someone different* Gerontologists reflect on the stages of the life cycle. Some refer to the first stage as the stage of formation which is the time to grow an identity before we are consumed by busyness. Properly balanced, the second stage is the time of one's major contribution to work or home or community. This consuming busyness, which demands so much of us and is so overarching, is, however, only one stage of our journey. A third stage is the opportunity to be someone different. If there are things about our lives that we want to change, then we should stop complaining and get on and change them. There are fewer restrictions on how life should be lived. If we have spent the first part of our life living in other people's ways, do it now in your own way or, in the words of the professionals, seek the enhanced flexibilities in lifestyle choices.

6   *Get philosophical* In a materialistic world we live too often on
    the surface. Successfully ageing is about thinking through
    what you believe. Who have I been? Who am I now? Who will I
    be? What will become of me? What bits of the past do we need
    to leave behind as properly dead and gone, and how might we
    shape the future – by doing philosophy? Are you free? Are you
    hopeless? Who makes this journey with you?

7   *Prepare for death* You can't put it off – and don't leave it to
    chance. Think about how you want your life celebrated.
    Thinking about change, loss, diminishment and ultimately
    death will help you face these changes and difficulties as they
    emerge through the course of ageing.[8]

This brings us full circle back to ourselves as the final case study
in this book. These initial thoughts about 'successful ageing' give
us an opportunity to reflect on its shape for us and the opportunity that we have to influence the direction of our pilgrimage
into age.

Age statistics

1 How many people over state pension age are there in the UK today?
   More than 11 million or 16 per cent of the total population
   (Population Trends (PT 126) National Statistics, 2006)

2 How many of these are over 85?
   Nearly 1.2 million
   (Population Trends (PT 126) National Statistics, 2006)

3 How many are centenarians?
   11,000
   (Population projections by the Government Actuary – based on GAD, 2005)

4 Compare this with 300 in 1951 and 4,400 in 1991.
   (Debate of the Age: Ten Key Facts, April/May 1998)

5 Is this population growing as a proportion of the total population?
   Population over 65 grew by 31 per cent between 1971 and 2007 whereas the
   population under 16 declined by 19 per cent
   (National Statistics online <www.statistics.gov.uk>)

6 In 2001 there were more people over 60 (21 per cent of the population) than
   under 16 (20 per cent)
   (Census 2001 (ONS, 2003))

7 By 2021 there will be more people over 80 than under five.
   (Speech by Liam Byrne MP, July 2006)

8 How many older people (i.e. of pensionable age) will there be in 2026?
   13.9 million
   (National Population Projections 2004 – based on National Statistics, 2006)

9 How many will there be in 2031?
   15.3 million
   (General Household Survey Results for 2005 – National Statistics, 2006)

10 How many people in the UK have dementia?
   Nearly 700,000
   1:5 million over 80; 1:20 over 65
   (Dementia UK: Summary of key findings PSSRU, 2007)

11 How many people in the UK is it estimated will have dementia in 2021 and 2051?
Nearly 950,000 and 1.7 million
(General Household Survey Results for 2005 – National Statistics, 2006)

12 What proportion of older people live alone?
29 per cent of men over 75 and 60 per cent of women over 75
(General Household Survey Results for 2005 – National Statistics, 2006)

13 What proportion of older people have a limiting long-term health condition?
37 per cent of those 65–74, 47 per cent aged 75 and over
(General Household Survey Results for 2002 – National Statistics, 2003)

14 Are older people living in poverty, defined as household income less than 60 per cent of median income of population as a whole?
1.8 million live in poverty
(Households below average income 1994–5 to 2005–6: Department of Work and Pensions, 2006)

15 Do older people use the Internet?
In 2006 28 per cent aged 65 and over had access to the Internet
(The Consumer Experience: research report OfCom, 2006)

16 What proportion of hospital beds are occupied by older people?
Two thirds
(Speech by Liam Byrne MP, July 2006)

17 What is the role of older people as carers?
Nearly 350,000 people aged 65 and over provide 50 hours or more of care a week
(Census 2001 National Report for England and Wales – National Statistics, 2002)

18 What is the life expectancy of people of 60 today?
A man can expect to live to 80.5 and a woman to 83.6
(Interim Life Tables (ONS, 2007))

APPENDIX TWO

Narrative biography and older people

Throughout this book we have framed a number of questions and issues that need to be addressed as part of our understanding of the older person, their world, their hope and aspirations for life, their reflections on the past and the world around them. Part of the task of pastoral care is to enable older people to articulate what some of these areas of narrative might look like.

Narrative biography, life history and reminiscence work are all seen as key concepts in gerontology and care. The life stories and spiritual beliefs of older people and how these link to older people's experiences at the end of life and in bereavement need to be better understood. As professionals work together to deliver person-centred care it is important that we should listen to older people and recognize their individual differences and specific needs.

Nowhere is this approach more important than in care and relationships with older people with dementia, who may be losing their awareness of themselves and their personal history. How can one maintain one's personhood when one cannot always remember who one is?

Tom Kitwood comments in this way:

If personhood is to be maintained, it is essential that each individual is appreciated in his or her uniqueness. Where there is empathy without personal knowledge, care will be aimless and unfocussed. Where there is personal knowledge without empathy, care will be detached and cold. But when empathy and personal knowledge are brought together, miracles can happen. (*Dementia Reconsidered*, Maidenhead: Open University Press, 1997, p. 19)

Knowing more about each person allows care to be delivered in a more individually tailored and responsive fashion and often offers explanations from the past for actions and attitudes today.

What particular questions or areas should be explored with older people in order to build up a sensitive understanding of their spiritual needs? You will be able to generate your own questions but the principle that questions must be open and not have a clear answer should guide the engagement and process of listening.

Fairly specific topics might include –

- Childhood – Where were you born? Where did you live? Memories you may have.
- Schooling – Was it enjoyable and what particular subjects were favourite or important?
- Places you have lived.
- Work – What jobs did you have? Did you enjoy the world of work?
- Relationships – marriage, children, friends. Who have been important people in your life?
- Social – hobbies, interests, pets, likes and dislikes in food or music.

More general areas for exploration might be –

- What is life like for you now?
- How would you like it to be?
- What makes you happy?
- What makes you sad?
- What makes you cross?
- What would you do if you were offered a chance to do anything?
- What makes you laugh?

Here are some questions which have worked within the context of the life and community here at Temple Balsall.

GOOD QUESTIONS

- Are you conscious of your age?
- What keeps you going in life?
- Tell me how you spend your time.
- How would you like to be remembered?
- What do you get angry about?
- What are the qualities you think your parents gave you?
- What were you doing when the war began?

MORE QUESTIONS

- Do you think that others understand being old?
- Are there advantages in getting older?
- Do you pray?
- What most upsets you about the world today?
- What gives most pleasure?
- Do you think we should try to be good?

FURTHER QUESTIONS

- Do you feel hope?
- Do you feel wiser now?
- In what ways do you sense God?
- Would you like to go on for ever?
- Has your spirituality changed since you got older?
- What do you see when you look into the mirror?

Following some group work with older people here are some of the more playful questions which older people have enjoyed asking one another.

- When were you happiest?
- What is your greatest fear?
- Which living person do you most admire and why?
- What is the trait you most deplore in yourself?
- What is the trait you most deplore in others?
- Aside from property or a car, what is the most expensive thing you've bought?
- What is your most treasured possession?
- What makes you depressed?
- Would you rather be clever and ugly, or thick and attractive?
- Who would play you in the film of your life?
- What is your most unappealing habit?
- What is your favourite word?
- What is your favourite smell?
- Is it better to give or receive?
- What is your guiltiest pleasure?
- To whom would you most like to say sorry and why?
- What or who is the greatest love of your life?
- Which living person do you most despise and why?
- Who would you invite to your dream dinner party?
- If you could go back in time, where would you go?
- When did you last cry and why?
- How do you relax?
- How often do you have sex?
- What is the closest you've ever come to death?
- What do you consider your greatest achievement?
- What keeps you awake at night?
- Where would you most like to be right now?

CONCLUSION

We should note that reminiscence can result in the resurfacing of unpleasant and unhappy memories, but this is not always a bad thing. Older people may need someone to help them acknowledge grief and put things right from the past. As ever, pastoral sensitivity of the highest quality is required.

With people with dementia, direct questions rarely succeed, so a more open-ended approach is needed with, for example, the use of triggers in the form of a reminiscence or memory box, photographs, memorabilia or the involvement of a close family member.

Memory box

The memory box, in particular for people with dementia, was launched in 1995 by Faith in Elderly People, Leeds. Believing that our identity is closely related to what we have been and done and that in dementia childhood memories often remain vivid when more recent memory is hazy, they suggested that to help retain identity, people should make their own memory box. This box would contain meaningful items which say something about the person whose box it is. The items can be looked at over and over again by their owner but can also provide clues for visitors and professional carers as to what is important in the person's life.

It is never too early to start making a memory box and this can be an enjoyable activity either in retirement or when one is younger. Close relatives may need to help where the person is already suffering memory loss.

Some ideas for a memory box:

- Photos of people or places of significance.
- Important letters or diaries (people with dementia can sometimes read even when they no longer speak).
- CDs of favourite music (to ensure that those who enjoy Mozart don't need to suffer Elvis – and vice versa).
- Painting equipment or items connected with other creative hobbies.
- Football programmes, a golf ball or other reminders of sporting interests.
- Packets of seeds to encourage conversation about gardening.
- A Bible, prayer book, cross or candle to signify a religious allegiance.
- If possible some notes about the significance of the items to their owner.

The memory box has a considerable number of practical uses:

- For the person themselves to sit quietly handling the items and remembering past experiences.
- To share with other people, remembering together, talking about the past and thus engaging in conversation. These other people may be contemporaries or visitors who may not have known the person when they were younger.
- To share with children and younger people memories of the past.
- To take into hospital or a care home so that carers and new people in the person's life can find clues as to their identity and what is important to them.

There are numerous stories of instances where carers' attitudes have been radically changed and care practices improved through the greater understanding brought about through a memory box.

Useful organizations

ADVICE AND SUPPORT

Action on Elder Abuse
Aims to prevent abuse by raising awareness, encouraging education, promoting research and collecting and disseminating information
Astral House, 1268 London Road, London SW16 4ER
Tel.: 020 8765 7000
Helpline: 0808 808 8141
Website: www.elderabuse.org.uk

Age Concern local branches
Provide information and advice and a varied range of services for older people
Website: www.ageconcern.org.uk
Click on 'Find your Age Concern' for details of local branches

Alzheimer's Society
Provides information and local support to help people with dementia and their carers cope with the day-to-day realities of dementia. It funds research and campaigns on issues connected with dementia
Devon House, 58 St Katharine's Way, London E1W 1JX
Tel.: 020 7423 3500
Helpline: 0845 300 0336 (Monday to Friday: 8.30 a.m. to 6.30 p.m.)
Website: www.alzheimers.org.uk

Alzheimer Scotland
22 Drumsheugh Gardens, Edinburgh EH3 7RN
Tel.: 0131 243 1453
Website: www.alzscot.org

Alzheimer's Society North Wales
Cymdeithas, North Wales Area Office, 6a Llys Onnen, Parc Menai, Bangor LL57 4DF
Tel.: 01248 671137
Website: www.alzheimers.org.uk
Email: nwa@alzheimers.org.uk

Alzheimer's Society South Wales

Cymdeithas, Third Floor, Baltic House, Mount Stuart Square, Cardiff CF10 5FH
Tel.: 029 2048 0593
Website: www.alzheimers.org.uk
Email: SDAreaOffice-SouthWales@alzheimers.org.uk

Alzheimer's Northern Ireland

86 Eglantine Avenue, Belfast BT9 6EU
Tel.: 028 9066 4100
Helpline: 0845 300 0336
Website: www.alzheimers.org.uk

Arthritis Care

A user-led organization supporting people with arthritis
18 Stephenson Way, London NW1 2HD
Tel.: 020 7380 6500
Helpline: 0845 600 6868
Website: www.arthritiscare.org.uk

British Heart Foundation

Invests in pioneering research and provides support and care for heart patients
14 Fitzhardinge Street, London W1H 6DH
Tel.: 020 7935 0185
Heart Information Line: 08450 70 80 70 (Monday, Tuesday, Friday: 9 a.m. to 5
p.m.; Wednesday and Thursday: 8 a.m. to 6 p.m.)
Website: www.bhf.org.uk

Carers UK

Improves carers' lives through research, information, provision of services and
campaigning
32–36 Loman Street, Southwark, London SE1 0EE
Tel.: 020 7922 8000
Carers Line: 0808 808 7777 (Helpline: Wednesday, Thursday: 10 a.m. to 12 noon,
2 p.m. to 4 p.m.)
Website: www.carersuk.org

Cinnamon Trust

A specialist national charity for older people and their pets. Has a register of pet-
friendly care homes
10 Market Square, Hayle, Cornwall TR27 4HE
Tel.: 01736 757900
Website: www.cinnamon.org.uk

Citizens Advice

Operating name of the **National Association of Citizens Advice Bureaux**
Provides from more than 300 locations free advice which helps people resolve
their legal, financial and other problems
Myddelton House, 115–123 Pentonville Road, London N1 9LZ
Tel.: 08451 264264
Website: www.citizensadvice.org.uk

Counsel and Care

Provides advice, information and financial support for those looking for the best care and support for older people. Influences national policies on services and funding
Twyman House, 16 Bonny St, London NW1 9PG
Tel.: 020 7241 8555
Helpline: 0845 300 7585
Website: www.counselandcare.org.uk

Crossroads Association

Provides breaks for carers to meet their individual needs. Branches in most parts of England and Wales
10 Regent Place, Rugby, Warwickshire CV21 2PN
Tel.: 0845 450 0350
Website: www.crossroads.org.uk

Cruse Bereavement Care

Promotes the well-being of bereaved people, providing counselling and support
PO Box 800, Richmond, Surrey TW9 1RG
Tel.: 020 8939 9530
Helpline: 0844 477 9400
Website: www.crusebereavementcare.org.uk

Diabetes UK

Helps people with diabetes, funding research and campaigning
Macleod House, 10 Parkway, London NW1 7AA
Tel.: 020 7424 1000
Helpline: 0845 120 2960
Website: www.diabetes.org.uk

Elderly Accommodation Counsel

Helps older people to make decisions about housing and support needs through its other website <www.housingcare.org>. Keeps registers of housing with care and care homes
Third Floor, 89 Albert Embankment, London SE1 7PT
Tel.: 020 7820 1343
Website: www.eac.org.uk

Hospice Information Service

Provides advice and information service for health professionals and members of the public on UK and international palliative care
St Christopher's Hospice, 51–59 Lawrie Park Road, London SE26 6DZ
Tel.: 020 7520 8232
Helpline: 0870 903 3903
Website: www.hospiceinformation.info/

Macular Disease Society

Provides information and support for those with central vision impairment and funds research
PO Box 1870, Andover, Hants SP10 9AD

Tel.: 01264 350551
Helpline: 0845 241 2041
Website: www.maculardisease.org

National Association of Providers of Activities

Develops expertise in activity provision for older people, through training, setting and disseminating standards and supporting activity providers
Bondway Commercial Centre, Unit 5.12, Fifth Floor, 71 Bondway, London SW8 1SQ
Tel.: 020 7078 9375
Website: www.napa-activities.net

Nursing Home Fees Agency

Helps people to understand methods of funding long-term care
St Leonard's House, Mill Street, Eynsham, Oxford OX29 4JX
Tel.: 01865 733000
Helpline: 0800 99 88 33
Website: www.nhfa.co.uk

Parkinson's Disease Society UK

Provides support, information and advice for people with Parkinson's Disease
215 Vauxhall Bridge Road, London SW1V 1EJ
Tel.: 020 7931 8080
Helpline: 0808 800 0303
Website: www.parkinsons.org.uk

Princess Royal Trust for Carers

Provides comprehensive care support services through an independently managed network of 129 Carers Centres
Unit 14, Bourne Court, Southend Road, Woodford Green, Essex IG8 8HD
Tel.: 0844 800 4361
Website: www.carers.org

Relatives and Residents Association

Supports older people finding or living in care homes and their families and friends
24 The Ivories, 6–18 Northampton Street, London N1 2HY
Tel.: 020 7359 8148
Helpline: 020 7359 8136
Website: www.relres.org

Royal National Institute for Deaf People

Campaigns, provides advice and training and supports research into hearing loss
19–23 Featherstone Street, London EC1Y 8SL
Tel.: 020 7296 8000
Helpline: 0808 808 0123 (freephone)
Textphone: 0808 808 9000
Website: www.rnid.org.uk

Royal National Institute of Blind People
Provides information, advice and support for people with sight loss
105 Judd Street, London WC1H 9NE
Tel.: 020 7388 1266
Helpline: 0845 766 9999
Website: www.rnib.org.uk

Stroke Association
Combats stroke through funding research and helping stroke patients and their families
Stroke House, 240 City Road, London EC1V 2PR
Tel.: 020 7566 0300
Helpline: 0845 303 3100
Website: www.stroke.org.uk

University of the Third Age
A network of self-help, self-managed lifelong learning co-operatives for older people
Third Age Trust, The Old Municipal Buildings, 19 East Street, Bromley BR1 1QE
Tel.: 020 8466 6139 (9.30 a.m. to 1.30 p.m., Monday and Friday; 9.30 a.m. to 5 p.m., Tuesday, Wednesday, Thursday)
Website: www.u3a.org.uk

COUNSELLING

Relate
Promotes health, respect and justice in couple and family relationships through counselling, therapy and relationship assistance using professionally trained counsellors
Premier House, Carolina Court, Lakeside, Doncaster DN4 5RA
Tel.: 0300 100 1234
Website: www.relate.org.uk

Samaritans
Provides confidential emotional support to any person who is suicidal or despairing
Chris, PO Box 90 90, Stirling FK8 2SA
Helpline: 08457 90 90 90
Website: www.samaritans.org

POLICY ORGANIZATIONS

Age Concern England
A national charitable movement concerned with the needs and aspirations of older people. Produces an excellent series of information leaflets on matters of concern to older people
Astral House, 1268 London Road, London SW16 4ER
Tel.: 020 8765 7000
Free helpline: 0800 00 99 66
Website: www.ageconcern.org.uk

Age Concern Scotland
Causewayside House, 160 Causewayside, Edinburgh EH9 1PR
Tel.: 0845 833 0200
Helpline: 0845 125 9732
Website: www.ageconcernscotland.org.uk

Age Concern Cymru
13/14 Neptune Court, Vanguard Way, Cardiff CF24 5PJ
Tel.: 029 2043 1555
Website: www.accymru.org.uk

Age Concern Northern Ireland
3 Lower Crescent, Belfast BT7 1NR
Tel.: 028 9024 5729
Helpline: 028 9032 5055
Website: www.ageconcernni.org

Better Government for Older People (BGOP)
Composed of a broad range of organizations that work in alliance locally, region-
ally and nationally. Provides members with impetus and practical support to
bring about the changing public service agenda for older people
25–31 Ironmonger Row, London EC1V 3QP
Tel.: 020 7553 6530
Website: www.bgop.org.uk

Bradford Dementia Group
Part of the University of Bradford; has a mission to improve the lives of people
with dementia and their families through excellence in research, education and
training
School of Health Studies, 25 Trinity Road, Bradford BD5 0BB
Tel.: 01274 236367
Website: www.bradford.ac.uk/acad/health/bdg

The British Society of Gerontology
A membership organization that aims to promote the understanding of ageing
and later life through research and communication between different disciplines
See website for current officers' contact details
Website: www.britishgerontology.org

Centre for Policy on Ageing
Focuses on enhancing the exchange of knowledge and information to keep policy
makers, practitioners and researchers better informed about current issues
affecting older people
25–31 Ironmonger Row, London EC1V 3QP
Tel.: 020 7553 6500
Website: www.cpa.org.uk

Coalition for Quality in Care
Promotes the well-being of older people receiving long-term care in a range of
settings

Twyman House, 16 Bonny St, London NW1 9PG
Tel.: 020 7241 8521
Website: www.coalitionforqualitycare.org.uk

Continuing Care Coalition

An independent coalition of commercial, charitable and public service organizations that have a common interest in improving the care of older people in the UK
Twyman House, 16 Bonny St, London NW1 9PG
Tel.: 020 7241 8521
Website: www.ccc-ltc.org.uk

English Community Care Association

A representative body for community care in England working on behalf of small, medium and large providers in the independent sector (private and voluntary)
Second Floor, Monmouth House, 38–40 Artillery Lane, London E1 7LS
Tel.: 08450 577 677
Website: www.ecca.org.uk

Help the Aged

A leading charity for and concerning older people with a research and policy department
207–221 Pentonville Road, London N1 9UZ
Tel.: 020 7278 1114
Website: www.helptheaged.org.uk

The King's Fund

An independent charitable foundation working for better health, especially in London. It is involved in research, policy analysis and development and has an important library which is open to the public
11–13 Cavendish Square, London W1G 0AN
Tel.: 020 7307 2400
Website: www.kingsfund.org.uk

National Care Forum

Represents the views of not-for-profit health and social care organizations who provide care services for older people
3 The Quadrant, Coventry CV1 2DY
Tel.: 0247 624 3619
Website: www.nationalcareforum.org.uk

The National Institute of Adult Continuing Education

Exists to encourage adults to engage in learning of all kinds and has an Older and Bolder programme which focuses on the learning needs and achievements of older adults
Renaissance House, 20 Princess Road West, Leicester LE1 6TP
Tel.: 0116 204 4200
Website: www.niace.org.uk

Social Care Institute for Excellence
Collects, synthesizes and disseminates knowledge about what works in social care
Goldings House, 2 Hay's Lane, London SE1 2HB
Tel.: 020 7098 6840
Website: www.scie.org.uk

CHURCH-RELATED ORGANIZATIONS

Christian Council on Ageing
Aims to assist churches and individual Christians to respond to the pastoral needs of older people
3 Stuart Street, Derby DE1 2EQ
Tel.: 0845 094 4161
Website: www.ccoa.org.uk

Church Army's Research Unit
Includes work exploring evangelism, spiritual needs and fresh expressions of church among older people
The Sheffield Centre, Wilson Carlile Campus, Cavendish Street, Sheffield S3 7RZ
Tel.: 0114 272 7451
Website: www.churcharmy.org.uk/sheffieldcentre

Faith in Elderly People, Leeds
A local ecumenical group concerned with the needs, including the spiritual needs, of older people
29 Silverdale Avenue, Guiseley, Yorks LS20 8BD.
Tel.: 01943 879320

Faith in Older People
Aims to celebrate the lives of older people and support them in their various needs by using a network provided by faith communities throughout Scotland and offering support and training to lay and ordained members of all faith communities
21a Grosvenor Crescent, Edinburgh EH12 5EL
Tel.: 0131 364 7981
Website: www.faithinolderpeople.org.uk

Leveson Centre for the Study of Ageing, Spirituality and Social Policy
A local and national focus for practical education, training and research on the role of older people in the twenty-first century
Temple House, Fen End Road, Temple Balsall, Knowle, Solihull B93 0AN
Tel.: 01564 778022
Website: www.levesoncentre.org.uk

MHA Care Group
Provides care, housing and support services for older people throughout Britain and promotes the importance of the spiritual needs of older people
Epworth House, Stuart Street, Derby DE1 2EQ

Tel.: 01332 296200
Website: www.mha.org.uk

Outlook Trust
An interdenominational body dedicated to evangelism among the over-55s
The Wycliffe Centre, Horsleys Green, High Wycombe, Bucks HB14 3XL
Tel.: 01494 485222
Website: www.outlook-trust.org.uk

PARCHE (Pastoral Action in Residential Care Homes for the Elderly)
An ecumenical project which aims to meet the spiritual needs of older people in
residential care in Eastbourne through providing regular services and visits in
care homes and retirement housing schemes
St Elizabeth's Church Centre, 268 Victoria Drive, Eastbourne BN20 8QX
Tel.: 01323 438527
Website: www.parche.org.uk

Pastoral Care Project, Nuneaton
Focuses upon spiritual care and demonstrates that effective care of people with
dementia requires the input of a multi-disciplinary team of professionals and
volunteers with the contribution of family, friends and church
St Gerard's, Father Hudson's Campus, Coventry Road, Coleshill B46 3EB
Tel.: 01675 434035
Website: www.pastoralcareproject.org.uk

PSALM (Project for Seniors and Lifelong Ministry)
Develops opportunities for continuing work and ministry by and for older people
in London. It includes training programmes and seminars and a developing
network of parish workers/volunteers
The Gallery, St Pancras Church, Euston Road, London NW1 2BA
Tel.: 020 7388 1461
www.stpancraschurch.org

GOVERNMENT DEPARTMENTS

Department for Work and Pensions
Responsible for benefits and the Government welfare reform agenda
The Adelphi, 1–11 John Adam Street, London WC2N 6HT
Tel.: 020 7712 2171
Website: www.dwp.gov.uk

Department of Health
Improves health and well-being and promotes health and social care policy
Richmond House, 79 Whitehall, London SW1A 2NS
Tel.: 020 7210 4850
Website: www.dh.gov.uk

OTHER USEFUL WEBSITES

Keychange
www.keychange.org.uk/elderly.asp

Mission Care
www.missioncare.org.uk

National Council for Palliative Care
www.ncpc.org.uk

RISE – Reaching the Isolated Elderly
www.regenerate-rise.co.uk

Sheffield Centre
www.encountersontheedge.co.uk

Notes

Introduction

1   For more information about the work of the Foundation of Lady Katherine Leveson please see <www.leveson.org.uk> or write to Temple House, Fen End Road West, Temple Balsall, Knowle, Solihull B93 0AN.

2   See J. Woodward and S. Pattison, eds, *The Blackwell Reader in Pastoral and Practical Theology* (Oxford: Blackwell, 2000).

3   See my earlier books: J. Woodward, ed., *Embracing the Chaos*: *Theological Reflections on AIDS* (London: SPCK, 1990); J. Woodward, *Encountering Illness* (London: SCM Press, 1995).

4   For more information about the Australian context and thinking see <www.agedcareaustralian.gov.au>, <www.health.gov.au> or <www.seniors. gov.au>. Or see A. Borowski, S. Encel, E. Ozanne, eds, *Ageing and Social Policy in Australia* (Cambridge: CUP, 1997).

5   For an overview of my interest in pastoral theology and reflective ministry see <www.jameswoodward.info>.

6   I welcome feedback and suggestions for improvement of both thought and practice via the Leveson Centre web page: <www.levesoncentre.org.uk> or my web page: <www.jameswoodward.info>.

1 An ageing society?

1   *Older People in the United Kingdom: Key Facts and Statistics 2007* <www.ageconcern.org.uk>. For a more detailed and accessible account of age statistics see Appendix 1 (p. 207).

2   See G. Cohen, *The Creative Age: Awakening Human Potential in the Second Half of Life* (London: Avon Books, 2000) or H. Moody, *Aging: Concepts and Controversies* (Thousand Oaks, CA: Pine Forge Press, 1994).

3   A. Tinker, *Older People in Modern Society* (London: Longman, 1996). See U. Kroll, *Living Life to the Full: A Guide to Spiritual Health in Later Years* (London: Continuum, 2006); A. Tinker, *85 Not Out* (London: Age Concern, Institute of Gerontology, King's College London, 2000).

4   J. Vincent, *Old Age* (London: Routledge, 2003); H. Moody and D. Carroll, *The Five Stages of the Soul* (London: Rider, 1998); A. Walker and C. Hennessy, eds, *Understanding Quality of Life in Old Age* (Maidenhead: Open University Press, 2004); D. Draaisma, *Why Life Speeds Up As You Get Older* (Cambridge: CUP, 2006); S. MacLaine, *Sage-ing While Age-ing* (Pymble, NSW, Australia: Simon & Schuster, 2007).

5   B. Friedan, *The Fountain of Age* (New York: Vintage, 1993). See <www.u3a.org.uk>.
6   J. Grubuim and J. Holstein, eds, *Ageing and Everyday Life* (Oxford: Blackwell, 2000).
7   A. Blaikie, *Ageing and Popular Culture* (Cambridge: CUP, 1999).

2 Theories of ageing

1   For a fuller discussion of this approach see B. Myerhoff, *Remembered Lives: The Work of Ritual, Storytelling, and Growing Older* (Ann Arbor: University of Michigan Press, 1992).
2   See J. Reed, D. Stanley and C. Clarke, *Health, Well-being and Older People* (Bristol: Policy Press, 2004).
3   See M. Sidell, *Health in Old Age: Myth, Mystery and Management* (Maidenhead: Open University Press, 1995).
4   See D. Gibson, *Aged Care: Old Policies, New Problems* (Cambridge: CUP, 1998).
5   S. Carmody and S. Forster, eds, *Nursing Older People* (Abingdon: Radcliffe Publishing, 2003).
6   P. Thompson, C. Itzin and M. Abendstein, *I Don't Feel Old: The Experience of Later Life* (Oxford: OUP, 1990).
7   A. Milne, E. Hatzidimitriadov, J. Wiseman, 'Health and quality of life among older people in rural England', *Journal of Social Policy* (2007), 36: 477–95.
8   G. Wenger, *Old People's Health and Experience of the Caring Services: Accounts from Rural Communities in North Wales* (Liverpool: Liverpool University Press, 1988).
9   R. Williams, *The Protestant Legacy: Attitudes to Death and Illness Among Older Aberdonians* (Oxford: OUP, 1990).
10 See note 6; M. Blaxter, *Health and Lifestyles* (London: Routledge, 1990).

3 Images of old age

1   For a fuller discussion of this see M. Featherstone and A. Wernick, *Images of Ageing: Cultural Representations of Later Life* (London: Routledge, 1995).
2   P. Coleman and A. O'Hanlon, *Ageing and Development* (London: Edward Arnold, 2004).
3   Many of Rembrandt's paintings are available via the Internet.
4   J. Rose, *Demons and Angels: A Life of Jacob Epstein* (Cambridge, MA: Da Capo Press, 2002).
5   P. Berger and T. Luckmann, *The Social Construction of Reality* (London: Allen Lane, 1966). This work has been developed by Giddens – see, for example, A. Giddens, *Modernity and Self Identity: Self and Society in Late Modern Age* (Cambridge and Oxford: Polity, 1991).
6   E. Erikson, *The Life Cycle Completed: A Review* (New York: W.W. Norton, 1982).
7   B. Bytheway, *Ageism* (Maidenhead: Open University Press, 1995).
8   See Diocese of Hereford Policy for Older People, July 2006.
9   Ann Morisy, 'New Ageing', *Third Way* (Winter 2008), 31(1).
10 T. Cole and S. Gadow, eds, *What Does It Mean To Grow Old? Reflections from the Humanities* (Durham, NC: Duke University Press, 1986).
11 K. Woodward, *Figuring Age: Women, Bodies, Generations* (Bloomington: Indiana University Press, 1999). For an excellent set of images of older

women see E. and C. Handy, *Reinvented Lives: Women at Sixty – a Celebration* (London: Hutchinson, 2002).

4 Health and well-being in age

1 For an American perspective on this question see H. Simmonds and C. MacBean, *Thriving after 55: Your Guide to Fully Living the Rest of Your Life* (Richmond, VA: Prime Press, 1999).
2 B. McPherson, *Aging as a Social Process* (Oxford: OUP, 2004).
3 A. Walker and C. Hennessy, eds, *Understanding Quality of Life in Old Age* (Maidenhead: Open University Press, 2004).
4 See Appendix 2, Narrative biography and older people (pp. 209–12).
5 M. Sidell, *Health in Old Age: Myth, Mystery and Management* (Maidenhead: Open University Press, 1997).
6 S. Hooft, *Caring about Health* (Aldershot: Ashgate, 2006).
7 J. Johnson and R. Slater, eds, *Ageing and Later Life* (London: Sage, 1993).
8 A. Maslow, *Towards a Psychology of Being* (New York: Harper & Row, 1962).
9 Adapted from M. McClyment et al., *Health Visiting and Elderly People* (Philadelphia, PA: Churchill Livingstone, 1991).
10 V. Carver and P. Liddiard, eds, *An Ageing Population* (Maidenhead: Open University Press, 1985).
11 P. Ebersole and P. Hess, eds, *Towards Healthy Ageing* (St Louis, MO: Mosby, 1993).
12 H. Heath and I. Schofield, eds, *Healthy Ageing* (St Louis, MO: Mosby, 1999).
13 A. Campbell, *Moderated Love: A Theology of Professional Care* (London: SPCK, 1984); S. Pattison, *Pastoral Care and Liberation Theology* (Cambridge: CUP, 1994). For a consistent attempt to engage in context see any of the writings of Kenneth Leech.
14 This approach to understanding health and well-being has been shaped by my teaching with the Open University from 1991 to 2002 (Understanding Health and Social Care K100).
15 J. Woodward, *Befriending Death* (London: SPCK, 2005).

5 Diminishment: age-related changes

1 A. Bowling, *Measuring Disease* (Maidenhead: Open University Press, 1995).
2 J. Brookbank, *The Biology of Aging* (New York: Harper & Row, 1990).
3 J. Christianson and J. Grzybowski, *Biology of Aging* (St Louis, MO: Mosby, 1993).
4 R. Binstock and L. George, eds, *Handbook of Aging and the Social Sciences* (London: Academic Press, 1995).
5 H. Heath and I. Schofield, eds, *Healthy Ageing* (St Louis, MO: Mosby, 1999).
6 E. Schneider and I. Rowe, eds, *Handbook of the Biology of Ageing* (London: Academic Press, 1995).
7 C. Victor, *Health and Healthcare in Later Life* (Maidenhead: Open University Press, 1991).
8 S. Carmody and S. Forster, eds, *Nursing Older People* (Abingdon: Radcliffe, 2003).
9 I. Stuart-Hamilton, *The Psychology of Ageing* (London: Jessica Kingsley, 2006).
10 V. Tschudin, *Counselling and Older People* (London: Age Concern, 1999).
11 R. Slater, *The Psychology of Growing Old* (Maidenhead: Open University Press, 1995).

12 K. Morgan, *Gerontology: Responding to an Ageing Society* (London: Jessica Kingsley, 1992).
13 J. Johnson and R. Slater, eds, *Ageing and Later Life* (London: Sage, 1993).
14 D. Gibson, *Aged Care* (Cambridge: CUP, 1998).

6 The religious and spiritual needs of older people

1 See D. Willows and J. Swinton, eds, *Spiritual Dimensions of Pastoral Care: Practical Theology in a Multidisciplinary Context* (London: Jessica Kingsley, 2000); D. Stoter, *Spiritual Aspects of Health Care* (St Louis, MO: Mosby, 1995).
2 See S. Pattison, 'Dumbing down the spirit', in H. Orchard, ed., *Spirituality in Health Care Contexts* (London: Jessica Kingsley, 2001).
3 See T. Gordon, 'Clearing the dark corners of the mental attic', *Professional Social Work* (January 1997).
4 L. Moffitt, 'Helping to recreate a personal sacred space', *Journal of Dementia Care*, 4(3).
5 W. McSherry, *Making Sense of Spirituality in Nursing and Health Care Practice* (London: Jessica Kingsley, 2006).
6 A. Peberdy, 'Spiritual care of dying people', in D. Dickenson and A. Johnson, eds, *Death, Dying and Bereavement* (London: Sage, 1993).
7 A. Jewell, ed., *Ageing, Spirituality and Well Being* (London: Jessica Kingsley, 2004).
8 E. MacKinlay, *The Spiritual Dimension of Ageing* (London: Jessica Kingsley, 2001).
9 S. Cassidy, *Sharing the Darkness: The Spirituality of Caring* (London: Darton, Longman & Todd, 1989).
10 *Plato Charmides*, *c.*380 <sc>BC<xsc>, trans. Benjamin Jowett.
11 Quoted in H. Nouwen, *The Return of the Prodigal Son* (London: Darton, Longman & Todd, 2003), p. 72.
12 D. Wainwright, *Being rather than Doing: A Spirituality of Retirement*, Occasional paper 13 (Derby: Christian Council on Ageing, 2001).
13 Wainwright, *Being*, p. 5.
14 Cassidy, *Sharing*, p. 112.

7 Worship *with* older people

1 J. G. Davies, ed., *A New Dictionary of Liturgy and Worship* (London: SCM, 1986).
2 J. Woodward and L. Houlden, *Services for Weekdays* (London: SPCK, 2006).
3 See 'Taking services with and for older people' in the Further reading section. For further worship resources see <www.levesoncentre.org.uk> (Further reading section).

8 Older people and memory

1 In S. Benson and J. Killick, eds, *Creativity in Dementia Care*, Calendar 2004 (London: Hawker, 2004).
2 See the Alzheimer's Society web page <www.alzheimers.org.uk>.
3 J. Lee, *Just Love Me: My Life Turned Upside Down by Alzheimer's Disease* (West Lafayette, Ind.: Purdue University Press, 2003).
4 M. Goldsmith, *In a Strange Land: People with Dementia and the Local Church* (4M Publications, 2004). Available from 34 Cumberland Street, Edinburgh EH3 6SA.
5 T. Kitwood, *Dementia Reconsidered: The Person Comes First* (Maidenhead:

Open University Press, 1997).

6 Alzheimer's Society, *Home from Home* (London: Alzheimer's Society, 2007).

7 Christian Council on Ageing and Methodist Homes, *Visiting People with Dementia* (Derby: CCOA, 2001).

8 J. Treetops, *Holy, Holy, Holy: The Church's Ministry for People with Dementia*: *Suggestions for Action* (Leeds: Faith in Elderly People, 1996). Available from 29 Silverdale Avenue, Guiseley, Yorks LS20 8BD.

9 CCOA and Methodist Homes, *Worship for People with Dementia* (Derby: CCOA, 2001); C. Crosskey, *Older People, Faith and Dementia: Twenty-Four Practical Talks for Use in Care Homes*, Leveson Paper No. 7 (Solihull: The Leveson Centre and Sidcup, Kent: Church Army, 2004); P. Higgins and R. Allen, *Lighting the Way: Spiritual and Religious Care for Those with Dementia*, Leveson Paper No. 16 (Solihull: The Leveson Centre, 2007); G. Hammond and J. Treetops, *The Wells of Life: Moments of Worship with People with Dementia, Suggestions for Action* (Leeds: Faith in Elderly People, 2004). Available from 29 Silverdale Avenue, Guiseley, Yorks LS20 8BD.

9 Older people: intimacy, relationships and sexuality

1 M. Abrahams, *Beyond Three Score Years and Ten* (England: Age Concern, 1978).

2 <www.leveson.org.uk>.

3 WHO draft working definition (October 2002) <www.who.int/en/>.

4 V. C. Pangman, 'Sexuality and the chronically ill older adult: social justice issues, 18(1): 51.

5 N. Woods, *Human Sexuality in Health and Illness* (St Louis, MO: Mosby, 1983).

6 See Kingsberg's research (Healthywomen Sexuality Center) at <www.healthywomen.org/>.

10 Sharing our story: pastoral engagement with older widows

1 See P. Chambers, *Older Widows and the Life Course* (Aldershot: Ashgate, 2005).

2 S. Llewelyn and K. Osborne, *Women's Lives* (London: Routledge, 1990); M. Maynard and J. Purvis, eds, *Researching Women's Lives from a Feminist Perspective* (London: Taylor & Francis, 1994).

3 J. Bowlby, *Attachment and Loss* (New York: Basic Books, 1980); A. Bowling and A. Cartwright, *Life after a Death* (London: Tavistock, 1982).

4 See K. Fischer, *Moving On: A Spiritual Journey for Women of Maturity* (London: SPCK, 1996).

5 W. Bridges, *Transitions: Making Sense of Life's Changes* (London: Nicholas Brealey, 1996).

6 A. Deveson, *Coming of Age* (Carlton North, Victoria, Australia: Scribe Publications, 1994).

7 G. Sheehy, *New Passages* (New York: HarperCollins, 1997); D. van den Hoonaard, *The Widowed Self: The Older Woman's Journey Through Widowhood* (Waterloo, Ontario, Canada: Laurier University Press, 2001).

11 Men and age: images, questions and reconstructions

1   For an example of exploring experience within this perspective see R. Dass, *Still Here: Embracing Ageing, Changing and Dying* (London: Hodder, 2000).

2   M. LaMont, *A Graceful Age: Reflections for the Wisdom Years* (Winona, Minn.: St Mary's Press, 1999).

3   K. Mann, *Approaching Retirement* (Bristol: Policy Press, 2001).

4   C. Brister, *Spiritual Wisdom for a Successful Retirement: Living Forward* (Philadelphia, PA: Haworth Press, 2001).

5   See M. Pyke, *Long Life* (London: J.M. Dent, 1980). Some of these issues are discussed in J. Eldred, *A Telling Minority: Spirituality of Older Men* (Leeds: MHA Care Group, 2004).

12 Lifelong learning and older people

1   See the work of the centre at <www.levesoncentre.org.uk> and the work of the National Institute of Adult Continuing Education at <www.niace.org.uk>.

2   For further information about the University of the Third Age see <www.u3a.org.uk>.

3   H. Moody, *The Five Stages of the Soul* (London: Rider, 1998).

4   E. MacKinlay, *Spiritual Growth and Care in the Fourth Stage of Life* (London: Jessica Kingsley, 2006).

5   A. Tuckett and A. McAulay, eds, *Demography and Older Learners: Approaches to a New Policy Challenge* (Leicester: NIACE, 2005).

6   A. Withnall, V. McGivney and J. Soulsby, *Older People Learning: Myths and Realities* (Leicester: NIACE, 2004).

7   S. Carlton and J. Soulsby, *Learning to Grow Older and Bolder* (Leicester: NIACE, 1999).

8   Withnall, McGivney and Soulsby, *Older People Learning*.

9   A. Walker and C. Hennessy, *Understanding Quality of Life in Old Age* (Maidenhead: Open University Press, 2004).

10 H. Moody, *Aging: Concepts and Controversies* (Thousand Oaks, CA: Pine Forge Press, 1994).

11 J. Fisher and H .Simmons, *A Journey Called Aging: Challenges and Opportunities in Older Adulthood* (Philadelphia, PA: Haworth, 2007).

13 Retirement

1   Department for Work and Pensions, *Households Below Average Income 2004/5* (2006).

2   Department for Work and Pensions, *Pensioners' Income Series 2004/5* (2006).

3   Department for Work and Pensions, *Personal Accounts: A New Way to Save* (2006).

4   Resolution Foundation, *Closing the Advice Gap: Providing Financial Advice to People on Low Incomes* (2006).

5   R. Prasad, 'Lynchpins of family spend three days a week with grandchildren', *Guardian* (14 December 2000).

6   D. Wainwright, *Being rather than Doing: A Spirituality of Retirement*, Occasional paper 13 (Derby: Christian Council on Ageing, 2001).

7   J. Woodward, *Befriending Illness*, Leveson Paper No. 13 (Solihull: The Leveson Centre for the Study of Ageing, Spirituality and Social Policy, 2006).

14 Older people: illness, healing and death

1 P. Tillich, *The Courage to Be* (New Haven: Yale University Press, 2001).

2 J. V. Taylor, *The Go-Between God* (London: SCM, 1979).

3 W. H. Vanstone, *The Stature of Waiting* (London: Darton, Longman & Todd, 1982).

4 D. Potter, *Seeing the Blossom: Two Interviews and a Lecture* (London: Faber, 1994).

5 J. Polkinghorne, *One World: The Interaction between Science and Theology* (London: SPCK, 1996).

6 A. Farrer, *A Science of God?* (London: Geoffrey Bles, 1966).

7 G. Kaufman, *God, Mystery and Diversity* (Philadelphia: Fortress Press, 1989).

8 L. Houlden, *The Strange Story of the Gospels* (London: SPCK, 2002).

9 E. Becker, *The Denial of Death* (Glencoe: Free Press, 1985).

10 N. P. Harvey, *Death's Gift* (London: Darton, Longman & Todd, 1984).

11 J. Woodward, *Befriending Death* (London: SPCK, 2005).

12 M. Ignatieff, *Scar Tissue* (London: Hodder, 2002).

13 Potter, *Seeing the Blossom*.

15 Ageing and social policy

1 Social Caring (February, 2007).

2 Government Actuaries Department (2004).

3 Department of Health and Social Security, *Community Care: An Agenda for Action* (Norwich: Stationery Office Books, 1988).

4 *The NHS Plan: A Plan for Investment, a Plan for Reform* (Norwich: Stationery Office Books, 2000).

5 *Putting People First: A Shared Vision and Commitment to the Transformation of Adult Social Care* (London: Department of Health, 2007).

6 *National Service Framework (NSF) for Older People* (London: Department of Health, 2001).

7 Department of Health, *Our Health, Our Care, Our Say: A New Direction for Community Services* (Norwich: Stationery Office Books, 2006).

8 See the In Control website <www.in-control.org.uk>.

9 *Fair Access to Care Services: Guidance on Eligibility Criteria for Adult Social Care* (London: Department of Health, 2003)

10 Royal Commission on Long Term Care, *With Respect to Old Age: Rights and Responsibilities* (Norwich: Stationery Office Books, 1999).

11 D. Wanless, *Securing Good Care for Older People: Taking a Long-term View* (the Wanless Report) (London: King's Fund, 2006).

12 Department of Health, *Care Homes for Older People: National Minimum Standards* (Norwich: Stationery Office Books, 2001).

13 *My Home Life: Quality of Life in Care Homes* (London: Help the Aged, 2006).

14 L. Buckner and S. Yeandle, *Valuing Carers: Calculating the Value of Unpaid Care* (London: Carers UK, 2007).

15 *A New Deal for Carers* (London: Department of Health, 2007).

16 In June 2008, the Department of Health produced a report, *Carers at the Heart of 21st-Century Families and Communities: A Caring System on Your Side, A Life of Your Own*.

17 *A New Pension Settlement for the 21st Century* (the Turner Report) (London: Pensions Commission, 2005).

18 Department for Work and Pensions, *Opportunity Age: Meeting the Challenges*

of Ageing in the 21st Century (Norwich: Stationery Office Books, 2005).

19 Social Exclusion Unit, *A Sure Start to Later Life: Ending Inequalities for Older People* (London: Office of the Deputy Prime Minister, 2006).

20 *Spotlight Report 2007: Spotlight on Older People in the UK* (London: Help the Aged, 2007).

16 A theology of ageing

1 I was very fortunate to be able to have long conversations with Michael Mayne about ageing at a conference organized by the Royal Society of Medicine in Cumberland Lodge, Windsor, in 2005.

2 See the research of Peter Coleman and Marie Mills <www.soton.ac.uk/~pgc/>.

3 Ian McEwan interview with Kate Kellaway, *Observer* (16 September 2001).

4 M. Mayne, *The Enduring Melody* (London: Darton, Longman & Todd, 2006).

5 P. Larkin, 'The Old Fools', *Collected Poems* (London: Faber, 1988).

6 H. Luke, *Old Age* (New York: Parabola Books, 1987).

7 J. Woodward, *Befriending Death* (London: SPCK, 2005).

8 M. Muggeridge, *The Chronicles of Wasted Time* (Vancouver: Regent College Publishing, 1999).

9 D. Nicholl, *The Testing of Hearts* (London: Darton, Longman & Todd, 1998).

17 Successful ageing

1 R. Gingold, *Successful Ageing* (Oxford: Oxford University Press, 1992).

2 H. Heath and I. Schofield, eds, *Healthy Ageing* (St Louis, MO: Mosby, 1999).

3 E. Cumming and W. Henry, *The Process of Disengagement* (New York: Basic Books, 1961).

4 J. Hockey and A. James, *Growing and Growing Old* (London: Sage, 1993).

5 See the WHO web page at <www.who.int>.

6 A. Antonovsky, *Health, Stress and Coping* (New York: Jossey-Bass, 1979).

7 H. Simmonds and C. MacBean, *Thriving after 55: Your Guide to Fully Living the Rest of Your Life* (Richmond, VA: Prime Press, 1999).

8 J. Woodward, *Befriending Death* (London: SPCK, 2005).

Further reading

General resources

Butler, Michael and Orbach, Ann (1993), *Being Your Age: Pastoral Care for Older People*. London: SPCK.

Church of England Board for Social Responsibility (1990), *Ageing*. London: Church House Publishing.

Collyer, Michael (2004), *Psalm Project for Seniors and Lifelong Ministry* (Discovering Faith in Later Life No. 3). Sidcup, Kent: Church Army.

Collyer, Michael (2004), *St Stephen's Seniors: Christ to Elderly and Lonely in East Twickenham* (Discovering Faith in Later Life No. 2). Sidcup, Kent: Church Army.

Collyer, Michael (2005), *The Outlook Trust: Christian Hope and Encouragement for Older People* (Discovering Faith in Later Life No. 4). Sidcup, Kent: Church Army.

Howse, Ken (1999), *Spirituality, Religion and Older People*. London: Centre for Policy on Ageing.

Jewell, Albert (2000), *Grow Old Along with Me*. Birmingham: National Christian Education Council.

Jewell, Albert (2001), *Older People and the Church*. Peterborough: Methodist Publishing House.

Knox, Ian S. (2002), *Older People and the Church*, Edinburgh: T.&T. Clark.

Merchant, Rob (2003), *Pioneering the Third Age*. Carlisle: Paternoster Press.

Santer, Mark (2000), *Valuing Age: An Agenda for Society and the Church* (Leveson Paper No 2). Solihull: The Leveson Centre.

Treetops, J. (1992), *A Daisy among the Dandelions: The Church's Ministry with Older People: Suggestions for Action*. Leeds: Faith in Elderly People. Available from 29 Silverdale Avenue, Guiseley, Yorks LS20 8BD.

Working with Older People: A Resource Directory for Churches, 2nd edn (2006). Details of over 100 church-related organizations working with older people (published in collaboration with MHA Care Group), £7.50 (in plastic wallet) or downloadable from the website: <www.levesoncentre.org.uk>.

Spiritual needs of older people

Airey, Jo et al. (2002), *Frequently Asked Questions on Spirituality and Religion*. Derby: Christian Council on Ageing and Methodist Homes. Leeds: Faith in Elderly People.

Jewell, Albert, ed. (1999), *Spirituality and Ageing*. London: Jessica Kingsley.

MacKinlay, Elizabeth (2001), *The Spiritual Dimension of Ageing*. London: Jessica Kingsley.

MacKinlay, Elizabeth (2006), *Spiritual Growth and Care in the Fourth Age*. London: Jessica Kingsley.

SCOP (2006), *Spiritual Care for Older People: The Extra Dimension*. Continuing series of sheets. Oxford: SCOP.

Wainwright, David (2001), *Being rather than Doing: A Spirituality of Retirement*, Occasional Paper 13. Derby: Christian Council on Ageing.

Wray, Martin (2005), Second Wind: Spirituality and the Second Half of Life (study course). Leeds: MHA Care Group.

Raising awareness

Bytheway, B. (1995), *Ageism*. Maidenhead: Open University Press.

Finney, J. (1992), *Finding Faith Today*. Swindon: British and Foreign Bible Society.

Green, M. (1990), *Evangelism through the Local Church*. London: Hodder & Stoughton.

Slater, Robert (1995), *The Psychology of Growing Old*. Maidenhead: Open University Press.

Taylor, R. (1996), *Love in the Shadows*. London: Scripture Union.

Taylor, Rhena (2004), *Three Score Years and Then? How to Reach Older People for Christ*. Available from OUTLOOK Trust. Tel.: 01494 485222.

Taking services with and for older people

Butler, Michael et al. (1999), *Worship in Residential Care* (Good Practice Guide No. 2), rev. edn. Derby: Christian Council on Ageing.

Carols that Live (large print). Available from PO Box 341, Enterprise House, Northampton NN3 2WZ.

Collyer, Michael (2004), *Taking the Church into Residential Care Homes in Eastbourne* (Discovering Faith in Later Life No. 1). Sidcup, Kent: Church Army.

Crosskey, Chris (2004), *Older People, Faith and Dementia: Twenty-four Practical Talks for Use in Care Homes* (Leveson Paper No. 7). Solihull: The Leveson Centre and Sidcup, Kent: Church Army.

Hammond, Gaynor and Treetops, Jackie (2004), *The Wells of Life: Moments of Worship with People with Dementia – Suggestions for Action*. Leeds: Faith in Elderly People, Leeds. Available from 29 Silverdale Avenue, Guiseley, Yorks LS20 8BD.

Higgins, Patricia and Allen, Richard (2007), *Lighting the Way: Spiritual and Religious Care for Those with Dementia* (Leveson Paper No. 16). Solihull: The Leveson Centre.

Hymns that Live (large print). Available from PO Box 341, Enterprise House, Northampton NN3 2WZ.

Johnson, Alison (2000), *Residential Care: A Christian Perspective*. Derby: Christian Council on Ageing.

Kirkbride, Susan (2005), *O Tidings of Comfort and Joy: Favourite Christmas Hymns* (CD), Stirling Dementia Services Development Centre. Available from tel.: 01786 467740 or email: <dementia@stir.ac.uk>.

Kirkbride, Susan (2005), *Restoring the Soul: A Selection of Favourite Hymns* (CD), Stirling Dementia Services Development Centre. Available from tel.: 01786 467740 or email: <dementia@stir.ac.uk>.

Knocker, Sally and Johnson, Alison (2005), *Creating Links between Care Settings and Local Faith Communities: A Practice Guide*, NAPA. Available from tel.: 020 078 9375 or email: <sue@napa-activities.co.uk>.

SCOP (2007), *Worship with Older People in a Care Setting*. Oxford: Spiritual Care of Older People.

Woodward, James and Houlden, Leslie (2006), *Services for Weekdays*. London: SPCK.

Woodward, James and Houlden, Leslie (2007), *Praying the Lectionary*. London: SPCK.

Running a holiday at home event

Collyer, Michael (2006), *Holiday at Home* (Discovering Faith in Later Life No. 5). Sidcup, Kent: Church Army.

What Shall We Do Now? Christian Resources for Older People (2002). London: Women's Network of the Methodist Church. Available from tel.: 0207 467 5175 or email: <network@methodistchurch.org.uk>.

Visiting and befriending

Butler, Michael, ed. (1997), *Visiting Older People*. Derby: Christian Council on Ageing.

Hammond, Gaynor (2002), *The Friendship Club*. Leeds: Faith in Elderly People. Available from 29 Silverdale Avenue, Guiseley, Yorks LS20 8BD.

Living with loss and change

Counsel and Care (1995), *Last Rights: A Study of How Death and Dying are Handled in Residential Care and Nursing Homes*. London: Counsel and Care.

A Good Death: Papers Presented at a Leveson Seminar (2003). (Leveson Paper No. 4). Solihull: The Leveson Centre.

A Good Funeral: Papers Presented at a Leveson Seminar (2006) (Leveson Paper No. 14). Solihull: The Leveson Centre.

Missinne, Leo (2004), *Journeying through Old Age and Illness* (Leveson Paper No. 10). Solihull: The Leveson Centre.

URC (2002) . . . *A Time to Die: A Resource Pack for Churches*. London: The United Reformed Church.

Woodward, James (2005), *Befriending Death*. London: SPCK.

Woodward, James (2006), *Befriending Illness*. (Leveson Paper No. 13). Solihull: The Leveson Centre.

The ministry of the Church to people living with dementia

Allen, Brian, ed. (2002), *Religious Practice and People with Dementia*. Derby: Christian Council on Ageing.

CCOA (2001), *Visiting People with Dementia*. Derby: Christian Council on Ageing and Methodist Homes.

CCOA (2001), *Worship for People with Dementia*. Derby: Christian Council on Ageing and Methodist Homes.

Crosskey, Chris (2004), *Older People, Faith and Dementia: Twenty-four Practical Talks for Use in Care Homes* (Leveson Paper No. 7). Solihull: The Leveson Centre and Sidcup, Kent: Church Army.

Froggatt, Alison and Moffitt, Laraine (1997), 'Spiritual needs and religious practice in dementia care', in Mary Marshall, ed., *State of the Art in Dementia Care*. London: Centre for Policy on Ageing.

Goldsmith, Malcolm (1998), *Dementia, Ethics and the Glory of God* (CCOA Occasional Paper No. 11). Derby: Christian Council on Ageing.

Goldsmith, Malcolm (2004), *In a Strange Land: People with Dementia and the Local Church*. Southwell, Notts.: 4M Publications. Available from 34 Cumberland Street, Edinburgh EH3 6SA.

Hammond, Gaynor and Treetops, Jackie (2004), *The Wells of Life: Moments of Worship with People with Dementia – Suggestions for Action*. Leeds: Faith in Elderly People, Leeds. Available from 29 Silverdale Avenue, Guiseley, Yorks LS20 8BD.

Higgins, Patricia and Allen, Richard (2007), *Lighting the Way: Spiritual and Religious Care for Those with Dementia* (Leveson Paper No. 16). Solihull: The Leveson Centre.

Killick, John and Allan, Kate (2001), *Communication and the Care of People with Dementia*. Maidenhead: Open University Press.

Murphy, Charles J. (1997), *Dementia Care and the Churches: Involving People and Premises*. Stirling: Dementia Services Development Centre.

Palliative Care for People with Dementia: Papers Presented at a Leveson Seminar (2005). Solihull: The Leveson Centre.

Saunders, J. (2002), *Dementia: Pastoral Theology and Pastoral Care*. Cambridge: Grove Books.

Seeing the Person beyond the Dementia: Papers Presented at a Leveson Seminar (2004). Solihull: The Leveson Centre.

Shamy, Eileen (2003), *A Guide to the Spiritual Dimension of Care for People with Alzheimer's Disease and Related Dementia* (previously published in New Zealand as *More than Body, Brain and Breath*). London: Jessica Kingsley.

Treetops, J. (1996), *Holy, Holy, Holy: The Church's Ministry for People with Dementia: Suggestions for Action*. Leeds: Faith in Elderly People, Leeds. Available from 29 Silverdale Avenue, Guiseley, Yorks LS20 8BD.

Worship for people with dementia (2001). Derby: Christian Council on Ageing and Methodist Homes.

Mixed economy: inherited and fresh expressions of church for older people

Collyer, Michael (2007), *Church for the Saga Generation: Cultural Shifts in Younger Old* (Discovering Faith in Later Life No. 6). Sidcup, Kent: Church Army.

Also available in the
New Library of Pastoral Care series

THE PASTORAL CARE OF PEOPLE WITH MENTAL HEALTH PROBLEMS

Marion L. S. Carson

As a minister or pastoral worker, it is highly likely that at some stage in your ministry you will find yourself caring for people with psychiatric problems and their families. *The Pastoral Care of People with Mental Health Problems* is an invaluable resource to help you provide support for those suffering from the most common problems, such as depression, Alzheimer's disease, anorexia, addiction to drugs or alcohol, post-traumatic stress disorder, bipolar disorder, schizophrenia and anti-social personality disorder.

As well as outlining the main psychiatric conditions and their treatments, the book examines the particular issues facing pastoral workers and discusses some of the ethical issues involved. Using a wealth of illustrations, it offers practical advice and guidance for the care of individuals and families who find their lives turned upside down by psychiatric illness, addressing questions such as:

- How can I help the family of a young girl who cuts herself?
- What is the difference between depression and an abnormal grief reaction?
- How can I distinguish between a symptom of mental illness and genuine religious revelation?

In cases of severe mental illness it will be necessary to work alongside medical, nursing and social work staff, and guidance is given on how best to do this.

The Pastoral Care of People with Mental Health Problems is the fruit of Marion Carson's many years of experience as a practising psychiatric nurse, her teaching in a theological college and her involvement in pastoral care provision in a local church setting.

ISBN: 978–0–281–05866–2

Also available in the
New Library of Pastoral Care series

ALL GOD'S CHILDREN
An Introduction to Pastoral Work with Children

Marian Carter

This helpful and practical book offers theological, sociological and psychological insights on childhood and the care and nurture of children within the Church. Marian Carter also includes questions to stimulate personal reflection and to encourage discussion and interaction in groups.

'This book shows the complexity and richness of the interplay between who children are (and how they can also teach us adults about our own spiritual maturity) and their pastoral care by adults. It should be read slowly and mindfully, but it can also be used as a handy reference for orientation in this rapidly growing and changing field.'

Jerome W. Berryman, Executive Director
The Center for the Theology of Childhood, Houston, Texas

'Marian Carter's *All God's Children* is a brilliant book. There are many books about how children develop. Advice abounds on how children should be brought up. There are plenty of handbooks to guide Sunday school teachers and clergy in their ministry to children. But there are very few serious studies of what, as Christians, we are to believe about children and of how childhood is to be understood from the perspective of Christian faith. Marian Carter's extraordinary achievement – and I know of no other book that has quite done this – is to ground an eminently practical discussion of how children should be nurtured, whether at home or in church, on a firm theological foundation. This is "applied theology" at its very best.'

John Pridmore, Vicar of St-John-at-Hackney
Committee member, Church of England's Strategy for Children

Marian Carter is a priest and a former teacher in primary and secondary education. She trained teachers and taught pastoral theology on the South West Ministerial Training Course and at the University College of St Mark and St John. She has written several publications on all-age learning and worship.

ISBN: 978–0–281–05888–4

Also available from SPCK in the
Library of Ministry series

COMMUNITY AND MINISTRY

An Introduction to Community Development
in a Christian Context

Paul Ballard and Lesley Husselbee

All clergy, ministers, church-related community workers and lay leaders need to understand how they and their churches may relate to the community in which they are set. This book provides a thorough and professional introduction to the subject, and includes discussion about:

- what community is
- community work and mission
- models of community work
- ethnic, cultural and religious diversity
- the local authority and voluntary agencies
- working with volunteers
- spirituality in community participation

'This book aims to take on the challenge of equipping people with the skills, understanding and information to critically explore the field of community and ministry. It is a timely publication given the increasing government acknowledgement of the contribution of faith communities in both urban and rural community development and regeneration.'

Jim Robertson, Chair of Enabling Group,
Churches' Community Work Alliance

Paul Ballard is Emeritus Professor in the School of Religious and Theological Studies, Cardiff University, where he taught Practical Theology. He has had active involvement in community development, as a consultant with church-based projects, and as a member of the Community Resource Unit of the British Council of Churches. With John Pritchard he has written *Practical Theology in Action* (SPCK, new edition 2006).

Lesley Husselbee is Tutor in Church and Community Education at Northern College, Manchester (which forms part of Luther King House College). She was Secretary for Training in the United Reformed Church (URC) and has also been Senior Lecturer in Urban Geography at the Roehampton Institute, London. She has published with the National Christian Education Council and Roots (an educational resource supported by Churches Together in Britain and Ireland).

ISBN: 978–0–281–05800–6

Also available from SPCK in the
Library of Ministry series

SUPPORTING NEW MINISTERS IN THE LOCAL CHURCH

A Handbook

Keith Lamdin and David Tilley

This book is designed to help those who supervise new ministers at the start of their ordained ministry. It will also be relevant and useful to all people taking up new appointments: the ministers themselves, ordinands on placement, youth ministers and pastoral assistants, preachers, Readers and lay ministers in all denominations.

It offers:

- ideas for good practice
- possibilities for solving problems
- different models of adult learning and supervision
- practical ways of working together with a curate

Professional supervision and mentoring is widely used in other professions, such as medicine, nursing, social work and legal practice. The Church also needs professional competence and has much to learn, as well as to share, in this area.

'This book offers both wisdom and the fruit of practical experience in the area of supervision of colleagues in ministry and will be a useful aid to those – incumbent or curate – embarking on this significant ministry.'

The Ven. Christopher Lowson,
Director of Ministry, Archbishops' Council

Keith Lamdin is Director of Stewardship, Training, Evangelism and Ministry in the Diocese of Oxford.

David Tilley has worked in the training of Methodist ministers and in Continuing Ministerial Education of clergy in the Coventry Diocese.

ISBN: 978–0–281–05879–2